Praise for *Effective SQL*

"Given the reputation of the authors, I expected to be impressed. Impressed doesn't cover it, though. I was blown away! Most SQL books tell you 'how.' This one tells you 'why.' Most SQL books separate database design from implementation. This one integrates design considerations into every facet of SQL use. Most SQL books sit on my shelf. This one will live on my desk."

—*Roger Carlson, Microsoft Access MVP (2006–2015)*

"It can be easy to learn the basics of SQL, but it is very difficult to build accurate and efficient SQL, especially for critical systems with complex requirements. But now, with this great new book, you can get up to speed and write effective SQL much more quickly, no matter which DBMS you use."

—*Craig S. Mullins, Mullins Consulting, Inc., DB2 Gold Consultant and IBM Champion for Analytics*

"This is a great book. It is written in language that can be understood by a relative beginner and yet contains tips and tricks that will benefit the most hardened workhorse. It will therefore appeal to readers across the whole range of expertise and should be in the library of anybody who is seriously concerned with designing, managing, or programming databases."

—*Graham Mandeno, database consultant and Microsoft MVP (1996–2015)*

"This book is an excellent resource for database designers and developers working with relational and SQL-based databases—it's an easy read with great examples that combine theory with practical examples seamlessly. Examples for top relational databases Oracle, DB2, SQL Server, MySQL, and PostgreSQL are included throughout. The book walks the reader through sophisticated techniques to deal with things such as hierarchical data and tally tables, along with explanations of the inner workings and performance implications of SQL using GROUP BY, EXISTS, IN, correlated and non-correlated subqueries, window functions, and joins. The tips you won't find anywhere else, and the fun examples help to make this book stand out from the crowd."

—*Tim Quinlan, database architect and Oracle Certified DBA*

"This book is good for those who need to support multiple dialects of SQL. It's divided up into stand-alone items that you just grab and go. I have been doing SQL in various flavors since 1992 and even I picked up a few things."

—*Tom Moreau, Ph.D., SQL Server MVP (2001–2012)*

"This book is a powerful, compact, and easily understandable presentation of how to use SQL—it shows the application of SQL to real-world questions in order to teach the construction of queries, and it explains the relationship of 'how data is stored' to 'how data is queried' so that you obtain results successfully and effectively."

—*Kenneth D. Snell, Ph.D., database consultant and former Microsoft Access MVP*

"It has been problematic for many that there is no book on going from a novice database administrator to a much more advanced status until now. *Effective SQL* is a road map, a guide, a Rosetta Stone, and a coach on moving from basic Structured Query Language (SQL) to much more advanced uses to solve real-world problems. Rather than stumble around reinventing the wheel or catching glimpses of the proper ways to use a database, do yourself a favor and buy a copy of this book. Not only will you see many different approaches it would take years to see as a database consultant, but you will get a detailed understanding of why the databases of many vendors do what they do. Save time, effort, and wear and tear on your walls from banging your head against them and get this book."

—*Dave Stokes, MySQL Community Manager, Oracle Corporation*

"*Effective SQL* is a 'must have' for any serious database developer. It shows how powerful SQL can be in solving real-world problems in a step-by-step manner. The authors use easy-to-understand language in pointing out every advantage and disadvantage of each solution presented in the book. As we all know, there are multiple ways of accomplishing the same thing in SQL, but the authors explain why a particular query is more efficient than others. The part I liked best about the book is the summary at the end of each section, which reemphasizes the take-away points and reminds the reader which pitfalls to avoid. I highly recommend this book to all my fellow database developers."

—*Leo (theDBguy™), UtterAccess Moderator and Microsoft Access MVP*

"I think this is the book that is relevant not only for developers, but also for DBAs, as it talks about writing efficient SQL and various ways of achieving a desired result. In my opinion, this is a must-have book. Another reason to have this book is that it covers most of the commonly used RDBMSs, and so if someone is looking to transition from one RDBMS to another, this is the book to pick up. The authors have done a fantastic job. My heartiest congratulations to them."

—*Vivek Sharma, technologist, Hybrid Cloud Solutions, Core Technology and Cloud, Oracle Asia Pacific*

Effective SQL

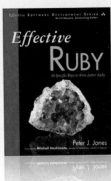

Effective SQL

61 Specific Ways to Write Better SQL

John L. Viescas

Douglas J. Steele

Ben G. Clothier

✦✦ Addison-Wesley

Boston • Columbus • Indianapolis • New York • San Francisco • Amsterdam • Cape Town
Dubai • London • Madrid • Milan • Munich • Paris • Montreal • Toronto • Delhi • Mexico City
São Paulo • Sydney • Hong Kong • Seoul • Singapore • Taipei • Tokyo

For information about buying this title in bulk quantities, or for special sales opportunities (which may include electronic versions; custom cover designs; and content particular to your business, training goals, marketing focus, or branding interests), please contact our corporate sales department at corpsales@pearsoned.com or (800) 382-3419.

For government sales inquiries, please contact governmentsales@pearsoned.com.

For questions about sales outside the U.S., please contact intlcs@pearson.com.

Visit us on the Web: informit.com/aw

Library of Congress Control Number: 2016955468

Some of the examples used in this book originally appeared in *SQL Queries for Mere Mortals®: A Hands-On Guide to Data Manipulation in SQL, Third Edition* (Addison-Wesley, 2014). These examples appear with permission from the authors and Pearson Education Inc.

ISBN-13: 978-0-13-457889-7
ISBN-10: 0-13-457889-9

1   16

Editor-in-Chief
Greg Wiegand

Senior Acquisitions Editor
Trina MacDonald

Development Editor
Songlin Qiu

Technical Reviewers
Richard Anthony Broersma Jr.
Craig S. Mullins
Vivek Sharma
Dave Stokes
Morgan Tocker

Managing Editor
Sandra Schroeder

Full-Service Production Manager
Julie B. Nahil

Project Editor
Anna Popick

Copy Editor
Barbara Wood

Indexer
Richard Evans

Proofreader
Anna Popick

Editorial Assistant
Olivia Basegio

Cover Designer
Chuti Prasertsith

Compositor
The CIP Group

For Suzanne, forever and always . . .

—John Viescas

To my gorgeous and intelligent wife, Louise.
Thanks once again for putting up with me while
I wrote this (and all the other times, too!).

—Doug Steele

Couldn't have done it without support from you both,
Suzanne and Harold!

—Ben Clothier

Contents

Foreword

In the 30 years since the database language SQL was initially adopted as an international standard, the SQL language has been implemented in a multitude of database products. Today, SQL is everywhere. It is in high-performance transaction-processing systems, in smartphone applications, and behind Web interfaces. There is even a whole category of databases called NoSQL whose common feature is (or was) that they don't use SQL. As the NoSQL databases have added SQL interfaces, "No" is now interpreted as "Not Only" SQL.

Because of SQL's prevalence, you are likely to encounter SQL in multiple products and environments. One of the (perhaps valid) criticisms of SQL is that while it is similar across products, there are subtle differences. These differences result from different interpretations of the standard, different development styles, or different underlying architectures. To understand these differences, it is helpful to have examples that compare and contrast the subtle differences in SQL dialects. *Effective SQL* provides a Rosetta Stone for SQL queries, showing how queries can be written in different dialects and explaining the differences.

I often claim that the best way to learn something is by making mistakes. The corollary to this claim is that the people who know the most have made the most mistakes and have learned from others' mistakes. This book includes examples of incomplete and incorrect SQL queries with explanations of why they are incomplete and incorrect. This allows you to learn from mistakes others have made.

SQL is a powerful and complex database language. As a database consultant and a participant in both the U.S. and international SQL Standards committees, I've seen a lot of queries that did not take advantage of SQL's capabilities. Application developers who fully learn SQL's power and complexities can take full advantage of SQL's capabilities not only to build applications that perform well, but also to build those applications efficiently. The 61 specific examples in *Effective SQL* assist in this learning.

—Keith W. Hare
Senior Consultant, JCC Consulting, Inc.;
Vice Chair, INCITS DM32.2—the U.S. SQL Standards Committee;
Convenor, ISO/IEC JTC1 SC32 WG3—the International SQL
Standards Committee

Acknowledgments

A famous politician once said that "it takes a village" to raise a child. If you've ever written a book—technical or otherwise—you know it takes a great team to turn your "child" into a successful book.

First, many thanks to our acquisitions editor and project manager, Trina MacDonald, who not only badgered John to follow up his successful *SQL Queries for Mere Mortals*® book with one for the Effective Software Development Series, but also shepherded the project through its many phases. John assembled a truly international team to help put the book together, and he personally thanks them for their diligent work. Special thanks to Tom Wickerath for his assistance both early in the project and later during technical review.

Trina handed us off to Songlin Qiu, our development editor, who ably helped us understand the ins and outs of writing an Effective Series book. Many thanks, Songlin, for your guidance.

Next, Trina rounded up a great set of technical editors who arduously went through and debugged our hundreds of examples and gave us great feedback. Thanks go to Morgan Tocker and Dave Stokes, MySQL; Richard Broersma Jr., PostgreSQL; Craig Mullins, IBM DB2; and Vivek Sharma, Oracle.

Along the way, series editor and author of the bestselling title *Effective C++, Third Edition*, Scott Meyers, stepped in and gave us invaluable advice about how to turn our items into truly effective advice. We hope we've made the father of the series proud.

Then the production team of Julie Nahil, Anna Popick, and Barbara Wood helped us whip the book into final shape for publication. We couldn't have done it without you!

And finally, many thanks to our families who put up with many long nights while we worked on the manuscript and examples. Their enduring patience is greatly appreciated!

—*John Viescas*
  Paris, France

—*Doug Steele*
  St. Catharines, Ontario, Canada

—*Ben Clothier*
  Converse, Texas, United States

About the Authors

 **John L. Viescas** is an independent database consultant with more than 45 years of experience. He began his career as a systems analyst, designing large database applications for IBM mainframe systems. He spent six years at Applied Data Research in Dallas, Texas, where he directed a staff of more than 30 people and was responsible for research, product development, and customer support of database products for IBM mainframe computers. While working at Applied Data Research, John completed a degree in business finance at the University of Texas at Dallas, graduating cum laude.

John joined Tandem Computers, Inc., in 1988, where he was responsible for the development and implementation of database marketing programs in Tandem's U.S. Western Sales region. He developed and delivered technical seminars on Tandem's relational database management system, NonStop SQL. John wrote his first book, *A Quick Reference Guide to SQL* (Microsoft Press, 1989), as a research project to document the similarities in the syntax among the ANSI-86 SQL Standard, IBM's DB2, Microsoft's SQL Server, Oracle Corporation's Oracle, and Tandem's NonStop SQL. He wrote the first edition of *Running Microsoft® Access* (Microsoft Press, 1992) while on sabbatical from Tandem. He has since written four editions of *Running*, three editions of *Microsoft® Office Access Inside Out* (Microsoft Press, 2003, 2007, and 2010)—the successor to the Running series, and *Building Microsoft® Access Applications* (Microsoft Press, 2005). He is also the best-selling author of *SQL Queries for Mere Mortals®, Third Edition* (Addison-Wesley, 2014). John currently holds the record for the most consecutive years being awarded MVP (Most Valuable Professional) for Microsoft Access from Microsoft, having received the award from 1993 to 2015. John makes his home with his wife of more than 30 years in Paris, France.

Douglas J. Steele has been working with computers, both mainframe and PC, for more than 45 years. (Yes, he did use punch cards in the beginning!) He worked for a large international oil company for more than 31 years before retiring in 2012. Databases and data modeling were a focus for most of that time, although he finished his career by developing the SCCM task sequence to roll Windows 7 out to over 100,000 computers worldwide.

Recognized by Microsoft as an MVP for more than 17 years, Doug has authored numerous articles on Access, was coauthor of *Microsoft® Access® Solutions: Tips, Tricks, and Secrets from Microsoft Access MVPs* (Wiley, 2010), and has been technical editor for a number of books.

Doug holds a master's degree in Systems Design Engineering from the University of Waterloo (Ontario, Canada), where his research centered on designing user interfaces for nontraditional computer users. (Of course, this was in the late seventies, so few people were traditional computer users at the time!) This research stemmed from his background in music (he holds an associateship in piano performance from the Royal Conservatory of Music, Toronto). He is also obsessed with beer and is a graduate of the Brewmaster and Brewery Operations Management program at Niagara College (Niagara-on-the-Lake, Ontario).

Doug lives with his lovely wife of more than 34 years in St. Catharines, Ontario. Doug can be reached at AccessMVPHelp@gmail.com.

Ben G. Clothier is a solution architect with IT Impact, Inc., a premier Access and SQL Server development shop based in Chicago, Illinois. He has worked as a freelance consultant with notable companies including J Street Technology and Advisicon and has worked on Access projects from small, one-person solutions to company-wide line-of-business applications. Notable projects include job tracking and inventory for a cement company, a Medicare insurance plan generator for an insurance provider, and order management for an international shipping company. Ben is an administrator at UtterAccess and was a coauthor, with Teresa Hennig, George Hepworth, and Doug Yudovich, of *Professional Access® 2013 Programming* (Wiley, 2013); a coauthor, with Tim Runcie and George Hepworth, of *Microsoft® Access in a Share-Point World* (Advisicon, 2011); and a contributing author of *Microsoft® Access® 2010 Programmer's Reference* (Wiley, 2010). He holds certifications for Microsoft SQL Server 2012 Solution Associate and MySQL 5.0 Certified Developer among others. He has been a Microsoft MVP since 2009.

Ben lives in San Antonio, Texas, with his wife, Suzanne, and his son, Harry.

About the Technical Editors

Richard Anthony Broersma Jr. is a systems engineer at Mangan, Inc., in Long Beach, California. He has 11 years of experience developing applications with PostgreSQL.

Craig S. Mullins is a data management strategist, researcher, and consultant. He is president and principal consultant of Mullins Consulting, Inc. Craig has been named by IBM as a Gold Consultant and an IBM Champion for Analytics. Craig has over three decades of experience in all facets of database systems development and has worked with DB2 since version 1. You may know Craig from his popular books: *DB2 Developer's Guide, Sixth Edition* (IBM Press, 2012) and *Database Administration: The Complete Guide to DBA Practices and Procedures, Second Edition* (Addison-Wesley, 2012).

Vivek Sharma is currently the designated "technologist" for the Oracle Core Technology and Hybrid Cloud Solutions Division at Oracle Asia Pacific. He has more than 15 years of experience working with Oracle technologies and started his career at Oracle as a developer working extensively on Oracle Forms and Reports before becoming a full-time Oracle DB performance architect. As an Oracle database expert, Vivek spends most of his time helping customers get the best out of their Oracle systems and database investments, and he is a member of the prestigious Oracle Elite Engineering Exchange and Server Technologies Partnership program. Sharma was declared "Speaker of the Year" in 2012 and 2015 by the Oracle India User Group Community. He writes articles on Oracle database technology on his blog, viveklsharma.wordpress.com, and for the Oracle Technology Network at www.oracle.com/technetwork/index.html.

Dave Stokes is a MySQL community manager for Oracle. Previously he was the MySQL certification manager for MySQL AB and Sun. He has worked for companies ranging alphabetically from the

American Heart Association to Xerox and done work ranging from anti-submarine warfare to Web developer.

Morgan Tocker is the product manager for MySQL Server at Oracle. He has previously worked in a variety of roles including support, training, and community. Morgan is based out of Toronto, Canada.

Introduction

Structured Query Language, or SQL, is the standard language for communicating with most database systems. We assume that because you are looking at this book, you have a need to get information from a database system that uses SQL.

This book is targeted at the application developers and junior database administrators (DBAs) who regularly work with SQL as part of their jobs. We assume that you are already familiar with the basic SQL syntax and focus on providing useful tips to get the most out of the SQL language. We have found that the mindset required is quite different from what works for computer programming as we move away from a procedural-based approach to solving problems toward a set-based approach.

A relational database management system (RDBMS) is a software application program you use to create, maintain, modify, and manipulate a relational database. Many RDBMS programs also provide the tools you need to create end-user applications that interact with the data stored in the database. RDBMS programs have continually evolved since their first appearance, and they are becoming more full-featured and powerful as advances occur in hardware technology and operating environments.

A Brief History of SQL

Dr. Edgar F. Codd (1923–2003), an IBM research scientist, first conceived the relational database model in 1969. He was looking into new ways to handle large amounts of data in the late 1960s and began thinking of how to apply mathematical principles to solve the myriad problems he had been encountering.

After Dr. Codd presented the relational database model to the world in 1970, organizations such as universities and research laboratories began efforts to develop a language that could be used as the foundation of a database system that supported the relational model. Initial work led to the development of several different languages in the early to mid-1970s. One such effort occurred at IBM's Santa Teresa Research Laboratory in San Jose, California.

IBM began a major research project in the early 1970s called System/R, intending to prove the viability of the relational model and to gain some experience in designing and implementing a relational database. Their initial endeavors between 1974 and 1975 proved successful, and they managed to produce a minimal prototype of a relational database.

At the same time they were working on developing a relational database, researchers were also working to define a database language. In 1974, Dr. Donald Chamberlin and his colleagues developed Structured English Query Language (SEQUEL), which allowed users to query a relational database using clearly defined English-style sentences. The initial success of their prototype database, SEQUEL-XRM, encouraged Dr. Chamberlin and his staff to continue their research. They revised SEQUEL into SEQUEL/2 between 1976 and 1977, but they had to change the name SEQUEL to SQL (Structured Query Language or SQL Query Language) for legal reasons—someone else had already used the acronym SEQUEL. To this day, many people still pronounce SQL as "sequel," although the widely accepted "official" pronunciation is "ess-cue-el."

Although IBM's System/R and SQL proved that relational databases were feasible, hardware technology at the time was not sufficiently powerful to make the product appealing to businesses.

In 1977 a group of engineers in Menlo Park, California, formed Relational Software, Inc., for the purpose of building a new relational database product based on SQL that they called Oracle. Relational Software shipped its product in 1979, providing the first commercially available RDBMS. One of Oracle's advantages was that it ran on Digital's VAX minicomputers instead of the more expensive IBM mainframes. Relational Software has since been renamed Oracle Corporation and is one of the leading vendors of RDBMS software.

At roughly the same time, Michael Stonebraker, Eugene Wong, and several other professors at the University of California's Berkeley computer laboratories were also researching relational database technology. They developed a prototype relational database that they named Ingres. Ingres included a database language called Query Language (QUEL), which was much more structured than SQL but made less use of English-like statements. However, it became clear that SQL was emerging as the standard database language, so Ingres was eventually converted to an SQL-based RDBMS. Several professors left Berkeley in 1980 to form Relational Technology, Inc., and in 1981 they announced the first commercial version of Ingres. Relational Technology has gone through several transformations. Formerly owned by Computer Associates International, Inc., and now part of Actian, Ingres is still one of the leading database products in the industry today.

Meanwhile, IBM announced its own RDBMS called SQL/Data System (SQL/DS) in 1981 and began shipping it in 1982. In 1983, the company introduced a new RDBMS product called Database 2 (DB2), which could be used on IBM mainframes using IBM's mainstream MVS operating system. First shipped in 1985, DB2 has become IBM's premier RDBMS, and its technology has been incorporated into the entire IBM product line.

With the flurry of activity surrounding the development of database languages, the idea of standardization was tossed about within the database community. However, no consensus or agreement as to who should set the standard or which dialect it should be based upon was ever reached, so each vendor continued to develop and improve its own database product in the hope that it—and, by extension, its dialect of SQL—would become the industry standard.

Customer feedback and demand drove many vendors to include certain elements in their SQL dialects, and in time an unofficial standard emerged. It was a small specification by today's standards, as it encompassed only those elements that were similar across the various SQL dialects. However, this specification (such as it was) did provide database customers with a core set of criteria by which to judge the various database programs on the market, and it also gave users knowledge that they could leverage from one database program to another.

In 1982, the American National Standards Institute (ANSI) responded to the growing need for an official relational database language standard by commissioning its X3 organization's database technical committee, X3H2, to develop a proposal for such a standard. After much effort (which included many improvements to SQL), the committee realized that its new standard had become incompatible with existing major SQL dialects, and the changes made to SQL did not improve it significantly enough to warrant the incompatibilities. As a result, they reverted to what was really just a minimal set of "least common denominator" requirements to which database vendors could conform.

ANSI ratified this standard, "ANSI X3.135-1986 Database Language SQL," which became commonly known as SQL/86, in 1986. In essence, it conferred official status on the elements that were similar among the various SQL dialects and that many database vendors had already implemented. Although the committee was aware of its shortcomings, at least the new standard provided a specific foundation from which the language and its implementations could be developed further.

The International Organization for Standardization (ISO) approved its own document (which corresponded exactly with ANSI SQL/86) as an international standard in 1987 and published it as "ISO 9075:1987 Database Language SQL." (Both standards are still often referred to as just SQL/86.) The international database vendor community could now work from the same standards as vendors in the United States. Despite the fact that SQL gained the status of an official standard, the language was far from being complete.

SQL/86 was soon criticized in public reviews, by the government, and by industry pundits such as C. J. Date for problems such as redundancy within the SQL syntax (there were several ways to define the same query), lack of support for certain relational operators, and lack of referential integrity.

Both ISO and ANSI adopted refined versions of their standards in an attempt to address the criticisms, especially with respect to referential integrity. ISO published "ISO 9075: 1989 Database Language SQL with Integrity Enhancement" in mid-1989, and ANSI adopted its "X3.135-1989 Database Language SQL with Integrity Enhancement," also often referred to as SQL/89, late that same year.

It was generally recognized that SQL/86 and SQL/89 lacked some of the most fundamental features needed for a successful database system. For example, neither standard specified how to make changes to the database structure once it was defined. It was not possible to modify or delete any structural component, or to make changes to the security of the database, despite the fact that all vendors provided ways to do this in their commercial products. (For example, you could CREATE a database object, but no ALTER or DROP syntax was defined.)

Not wanting to provide yet another "least common denominator" standard, both ANSI and ISO continued working on major revisions to SQL that would make it a complete and robust language. The new version (SQL/92) would include features that most major database vendors had already widely implemented, but it also included features that had not yet gained wide acceptance, as well as new features that were substantially beyond those currently implemented.

ANSI and ISO published their new SQL Standards—"X3.135-1992 Database Language SQL" and "ISO/IEC 9075:1992 Database Language

SQL," respectively—in October 1992. The SQL/92 document is considerably larger than the one for SQL/89, but it is also much broader in scope. For example, it provides the means to modify the database structure after it has been defined, supports additional operations for manipulating character strings as well as dates and times, and defines additional security features. SQL/92 was a major step forward from any of its predecessors.

While database vendors worked on implementing the features in SQL/92, they also developed and implemented features of their own, making additions to the SQL Standard known as "extensions." While the extensions (such as providing more data types than the six specified in SQL/92) provided more functionality within a given product and allowed vendors to differentiate themselves from one another, there were drawbacks. The main problem with adding extensions is that it causes each vendor's dialect of SQL to diverge further from the original standard, which prevents database developers from creating portable applications that can be run from any SQL database.

In 1997, ANSI's X3 organization was renamed the National Committee for Information Technology Standards (NCITS), and the technical committee in charge of the SQL Standard is now called ANSI NCITS-H2. Because of the rapidly growing complexity of the SQL Standard, the ANSI and ISO standards committees agreed to break the standard into 12 separate numbered parts and one addendum as they began to work on SQL3 (so named because it is the third major revision of the standard) so that work on each part could proceed in parallel. Since 1997, two additional parts have been defined.

Everything you read in this book is based on the current ISO Standard for the SQL database language—SQL/Foundation (document ISO/IEC 9075-2:2011)—as currently implemented in most of the popular commercial database systems. ANSI also adopted the ISO document, so this is truly an international standard. We also used the documentation from the latest versions of IBM DB2, Microsoft Access, Microsoft SQL Server, MySQL, Oracle, and PostgreSQL to provide, where necessary, syntax specific to each product. Although most of the SQL you will learn here is not specific to any particular software product, we do show you product-specific examples where appropriate.

Database Systems We Considered

Although you saw in the previous section that there are standards for SQL, that is not to say that all DBMSs are the same. The Web site DB-Engines collects and presents information on DBMSs and provides a monthly listing of them, ranked by their current popularity, at http://db-engines.com/en/ranking/relational+dbms.

For many months now, their rankings have presented six DBMSs as consistently the most popular, listed in alphabetical order here (the versions that we used for our testing are in parentheses):

1. IBM DB2 (DB2 for Linux, UNIX, and Windows v10.5.700.368)

2. Microsoft Access (Microsoft Access 2007—also compatible with versions 2010, 2013, 2016, and later)

3. Microsoft SQL Server (Microsoft SQL Server 2012—11.0.5343.0)

4. MySQL (MySQL Community Server 5.7.11)

5. Oracle Database (Oracle Database 11g Express Edition Release 11.2.0.2.0)

6. PostgreSQL (PostgreSQL 9.5.2)

That does not mean that the material presented in this book will not work on a DBMS not in that list of six. It simply means that we have not tested the material on other DBMSs or for different versions of the DBMSs listed. As you read this book, you will see that we have included advice (as Notes) when it is necessary to make changes. Those Notes apply only to the six DBMSs listed here. If you are using a different DBMS, check your documentation for compliance if you run into issues with any of our samples.

Sample Databases

To illustrate the concepts presented in this book, we use a number of sample databases, including the following:

1. **Beer Styles:** This is a fun attempt to catalog the details of 89 different styles of beer, based on the information presented by Michael Larson in his book *Beer: What to Drink Next* (Sterling Epicure, 2014).

2. **Entertainment Agency:** This database is designed to manage entertainers, agents, customers, and bookings. You would use a similar design to handle event bookings or hotel reservations.

3. **Recipes:** You can use this database to save and manage all your favorite recipes, as well as some of our favorites.

4. **Sales Orders:** This is a typical order-entry database for a store that sells bicycles, skateboards, and accessories.

5. **Student Grades:** This database lists students, the courses in which they are enrolled, and their performance in those courses.

We also provide a number of sample databases specific to a particular item, some of which are built by a code listing within the item. The schemas and sample data are available in the GitHub site associated with the book.

Where to Find the Samples on GitHub

Many technical books come with a CD-ROM containing the examples in electronic form. That can be limiting, so we decided to provide our examples in GitHub, at https://github.com/TexanInParis/Effective-SQL.

There, you will find high-level folders for each of the six DBMSs we considered. Within each of those high-level folders are ten folders corresponding to the ten chapters in the book, plus a folder for the sample databases.

Within each of the ten chapter folders, there are individual files, named to correspond to the listing numbers within each chapter. Note that not all listings are applicable to every DBMS. When that is the case, we highlight differences in the README files for each chapter. For Microsoft Access, the README file indicates which sample database contains the listings for the chapter.

The root folder on GitHub also contains the Listings.xlsx file that shows you which database contains each listing. That file also documents SQL samples that are applicable to each of the six database systems.

Each of the sample database folders, with the exception of the Microsoft Access folder that contains .accdb files in 2007 format, contains a number of SQL files. We used the 2007 format for Microsoft Access because it is compatible over all versions of the product since version 12 (2007). One set of these files creates the structure for each sample database, and the other set of files contains the data to populate the sample databases. (Note that some of the items in this book rely on specific data cases. The structures and data for those items are sometimes contained within the chapter listings.)

Note

In preparing the listings in this book for publication, we sometimes had issues fitting within the 63-character-per-line limit imposed by the physical page. It is possible that a listing could have been edited incorrectly. When in doubt, all the listings on GitHub were tested, so we are confident that they are correct.

Summary of the Chapters

As the title of the book suggests, 61 specific items are presented in this book. Each item is intended to stand by itself; you should not need to read other items in order to use the material presented in a specific item. There are, of course, times when the material in a specific item does build on material in other items. When that is the case, we have tried to present as much background material as we felt was necessary, but we do provide cross-references to other relevant items so that you can review the material yourself.

Although each item is, as already stated, intended to stand alone, we felt there were natural groupings of topics. The groupings we used are these ten:

1. **Data Model Design:** Because you cannot write effective SQL when you are working with a bad data model design, the items in this chapter cover some basics of good relational model design. If your database design violates any of the rules discussed in this chapter, you need to figure out what is wrong and fix it.

2. **Programmability and Index Design:** Simply having a good logical data model design is not sufficient to allow you to write effective SQL. You must ensure that you have implemented the design in an appropriate manner, or you may find that your ability to extract meaningful information from the data in an efficient manner using SQL will be compromised. The items in this chapter help you understand the importance of indexes, and how to ensure that they have been properly implemented.

3. **When You Can't Change the Design:** Sometimes, despite your best efforts, you are forced to deal with external data outside of your control. The items in this chapter are intended to help you deal with such situations.

4. **Filtering and Finding Data:** The ability to look for or filter out the data of interest is one of the most important tasks you can do in SQL. The items in this chapter explore different techniques you can use to extract the exact information you want.

5. **Aggregation:** The SQL Standard has always provided the ability to aggregate data. However, typically you are asked to provide "totals per customer," "count of orders by day," or "average sales of each category by month." It is the part after the "per," "by," and "of each" that requires additional attention. The items in this chapter present techniques to get the best performance out of your aggregation. Some of them also show how to use window functions to provide even more complex aggregations.

6. **Subqueries:** There are many different ways in which you can use subqueries. The items in this chapter are intended to show a variety of ways to get additional flexibility in your SQL through the use of subqueries.

7. **Getting and Analyzing Metadata:** Sometimes just data is not enough. You need data about data. You might even need data about how you are getting the data. In some cases, it might even be convenient to get the metadata using SQL. The items in this chapter tend to be quite product specific, but our hope is that we provide sufficient information so that you can apply the principles to your specific DBMS.

8. **Cartesian Products:** Cartesian Products are the result of combining all rows in one table with all rows in a second table. While perhaps not as common as other join types, the items in this chapter show real-world situations where it would not be possible to answer the underlying question without the use of a Cartesian Product.

9. **Tally Tables:** Another useful tool is the tally table, usually a table with a single column of sequential numbers, or a single column of sequential dates, or something more complex to aid in "pivoting" a set of summaries. While Cartesian Products are dependent on actual values in the underlying tables, tally tables allow you to cover all possibilities. The items in this chapter show examples of various problems that can be solved only through the use of a tally table.

10. **Modeling Hierarchical Data:** It is not uncommon to have to model hierarchical data in your relational database. Unfortunately, it happens to be one of SQL's weaker areas. The items in this chapter are intended to help you make the trade-off between data normalization, and ease of querying and maintenance of metadata.

Each database system has a variety of functions that you can use to calculate or manipulate date and time values. Each database system also has its own rules regarding data types and date and time arithmetic. Because of the differences, we also included an Appendix, "Date and Time Types, Operations, and Functions," to help you work with date and time values in your database system. We believe it accurately summarizes the data types and arithmetic operations supported, but we do recommend that you consult your database documentation for the specific syntax to use with each function.

Data Model Design

"You can't make a silk purse out of a sow's ear." This famous saying, attributed to English satirist Stephen Gosson in 1579, certainly applies to databases. You cannot begin to write "effective" SQL when you're working with a bad data model design. When your data model is not properly normalized with correct relationships defined, you will find it difficult, if not impossible, to extract meaningful information from the data using SQL. This chapter covers the basics of good relational model design. If your database design violates any of the rules discussed here, you need to figure out what is wrong and fix it.

If the design is not under your control, you will at least gain the understanding of why you are having such difficulty so that you can explain potential remedies to those who do have design control. You can use the information in this chapter to explain why it will be difficult or impossible to write the SQL that you have been asked to create to retrieve the information required. If you can't fix the design, there are a few things you can do in SQL to get around some of the problems. If that is the situation you face, read on to Chapter 3, "When You Can't Change the Design," to gather additional insights.

We do not try to cover all the nuances of database design, just the basics. If you want a deeper understanding of how to create a design that adheres to the relational model, get your hands on a good design book such as *Database Design for Mere Mortals, Third Edition*, by Michael J. Hernandez (Addison-Wesley, 2013).

Item 1: Verify That All Tables Have a Primary Key

Because adherence to the relational model requires that your database system be able to distinguish a single row of a table from all other rows, every table should have a column or set of columns as the primary key. The contents of a primary key must be unique for each row and cannot be null. (Refer to Item 10, "Factor in nulls when creating indexes," for more detail on nulls.) Without a primary key, it is impossible to ensure that you will match either exactly zero rows or one row when filtering. However, the "gotcha" is that it is legal to create a table without a primary key. In fact, simply having a column or set of columns that are not null and are unique across the rows does not mean that the database engine will be able to use the column(s) efficiently. You must explicitly tell the database engine about it by defining a primary key on one or more columns. Furthermore, it is not typically possible (or desirable) to model relationships between tables without a primary key defined.

When tables lack primary keys, all kinds of problems can ensue, including repeated and inconsistent data, slow-running queries, and inaccurate information in reports! Consider the example with an Orders table shown in Figure 1.1.

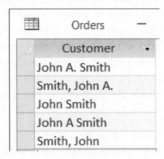

Figure 1.1 Example of inconsistent data

In Figure 1.1, all the values are certainly unique from a computer perspective, but it might be the case that they are all the same person, or at least rows 1, 2, and 4 (variations on John A. Smith) are the same. Although computers can process data much faster than any human brain, they are not very good at determining when certain data should be considered the same without a significant amount of programming. So even though we can define the Customer column as a primary key of the table, it does not follow that it is a good choice even though it has satisfied the uniqueness requirement.

So, what makes a good candidate for a primary key? The column(s) considered should have the following characteristics:

- Must hold unique values

- Can never be null

- Should be stable (i.e., there is no need to ever update the value)

- Should be as simple as possible (e.g., use an integer data type rather than floating point or character, and prefer a single column over multiple columns)

A common method of achieving this goal is to use an automatically generated meaningless numeric data value as a primary key. This has various names, depending on the relational database management system (RDBMS) software that you are using, such as IDENTITY in IBM DB2, Microsoft SQL Server, and Oracle 12c, AutoNumber in Microsoft Access, AUTO_INCREMENT in MySQL, and serial in PostgreSQL. In prior versions of Oracle, it was necessary to use a Sequence object to perform a similar service, but it was a stand-alone object rather than a column attribute. DB2, SQL Server, and PostgreSQL also support Sequence objects.

Referential integrity (RI) is a very important concept in relational databases. Enforced RI means there must be a matching record in a parent table for every record in a child table with a non-null foreign key.

In a well-designed Orders table, the customer information would come from a foreign key to a separate Customers table using the primary key of that table. If there are actually multiple different customers named John Smith, each customer row will have its own unique key, and it will be easy to identify the unique customer for each order.

In order to maintain RI between tables, any changes in the value of a primary key must be cascaded to all related child records in the related table(s). This cascading of updates causes locks to be placed on related tables, which can lead to serious problems in high-concurrency multi-user databases. Consider the example shown in Figure 1.2, taken from the Customers table of the sample Northwind database provided with Microsoft Access 2003.

	CustomerID	CompanyName	ContactName	ContactTitle
1	ALFKI	Alfreds Futterkiste	Maria Anders	Sales Representative
2	ANATR	Ana Trujillo Emparedados y helados	Ana Trujillo	Owner
3	ANTON	Antonio Moreno Taquería	Antonio Moreno	Owner
4	AROUT	Around the Horn	Thomas Hardy	Sales Representative
5	BERGS	Berglunds snabbköp	Christina Berglund	Order Administrator
6	BLAUS	Blauer See Delikatessen	Hanna Moos	Sales Representative

Figure 1.2 Sample data from the Customers table

In this example, we assume that it is a business rule that the text-based primary key, CustomerID, is related to the name of the company. If one of the companies were to change its name, the CustomerID should be updated to reflect the business rules for determining the key value. This would require cascading the change to related tables. If you use a meaningless key, you avoid the need to change or update its value, but you can still keep the text-based column to provide a display value that adheres to the business rule.

A common argument in favor of text-based primary keys is that they prevent the entry of duplicate values. For example, if you were to make CompanyName the primary key, you would ensure that there could be no duplicate names. However, it is just as easy to create a unique index on the CompanyName column in the Customers table to ensure that there can be no duplicate names. Integrity is ensured, but you can still use a generated numeric value as the primary key. This works especially well if you also adopt the advice in Item 2, "Eliminate redundant storage of data items," and Item 4, "Store only one property per column," which will help you avoid the problem we highlighted with Figure 1.1. On the other hand, it is true that using text-based primary keys often results in simpler SQL statements by avoiding the joins required to lookup tables to obtain the values associated with numeric keys (CompanyName, in the example in Figure 1.2).

The choice of numeric versus text-based primary keys has been known to cause great debate among database professionals. We do not take sides in this argument; the important point is to use a unique identifier in all tables that can be used as a primary key.

We also advise against using compound primary keys because they are less efficient, for two reasons:

1. When you define a primary key, most database systems enforce the definition with a unique index. A unique index on more than one column requires the database system to do more work.

2. Performing a join on a primary key is quite common, but doing so on multiple columns in a primary key is more complex and slower.

However, using a primary key that contains multiple columns can make sense in certain cases. Consider a table that links products and vendors where the table consists of a VendorID and a ProductID that point to the primary keys in the related tables. The table might contain other columns, such as an indicator of whether the vendor is the primary or secondary supplier for the product, and the price the vendor charges for the product.

You could create an additional generated numeric column to act as the artificial primary key, but you could also use the combination of the VendorID and ProductID columns as the primary key. You will always link to this table by the individual columns, so it is perhaps more efficient to define the compound primary key rather than use an additional column as the key. You will want to define the two columns together as unique, so it makes sense to avoid the additional column and define both as a compound primary key. Refer to Item 8, "When 3NF is not enough, normalize more," for an in-depth example where a compound primary key can be advantageous.

Things to Remember

✦ All tables should have a column (or set of columns) designated as a primary key.

✦ If you are concerned about duplicate values in a non-key column, you can define a unique index on the column to ensure integrity.

✦ Use as simple a key as possible, with values that do not need to be updated.

Item 2: Eliminate Redundant Storage of Data Items

Redundant storage of data causes many problems, including inconsistent data; insert, update, and delete anomalies; and wasted disk space. Normalization is a process that involves dividing information by subject to help eliminate problems associated with storing duplicate data. Note that by "redundant" we do not mean the apparent duplication of a primary key value from one table as a foreign key in another table. We are more concerned with cases where users enter the same piece of data in more than one place. Such redundancy is necessary to maintain the relational link between tables.

Although we cannot go into too much depth on the topic of database normalization because of space constraints, it is very important that people working with databases have a thorough understanding of this subject. There are many excellent resources available in books and on the Web that go into greater detail.

One goal of normalization is to minimize the need to repeat data, either in the same table or in different tables throughout a database. A few examples of the redundant storage of data are shown in the Customer Sales database shown Figure 1.3 on the next page.

An example of inconsistent data is the address for customer Tom Frank. In the second record, the numeric portion of his address is 7453, whereas in the sixth record, the numeric portion is 7435. Similar inconsistencies in data could be present in any of the columns.

An insertion anomaly is present because you cannot enter information for a given model of automobile until you have a sale that is entered with a customer record. Also, the design requires repeating most data when a customer purchases additional cars. This represents unnecessary data entry that is wasteful of disk space, memory, network resources, and even the time spent by a data entry clerk. In addition, repeating data entry greatly increases the risk of data entry errors, such as transposing numbers in an address as shown in the example in Figure 1.3.

CustomerSales						
SalesID ▾	CustFirstName ▾	CustLastName ▾	Address ▾	City ▾	Phone ▾	
1	Amy	Bacock	111 Dover Lane	Chicago	312-222-1111	...
2	Tom	Frank	7453 NE 20th St.	Bellevue	425-888-9999	...
3	Debra	Smith	3223 SE 12th Pl.	Seattle	206-333-4444	...
4	Barney	Killjoy	4655 Rainier Ave.	Auburn	253-111-2222	...
5	Homer	Tyler	1287 Grady Way	Renton	425-777-8888	...
6	Tom	Frank	7435 NE 20th St.	Bellevue	425-888-9999	...

▾	PurchaseDate ▾	ModelYear ▾	Model ▾	SalesPerson ▾
...	2/14/2016	2016	Mercedes R231	Mariam Castro
...	3/15/2016	2016	Land Rover	Donald Ash
...	1/20/2016	2016	Toyota Camry	Bill Baker
...	12/22/2015	2016	Subaru Outback	Bill Baker
...	11/10/2015	2016	Ford Mustang GT Convertible	Mariam Castro
...	5/25/2015	2015	Cadillac CT6 Sedan	Jessica Robin

Figure 1.3 Example of redundant storage of data in a single table

An update anomaly exists because if, for example, a salesperson gets married and changes his or her name, you would need to run an update query to update all occurrences of the person's name. This can present real challenges if you are dealing with a large number of records in a database that many people use concurrently. In addition, such an update will be successful only if all occurrences of the person's name are spelled exactly the same (meaning no inconsistent data) and if more than one person does not share the name.

A deletion anomaly exists because if a row is deleted, you may lose data you did not intend to remove from your database.

The customer sales data shown in Figure 1.3 can logically be divided into four tables:

1. Customers table (name, address, etc.)
2. Employees table (salesperson name, hire date, etc.)
3. AutomobileModels table (model year, model, etc.)
4. SalesTransactions table

This design allows you to enter customer, employee, and automobile model information once into the respective tables. All tables include a unique identifier that can be set as a primary key. The SalesTransactions table uses foreign keys to store the details of each sales transaction. See Figure 1.4.

Customers

CustomerID ▾	CustFirstName ▾	CustLastName ▾	Address ▾	City ▾	Phone ▾
1	Amy	Bacock	111 Dover Lane	Chicago	312-222-1111
2	Tom	Frank	7453 NE 20th St.	Bellevue	425-888-9999
3	Debra	Smith	3223 SE 12th Pl.	Seattle	206-333-4444
4	Barney	Killjoy	4655 Rainier Ave.	Auburn	253-111-2222
5	Homer	Tyler	1287 Grady Way	Renton	425-777-8888

Employees

EmployeeID ▾	SalesPerson ▾
1	Mariam Castro
2	Donald Ash
3	Bill Baker
4	Jessica Robin

AutomobileModels

ModelID ▾	ModelYear ▾	Model ▾
1	2016	Mercedes R231
2	2016	Land Rover
3	2016	Toyota Camry
4	2016	Subaru Outback
5	2016	Ford Mustang GT Convertible
6	2015	Cadillac CT6 Sedan

SalesTransactions

SalesID ▾	CustomerID ▾	ModelID ▾	SalesPersonID ▾	PurchaseDate ▾
1	1	1	1	2/14/2016
2	2	2	2	3/15/2016
3	3	3	3	1/20/2016
4	4	4	3	12/22/2015
5	5	5	1	11/10/2015
6	2	6	4	5/25/2015

Figure 1.4 Example of splitting data into tables by subject

The astute reader may have noticed that one duplicate customer record was eliminated in this process as a result of determining the correct address for customer Tom Frank.

We can create relationships (sometimes referred to as foreign key constraints) by joining the primary key from the three parent tables (Customers, AutomobileModels, and Employees) to the foreign key columns in the SalesTransactions child table, as shown in Figure 1.5 on the next page. We created the example shown in the figure using the relationships editor in Microsoft Access. Each relational database has a different way of representing relationships between tables.

You can easily re-create the original data, shown earlier in Figure 1.3, by constructing a virtual table (query) as shown in Listing 1.1 on the next page without the penalties imposed by storing redundant data. (Construction of the virtual table is a perfect use for a CTE, or common table expression, as discussed in Item 42, "If possible, use common table expressions instead of subqueries.")

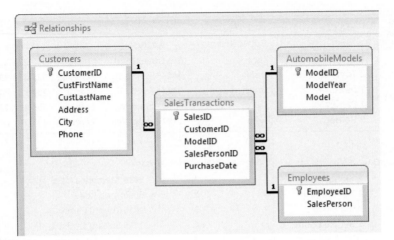

Figure 1.5 Four tables that have been related using primary keys joined to foreign key columns

Listing 1.1 An SQL statement that returns the original data

```
SELECT st.SalesID, c.CustFirstName, c.CustLastName, c.Address,
  c.City, c.Phone, st.PurchaseDate, m.ModelYear, m.Model,
  e.SalesPerson
FROM SalesTransactions st
  INNER JOIN Customers c
    ON c.CustomerID = st.CustomerID
  INNER JOIN Employees e
    ON e.EmployeeID = st.SalesPersonID
  INNER JOIN AutomobileModels m
    ON m.ModelID = st.ModelID;
```

Things to Remember

✦ A goal of database normalization is the elimination of redundant data and minimizing resource use when processing data.

✦ By eliminating redundant data, you eliminate insert, update, and delete anomalies.

✦ By eliminating redundant data, you minimize the occurrence of inconsistent data.

References

If you want to explore the correct ways to design a relational database, here are a couple of books we recommend; the first one is accessible to beginners and a good place for the novice to start:

◆ Hernandez, Michael J. *Database Design for Mere Mortals* (Addison-Wesley, 2013). ISBN-10: 0-321-88449-3.

◆ Fleming, Candace C., and Barbara von Halle. *Handbook of Relational Database Design* (Addison-Wesley, 1989). ISBN-10: 0-201-11434-8.

Item 3: Get Rid of Repeating Groups

It is common to see spreadsheets that include repeating groups of similar data. Often information workers simply import this data into a new database without any consideration of database normalization. An example of repeating groups of data is shown in Figure 1.6, with a DrawingNumber being associated with up to five Predecessors. The table has a one-to-many relationship between drawing numbers and predecessor values.

ID	DrawingNumber	Predecessor_1	Predecessor_2	Predecessor_3	Predecessor_4	Predecessor_5
1	LO542B2130	LS01847409	LS02390811	LS02390813	LS02390817	LS02390819
2	LO426C2133	LS02388410	LS02495236	LS02485238	LS02495241	LS02640008
3	LO329W2843-1	LS02388418	LS02640036	LS02388418		
4	LO873W1842-1	LS02388419	LS02741454	LS02741456	LS02769388	
5	LO690W1906-1	LS02742130				
6	LO217W1855-1	LS02388421	LS02769390			

Figure 1.6 Repeating groups of data in a single table

The example in Figure 1.6 shows a single attribute, Predecessor, as a repeating group. We also have a duplicate Predecessor value, for ID = 3, which was not intended. Another example could be columns named January, February, March (or Jan, Feb, Mar), and so on. However, repeating groups are not limited to single attributes. For example, if you were to see columns named Quantity1, ItemDescription1, Price1, Quantity2, ItemDescription2, Price2 . . . QuantityN, ItemDescriptionN, PriceN, you should recognize them as a repeating group pattern.

Repeating groups are difficult to query and create reports grouped by the attributes. In the example in Figure 1.6, if you later had a need to add Predecessor values or reduce the number of allowed Predecessors, the current design would require adding or removing table columns. You would also need to modify the design of all queries (views), forms, and reports that depend on the data in this table. A useful mnemonic to remember is:

> Columns are expensive.

> Rows are cheap.

A red flag should be raised in your mind if the table design requires adding or removing columns to accommodate future data requirements with similar data. A much better design involves adding or removing rows as needed. For this example, we create a Predecessors table that uses the ID value as a foreign key. For clarity, we also rename the existing ID column DrawingID, as shown in Figure 1.7.

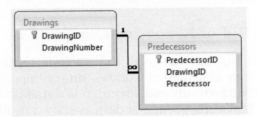

Figure 1.7 A normalized design that accommodates the one-to-many relationship

UNION queries are useful for dealing with repeating groups. We can use a UNION query to "normalize" our data in a read-only view if we do not have the ability to create a properly normalized design. We can also use a similar UNION query as the source for an append query to add records to a new Predecessors table, as shown in Listing 1.2.

Listing 1.2 A UNION query that normalizes the data

```
SELECT ID AS DrawingID, Predecessor_1 AS Predecessor
FROM Assignments WHERE Predecessor_1 IS NOT NULL
UNION
SELECT ID AS DrawingID, Predecessor_2 AS Predecessor
FROM Assignments WHERE Predecessor_2 IS NOT NULL
UNION
SELECT ID AS DrawingID, Predecessor_3 AS Predecessor
FROM Assignments WHERE Predecessor_3 IS NOT NULL
UNION
SELECT ID AS DrawingID, Predecessor_4 AS Predecessor
FROM Assignments WHERE Predecessor_4 IS NOT NULL
UNION
SELECT ID AS DrawingID, Predecessor_5 AS Predecessor
FROM Assignments WHERE Predecessor_5 IS NOT NULL
ORDER BY DrawingID, Predecessor;
```

Note

If we had a case where we needed to bring all the data together, including duplicates within a row, we could add the ALL keyword after each occurrence of the UNION keyword, as in UNION ALL. However, in this case we really do want to eliminate the duplicate Predecessor that was inadvertently entered for ID 3.

A UNION query requires that the columns be of the same data type, and in the same order, for each SELECT statement. This means that it is really not necessary to include AS DrawingID or AS Predecessor after the first instance: the UNION query takes its column names from the first SELECT.

Each SELECT statement can have different predicates for its WHERE clause. Depending on the data, we may also have to exclude zero-length strings (ZLSs) and/or other nonprintable formats, such as a single space (' ').

A UNION query can use a single ORDER BY clause at the end. We can specify the ordinal references, as in ORDER BY 1, 2. This would be the same as ORDER BY DrawingID, Predecessor in Listing 1.2.

Things to Remember

+ A goal of database normalization is the elimination of repeating groups of data and minimizing the schema change.

+ By eliminating repeating groups of data, you can use indexing to prevent accidental duplication of data, and you greatly simplify any queries needed.

+ Removing repeating groups of data makes the design more flexible because adding a new group simply requires adding another row of data, not changing the table design to add more columns.

Item 4: Store Only One Property per Column

In relational terminology, a relation (table) should describe one and only one subject or action. Attributes (columns) contain the data pertaining to one and only one property (often referred to as "atomic" data) that describes the subject defined by the relation. An attribute can also be a foreign key containing an attribute from another relation, and this foreign key provides the relationship to some tuple (row) in another relation.

It is not a good idea to store more than one property value in a single column because that makes it difficult to isolate that property value when performing searches or aggregating values. Fundamentally, you should consider putting important individual properties in their own columns. You can see an example of a table containing multiple properties in columns in Table 1.1 on the next page. (By the way, those are real addresses in the sample data, but not the actual addresses of the named authors.)

Table 1.1 A table containing multiple attributes in several columns

AuthID	AuthName	AuthAddress
1	John L. Viescas	144 Boulevard Saint-Germain, 75006, Paris, France
2	Douglas J. Steele	555 Sherbourne St., Toronto, ON M4X 1W6, Canada
3	Ben Clothier	2015 Monterey St., San Antonio, TX 78207, USA
4	Tom Wickerath	2317 185th Place NE, Redmond, WA 98052, USA

A table like this has several problems:

- It is difficult if not impossible to search on last name. Assuming the table contains more than just the four sample rows, and you want to search for someone with a last name of Smith, a LIKE search using wildcards may also return Smithson or Blacksmith.

- You can search for first name, but you have to use the less efficient LIKE or pull out the name as a substring. A LIKE with a trailing wildcard may be processed efficiently, but because the name might have a salutation (such as Mr.), you have to use a leading wildcard to ensure that you find the name you want, and that will cause a data scan.

- You cannot easily search for street name, city, state/province, or postal code.

- When attempting to group the data (perhaps joined with another table that lists assigned chapters and page counts), it is tough to extract the state/province, postal code, or country to do the grouping.

You are more likely to see data like this when you have imported information from an external data source such as a spreadsheet. But it is also not uncommon to find such a badly designed table in a production database.

A more correct solution would be to create a table similar to that shown in Listing 1.3.

Listing 1.3 SQL to create an Authors table with the attributes separated

```
CREATE TABLE Authors (
  AuthorID int IDENTITY (1,1),
  AuthFirst varchar(20),
  AuthMid varchar(15),
  AuthLast varchar(30),
  AuthStNum varchar(6),
  AuthStreet varchar(40),
  AuthCity varchar(30),
  AuthStProv varchar(2),
  AuthPostal varchar(10),
  AuthCountry varchar(35)
);

INSERT INTO Authors (AuthFirst, AuthMid, AuthLast, AuthStNum,
    AuthStreet, AuthCity, AuthStProv, AuthPostal, AuthCountry)
  VALUES ('John', 'L.', 'Viescas', '144',
    'Boulevard Saint-Germain', 'Paris', ' ', '75006', 'France');

INSERT INTO Authors (AuthFirst, AuthMid, AuthLast, AuthStNum,
    AuthStreet, AuthCity, AuthStProv, AuthPostal, AuthCountry)
  VALUES ('Douglas', 'J.', 'Steele', '555',
    'Sherbourne St.', 'Toronto', 'ON', 'M4X 1W6', 'Canada');

--  ... additional rows.
```

Note that we have used a character data type for street number because it is common for a street "number" to also include letters or other characters. For example, some street numbers include ½. In France, street numbers often contain the characters *bis* attached to a number. The same consideration applies to postal codes that are numeric in the United States but include letters and spaces in places like Canada and the United Kingdom.

Using the suggested table design, the data can now be split into one attribute per column as shown in Table 1.2 on the next page.

Now it is simple to perform searches or groupings on any one or more of the individual properties because there is only one property per column.

If you need to recombine the properties, to create a mailing list, for example, it is a simple matter of using concatenation in SQL to get back the original data. Listing 1.4 on the next page shows one way to do it.

Table 1.2 A properly designed Authors table with one attribute per column

AuthID	AuthFirst	AuthMid	AuthLast	AuthStNum	AuthStreet	...
1	John	L.	Viescas	144	Boulevard Saint-Germain	...
2	Douglas	J.	Steele	555	Sherbourne St.	...
3	Ben		Clothier	2015	Monterey St.	...
4	Tom		Wickerath	2317	185th Place NE	...

...	AuthCity	AuthStProv	AuthPostal	AuthCountry
...	Paris		75006	France
...	Toronto	ON	M4X 1W6	Canada
...	San Antonio	TX	78207	USA
...	Redmond	WA	98052	USA

Listing 1.4 Reassembling the original data using concatenation in SQL

```
SELECT AuthorID AS AuthID, CONCAT(AuthFirst,
  CASE
    WHEN AuthMid IS NULL
    THEN ' '
    ELSE CONCAT(' ', AuthMid, ' ')
  END, AuthLast) AS AuthName,
  CONCAT(AuthStNum, ' ', AuthStreet, ' ',
      AuthCity, ', ', AuthStProv, ' ',
      AuthPostal, ', ', AuthCountry)
    AS AuthAddress
FROM Authors;
```

Note

IBM DB2, Microsoft SQL Server, MySQL, Oracle, and PostgreSQL all support the CONCAT() function; however, DB2 and Oracle accept only two arguments, so you must nest CONCAT() functions to concatenate multiple strings. The ISO Standard defines only the operator || to perform concatenation. DB2, Oracle, and PostgreSQL accept the || concatenation operator, and MySQL accepts it if the server sql_mode includes PIPES_AS_CONCAT. In SQL Server, you can use + as a concatenation operator. Microsoft Access does not support the CONCAT() function, but you can concatenate strings using either & or +.

We earlier noted that Listing 1.3 is one of several possible "more correct" designs, and you might be wondering why we recommend separating the street number from the rest of the street address. In truth, in most applications, including the street number with the street name will work just fine. You must carefully consider the needs of your application. For a land survey database, separating the street number from the street name (and perhaps the designation as to "street," or "avenue," or "boulevard") could be crucial. In some other applications, it may be important to separate the country code, area code, and local phone number parts of a phone number. You need to decide what parts are important enough to dictate a finer granularity when identifying attributes.

It is clear that separating properties into individual columns makes it easy to perform searches or groupings on the individual bits of data. It is also simple to reassemble those pieces when needed for a report or a printed list.

Things to Remember

+ Correct table design assigns each individual property to its own column, because when a column contains multiple properties, searching and grouping become difficult if not impossible.

+ For some applications, the need to filter the parts in columns such as address or phone number may dictate the level of granularity.

+ When you need to reassemble properties for a report or a printed listing, use concatenation.

Item 5: Understand Why Storing Calculated Data Is Usually a Bad Idea

You might sometimes be tempted to store calculated data, especially when the calculation depends on data in a related table. Consider the example in Listing 1.5.

Listing 1.5 Sample table definition SQL

```
CREATE TABLE Orders (
  OrderNumber int NOT NULL,
  OrderDate date NULL,
  ShipDate date NULL,
  CustomerID int NULL,
  EmployeeID int NULL,
  OrderTotal decimal(15,2) NULL
);
```

At first glance, including the `OrderTotal` in the `Orders` table (presumably the sum of `Quantity` * `Price` from the related `Order_Details` table) seems like a good idea because it won't be necessary to fetch the related rows and perform the calculation each time you want all the orders and the amount due. The type of calculated field might be fine in a data warehouse but could have significant performance impact in an active database. (See also Item 9, "Use denormalization for information warehouses.") You may find it difficult to maintain data integrity because you must be sure to recalculate the value each time any related `Order_Details` row is changed, inserted, or deleted.

The good news is that many modern database systems provide a way to maintain such a field so that code running on the server performs the calculation for you. The most primitive way to ensure that a calculated column remains current is to attach a trigger to the table containing the source columns for the calculation. A trigger is code you write that runs when the target table is inserted, updated, or deleted. In the example in Listing 1.5, you would need a trigger on the `Order_Details` table to recalculate the `OrderTotal` column value. But triggers can be expensive and difficult to write correctly. (See also Item 13, "Don't go overboard with triggers.")

Potentially better than triggers, several database systems give you a method for defining a calculated column when you create the table. We say this is better than triggers because defining the calculated column as part of the table definition can avoid the complex code often required in a trigger. Several RDBMSs, especially in more recent versions, already support defining a calculated column. For instance, Microsoft SQL Server gives you the AS keyword followed by an expression that defines the computation you require. When the calculation uses only columns from the same table, you can simply write the expression on the other columns as the definition of the calculated column. If the calculation depends on values in a related table, some systems allow you to write a function to perform the calculation, then call that function in the AS clause you use to define the column when you create or alter the target table. Listing 1.6 shows a sample function and table definition using Microsoft SQL Server. Note that because the function depends on data from another table, it is nondeterministic, so you cannot build an index on the calculated field.

Deterministic versus Nondeterministic

A deterministic function is one that always returns the same result any time it is called with a specific set of input values. A nondeterministic function may return different results each time it is called with a

specific set of input values. For instance, the SQL Server DATEADD()
built-in function is deterministic because it always returns the same
result for any given set of values for its three parameters, whereas
GETDATE() is nondeterministic because it is always invoked with the
same argument, yet the value it returns can change each time it is executed. (This assumes that the three parameters for DATEADD() are also
deterministic. For example, you cannot use GETDATE() as one of the
parameters.) See the Appendix, "Date and Time Types, Operations,
and Functions," for details about date and time functions provided by
your database system.

Listing 1.6 Sample function and table definition SQL for Microsoft
SQL Server

```
CREATE FUNCTION dbo.getOrderTotal(@orderId int)
RETURNS money
AS
BEGIN
  DECLARE @r money
  SELECT @r = SUM(Quantity * Price)
  FROM Order_Details WHERE OrderNumber = @orderId
  RETURN @r;
END;
GO
CREATE TABLE Orders (
  OrderNumber int NOT NULL,
  OrderDate date NULL,
  ShipDate date NULL,
  CustomerID int NULL,
  EmployeeID int NULL,
  OrderTotal money AS dbo.getOrderTotal(OrderNumber)
);
```

It is actually a very bad idea to do it this way. Because the function is
nondeterministic, the column cannot be PERSISTED as a real column
in the table. You cannot build an index on the column, and you will
encounter lots of server overhead anytime you reference that column
because the server must call the function for each and every row. It
would be much more efficient to join the table with a subquery that
does the calculation grouped on the OrderID column any time you
need the result.

In IBM DB2, there is a similar facility, but the keyword is GENERATED.
However, DB2 absolutely disallows creating a calculated column on

a function that calls a query—again, because it makes the function nondeterministic. You can, however, define a column using a function call or expression that is deterministic. Listing 1.7 shows how to define an expression that calculates quantity times price to return an extended price value to create a column in the Order_Details table.

Listing 1.7 Sample table column definition SQL using an expression for DB2

```
-- Turn off integrity so we can change the table
SET INTEGRITY FOR Order_Details OFF;
-- Create the calculated column using an expression
ALTER TABLE Order_Details
  ADD COLUMN ExtendedPrice decimal(15,2)
    GENERATED ALWAYS AS (QuantityOrdered * QuotedPrice);
-- Turn integrity back on
SET INTEGRITY FOR Order_Details
IMMEDIATE CHECKED FORCE GENERATED;
-- Index the calculated column
CREATE INDEX Order_Details_ExtendedPrice
  ON Order_Details (ExtendedPrice);
```

Because the expression is now deterministic, you can create the column on the table and index it. Listing 1.7 shows an example for DB2, but we have included examples for other database systems in the listing files (as Listing 1.007 on GitHub at https://github.com/TexanInParis/Effective-SQL).

If you want to have a calculated column in Oracle (called a "virtual column"), use GENERATED [ALWAYS] AS. The SQL to create the ExtendedPrice column in the Order_Details table in Oracle might look like Listing 1.8.

Listing 1.8 Sample table definition SQL with inline expression for Oracle

```
CREATE TABLE Order_Details (
  OrderNumber int NOT NULL,
  OrderNumber int NOT NULL,
  ProductNumber int NOT NULL,
  QuotedPrice decimal(15,2) DEFAULT 0 NULL,
  QuantityOrdered smallint DEFAULT 0 NULL,
  ExtendedPrice decimal(15,2)
    GENERATED ALWAYS AS (QuotedPrice * QuantityOrdered)
);
```

At this point you are probably wondering why the title of this item is "Understand why storing calculated data is usually a bad idea" when we have just gone to great lengths to show you how to do it. Now for the bad news: if this table is meant to be used in a high-volume online data entry system, adding a calculated column like this may result in significant overhead on the server that can negatively affect response times.

If you are using IBM DB2, Microsoft SQL Server, or Oracle, you may also be able to define an index on the calculated column, which will generally help queries that depend on the calculated results to perform faster. Remember that you won't be able to create an index on the example from Listing 1.6 in SQL Server (nor could you for other database systems) because it is nondeterministic—it depends on a lookup to another table in the database. (See also Item 17, "Know when to use calculated results in indexes.")

With SQL Server, you must take the additional step of specifying the PERSISTED keyword on the expression, whereas with DB2, it is persisted automatically once you create an index on the expression.

In the case of Listing 1.7, the overhead occurs whenever the value of the called function might change—whenever you update, insert, or delete a row in Order_Details. Someone sitting at a terminal entering many order items may experience unacceptable response times because the function must be executed to calculate and store the value for the index. In Listing 1.6 or Listing 1.8, the overhead occurs every time you fetch that column from the Orders table, so response times may be unacceptable when performing a SELECT that includes the calculated column and asks for many rows.

Things to Remember

+ Many systems let you define calculated columns when you define your table, but you need to be aware of the performance implications, particularly when using nondeterministic expressions or functions.

+ You can also define calculated columns as regular columns and then maintain them with triggers, but the code to do so may be complex.

+ Calculated columns cause additional overhead in your database system, so use them only when the benefits outweigh the costs.

+ Most of the time, you will want to create an index on the calculated columns to reap some benefits in exchange for increased storage and slower updates.

+ Using views to define calculations is often a desirable alternative to actually storing calculations on a table for cases where indexing does not apply.

Item 6: Define Foreign Keys to Protect Referential Integrity

When you design a database schema correctly, you have foreign keys in many of your tables that contain the primary key value of the related parent table. For example, the Orders table in a Sales Orders database should have a CustomerID or CustomerNumber column that points to the related primary key of the Customers table so that you can identify the customer who placed each specific order.

Figure 1.8 shows a possible layout for a "typical" Sales Orders database.

Note

Figure 1.8 was created using the diagramming tool in Microsoft SQL Server Management Studio. Similar tools exist in DB2, MySQL, Oracle, and Microsoft Access, and in modeling tools such as Erwin and Idera ER/Studio.

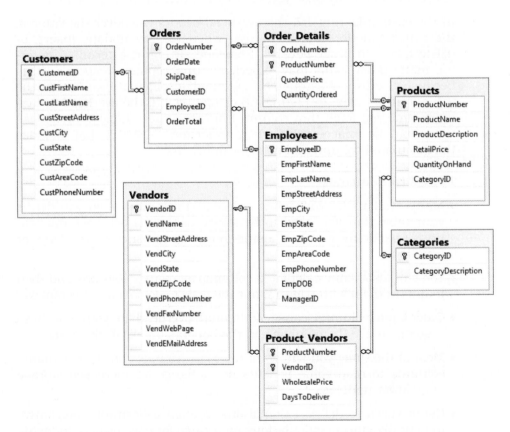

Figure 1.8 Table design for a typical Sales Orders database

The diagram clearly shows the relationships among the various tables. The key symbol on one end of each relationship line indicates that the relationship is from the primary key of one table, and the infinity symbol on the other end of the line indicates a "many" relationship to a foreign key in the second table.

The database system knows the relationships between the tables because we defined Declarative Referential Integrity (DRI) constraints. These relationship definitions serve two purposes:

1. The graphical query designer for the database knows how to correctly construct JOIN clauses when you use the designer to create a new view or stored procedure.

2. The database system knows how to enforce data integrity when inserting or changing a table on the "many" side of a relationship or changing or deleting a table on the "one" side of a relationship.

It is the second point that is most important because you need to ensure that, for example, no Orders rows can be created that contain an invalid or missing CustomerID. If it is possible to change the CustomerID in the Customers table, you want to be sure that the value propagates (specified with the keyword ON UPDATE CASCADE) to all related Orders rows. And if a user attempts to delete a Customers row that has related rows in the Orders table, you want to ensure that either the deletion of the customer row is disallowed, or that all related rows in the Orders table are also deleted (specified with ON DELETE CASCADE).

To enable this important feature in your database system, you need to add a FOREIGN KEY constraint either when you define a "many" table using CREATE TABLE, or by adding the constraint after the fact using ALTER TABLE. Let's look at how to do this on the Customers and Orders tables.

First, let's create the Customers table. Listing 1.9 shows how.

Listing 1.9 Creating a Customers table

```
CREATE TABLE Customers (
   CustomerID int NOT NULL PRIMARY KEY,
   CustFirstName varchar(25) NULL,
   CustLastName varchar(25) NULL,
   CustStreetAddress varchar(50) NULL,
   CustCity varchar(30) NULL,
   CustState varchar(2) NULL,
   CustZipCode varchar(10) NULL,
   CustAreaCode smallint NULL DEFAULT 0,
   CustPhoneNumber varchar(8) NULL
);
```

Next, let's create the Orders table and then execute an ALTER TABLE to define the relationship. Listing 1.10 shows how.

Listing 1.10 Creating an Orders table and then altering it to define the relationship

```
CREATE TABLE Orders (
  OrderNumber int NOT NULL PRIMARY KEY,
  OrderDate date NULL,
  ShipDate date NULL,
  CustomerID int NOT NULL DEFAULT 0,
  EmployeeID int NULL DEFAULT 0,
  OrderTotal decimal(15,2) NULL DEFAULT 0
);

ALTER TABLE Orders
  ADD CONSTRAINT Orders_FK99
    FOREIGN KEY (CustomerID)
      REFERENCES Customers (CustomerID);
```

Note that if you first create the two tables, add data to both of them, and then decide to add the FOREIGN KEY constraint, your attempt to alter the Orders table might fail if data in the tables fails the referential integrity check. In some database systems it might succeed, but the constraint may be considered untrusted and thus not used by the optimizer, so simply having it defined is not necessarily a guarantee that it has been enforced for data that existed prior to the constraint's creation.

You can also define the constraint when you create the child table. Listing 1.11 shows how.

Listing 1.11 Defining a FOREIGN KEY constraint when you create a table

```
CREATE TABLE Orders (
  OrderNumber int NOT NULL PRIMARY KEY,
  OrderDate date NULL,
  ShipDate date NULL,
  CustomerID int NOT NULL DEFAULT 0
    CONSTRAINT Orders_FK98 FOREIGN KEY
      REFERENCES Customers (CustomerID),
  EmployeeID int NULL DEFAULT 0,
  OrderTotal decimal(15,2) NULL DEFAULT 0
);
```

On some database systems (notably Microsoft Access), defining a referential integrity constraint automatically creates an index on the foreign key column(s), so there may be an added performance benefit when performing a join. For those database systems that do not automatically create an index on a foreign key (such as DB2), it is good practice to create an index to optimize constraint checking.

Things to Remember

+ Making foreign keys explicit helps ensure data integrity between related tables by ensuring that no child row exists without a matching parent row.

+ Attempting to add a FOREIGN KEY constraint to tables that contain data will fail if data exists that violates the constraint.

+ In some systems, the performance of joins may be improved because defining a FOREIGN KEY constraint automatically builds indexes. On other systems, you must take care to create an index to cover the FOREIGN KEY constraint. Even without indexes, some systems' optimizer may treat a column differently and produce better query plans.

Item 7: Be Sure Your Table Relationships Make Sense

You can, in theory, create any relationship you want between two tables as long as the data types of each pair of related columns are the same. But just because you *can* do something does not mean you *should*. Consider the schema diagram of a database containing sales order information in Figure 1.9 on the next page.

At first glance it seems to make sense; there are several tables, each of which contains a single subject. Let's focus on three of the tables: Employees, Customers, and Vendors. If you study those three tables, you will see that they have lots of similar fields. Many times this is not perceived to be a problem because the data in the three tables is usually distinct.

But if this company could have vendors or employees who are also the customers of the company, this model violates the rules against duplicating data discussed earlier in Item 2, "Eliminate redundant storage of data items." Some might try to solve this conundrum by creating a single table, perhaps called Contacts, which then enumerates all kinds of contacts. However, this is not without problems. For one thing, EmployeeID, CustomerID, and VendorID now would all come from a single primary key ContactID that gives us no way to validate that this ID is in fact a bona fide vendor who happens to be a customer occasionally.

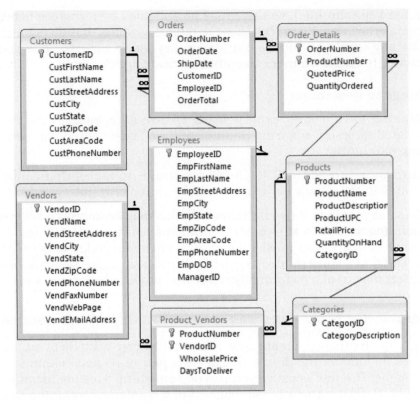

Figure 1.9 Schema diagram of a Sales Orders database

Some might solve this problem by adding Customers, Vendors, and Employees tables that contain a one-to-one relationship to the Contacts table. This has the benefit of easily keeping entity-specific data such as ManagerID or VendWebPage separate from other customer rows that need neither field. However, this means that the application using the database schema is now much more complicated because it must have the logic in place to verify whether an entity exists, and if so, whether it has the required domain-specific data filled out. After all, these extra tables would be for nothing if the application were permitted to blindly insert new records without searching for duplicates first. Understandably, not all companies want to spend more money and time for additional complexity. It is more typical that a company selling products usually does not have customers who are also vendors or employees, so occasional duplication in such rare situations is a small price to pay for simplification of the database schema.

Let's consider the scenario where we need to assign sales territories to employees and consequently map customers to employees based on those territories. One way to do this would be to create a relationship between the CustZipCode column in the Customers table and the EmpZipCode column in the Employees table. Both are the same data type and in the same domain. Instead of creating a relationship between the tables, you could perhaps do a join on the ZIP code columns in Employees and Customers to discover which customers live close to which employees.

Although it is possible to simply create a foreign key EmployeeID in the Customers table and thus relate the customer to an employee, this actually creates more problems. For one thing, suppose the customer moves to another sales territory? The data entry clerk might correctly update the customer's address but not realize or remember that the assigned employee needs to be updated for that customer, introducing a new source of errors.

It would be better to have a table called SalesTerritory that has a foreign key of EmployeeID, and the rows in the table would identify the ZIP codes (TerrZIP) assigned to that employee. Each ZIP code would be unique within the SalesTerritory table because you would not want to assign a ZIP code to more than one employee. It would then be valid to create a relationship from TerrZIP to the Customers table so that an employee could discover which customers are in his or her territory.

In contrast, if employees were assigned to customers according to some criterion other than the sales territory, having a foreign key EmployeeID in the Customers table might actually be a better choice to reflect the more arbitrary nature of the customer-employee assignment. This still works even if the sales territory is the default assignment, but the customers have the liberty of asking for some other employee. Like the previous example, this approach necessarily implies that there will be appropriate programming to help minimize data entry errors.

A similar problem exists when the company needs to list all products it sells but also provide detailed data on each product and all of its attributes. It might make sense for a lumber company to have a product table that has columns for linear feet, height, width, and wood types. After all, the company sells lumber. But when the company is a retail store selling a wide variety of products, adding several columns that are very sparsely used looks like a bad deal. Nor would we want to create one table for each product category so that we could store all the category-specific data. In this situation, some might find it preferable to create an Attribute column that accepts an XML or JSON document. This might be fine when no business rules dictate the ability to expose a product's attributes in the relational table. But in the event that it is necessary to be able to query on any attributes, creating a `ProductAttributes` table and thus transforming the columns into rows and relating them to a product in the `Products` table would achieve the goal.[1] Listing 1.12 illustrates a possible design for the tables.

Listing 1.12 Creating a relationship between the `Products` and `ProductAttributes` tables

```
CREATE TABLE Products (
  ProductNumber int NOT NULL PRIMARY KEY,
  ProdDescription varchar(255) NOT NULL
);

CREATE TABLE ProductAttributes (
  ProductNumber int NOT NULL,
  AttributeName varchar(255) NOT NULL,
  AttributeValue varchar(255) NOT NULL,
  CONSTRAINT PK_ProductAttributes
    PRIMARY KEY (ProductNumber, AttributeName)
);

ALTER TABLE ProductAttributes
  ADD CONSTRAINT FK_ProductAttributes_ProductNumber
    FOREIGN KEY (ProductNumber)
      REFERENCES Products (ProductNumber);
```

Although it would appear that we have solved the problem by storing the attributes as rows rather than columns, the queries to extract certain products with certain attributes are now much more complicated, especially if we need to work across multiple attributes.

Incidentally, the attributes problem illustrates the need for designers to be able to differentiate structured data from semistructured data. In a relational model, the data must be well defined up front, having all possible columns and data types enumerated before we can add any actual data. This is in contrast to semistructured data such as XML or JSON documents, where documents do not necessarily need to have identical schema, even at the level of a record. So if you find yourself struggling with defining the relationships, it might be worthwhile to ask whether you are, in fact, dealing with semistructured data and whether you really need to have it exposed directly in the relational model. The SQL Standards now cover using XML and JSON directly in SQL, which gives you even more options, but that discussion is beyond the scope of this book.

---

1. This is often referred to as the "entity-attribute-value" or EAV model.

The preceding discussion should illustrate the point that it is the business that dictates whether a data model is correct, and you need to factor in the application's design. This is often a challenge because people are more likely to allow the application to drive the data model design when it should actually be the other way around. In reality, choosing one data model over another usually entails significant changes in how one should design the applications that will use the database. These changes can influence the costs and time to market for the application.

Things to Remember

✦ Carefully examine whether it really makes sense to combine tables that appear to contain similar columns in order to simplify relationships.

✦ You can create a join between columns in two tables as long as the data types match (or can be implicitly casted), but a relationship is valid only if the columns are in the same domain. However, it is optimal to have the same data types on both sides of the join.

✦ Check whether you are in fact dealing with structured data before including it in your data model. If the data is semistructured, make the necessary provisions.

✦ It is usually helpful to clearly identify the goals of a data model to help you assess whether a given design justifies the added complexity or anomalies due to simplifications and the design of the applications using the data model.

Item 8: When 3NF Is Not Enough, Normalize More

A common myth is the idea that third normal form is usually sufficient for most applications. Many practitioners have heard and quoted that "3NF is usually enough," or maybe "Normalize until it hurts, then denormalize until it works." The problem with those pithy sayings is that they imply that higher normal forms require more modifications to achieve, but in fact it is more that for most data models, an entity that is already in third normal form likely already satisfies the higher normal forms. In fact, many reference tables in many databases today are already in 5NF or even 6NF, though people call it 3NF. Therefore, one actually needs to look for cases where a table is in third normal form but violates the higher normal forms. That is a rare subset, but it does happen, and when it does happen, it is very easy to make design mistakes that generate data anomalies even though the table seems to have satisfied the third normal form.

A warning flag that a design is in 3NF but could violate the higher normal forms is when a table is related to more than one other table. This is especially the case if it participates in more than one many-to-many relationship. Another sign is when a table contains composite keys that could violate the higher normal forms. Be wary when you are using surrogate keys and instead analyze the natural keys, as the later examples will make clearer.

As a quick reminder, the first three normal forms (as well as Boyce-Codd normal form) concern themselves with the functional dependency among a relation's attributes. By functional dependency, we mean that the attribute is dependent on the key of the relation. For example, a column storing a phone number that contains "466.315.0072" can be said to be functionally dependent on the column storing "Douglas J. Steele," as in asserting that this phone number belongs to him, and other attributes do not influence the association of that phone number to that person. If the phone number depended on some other attributes that are not a key, we are subject to data anomalies.

With the fourth normal form, we are now concerned with multivalued dependency. This deals with cases where two attributes are independent of each other but both depend on the same key of the relation. This then creates a number of possible combinations between two attributes. There is a special case where we could violate the fourth normal form. Consider products that a salesperson may sell in Table 1.3.

Table 1.3 A table containing products sold by salespeople

Salesperson	Manufacturer	Product
Jay Ajurap	Acme	Slicer
Jay Ajurap	Acme	Dicer
Jay Ajurap	Ace	Dicer
Jay Ajurap	Ace	Whomper
Sheila Nyu	A-Z Inc.	Slicer
Sheila Nyu	A-Z Inc.	Whomper

What is not implied from the table is the fact that each manufacturer produces only two products, and that the salesperson who carries a manufacturer must sell all products made by that manufacturer. Therefore, if Sheila decided to start selling Ace, we would need to insert two rows, one for Ace's Dicer product and another for

Ace's Whomper product. That can allow for data anomalies if we do not update the table properly. Therefore, to avoid this possibility, we should decompose the table into the tables illustrated in Figure 1.10.

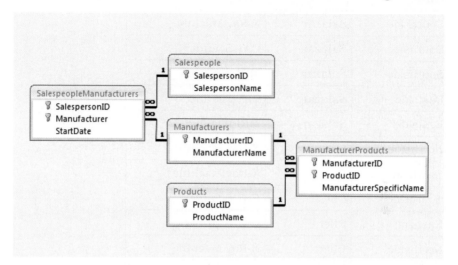

Figure 1.10 Schema diagram of a salesperson's inventory database

With this model, we only need to list all products that any salesperson might sell. We then map it to manufacturers that actually manufacture those products. We then infer the products a given salesperson actually sells by joining SalespeopleManufacturers with ManufacturerProducts to get back the same result as in Table 1.3. It is important to note that we are following a business rule that a salesperson must sell all products that a manufacturer produces. But in the real world, it is more likely that a salesperson sells only a subset of products produced by a manufacturer. In that case, the data in Table 1.3 no longer violates the fourth normal form. That illustrates the point why higher normal forms are rare; most business rules we have in place cause a data model to satisfy higher normal forms already.

The fifth normal form requires that the candidate keys imply all join dependencies. Consider the non-normalized data in Table 1.4 on the next page that lists offices, equipment, and doctors.

In this data model, we need to schedule doctors to offices where they can perform work on particular equipment. We assume that the doctors are trained on the equipment, so it makes no sense to send doctors to an office without any equipment that they are qualified to use. But not all doctors receive the same training; some might be relatively new, or might specialize a bit differently, so not all share the same set of skills.

Table 1.4 A table containing multiple attributes in several columns

Office	Doctor	Equipment
Southside	Salazar	X-Ray Machine
Southside	Salazar	CAT Scanner
Southside	Salazar	MRI Imaging
Eastside	Salazar	CAT Scanner
Eastside	Salazar	MRI Imaging
Northside	Salazar	X-Ray Machine
Southside	Chen	X-Ray Machine
Southside	Chen	CAT Scanner
Eastside	Chen	CAT Scanner
Northside	Chen	X-Ray Machine
Southside	Smith	MRI Imaging
Eastside	Smith	MRI Imaging

So, we have office locations, and we have equipment. Those overlap but are quite independent; an office having a particular piece of equipment has nothing to do with whether a doctor is trained to use that equipment. A possible attempt is to set up a data model with six tables, illustrated in Figure 1.11.

Note that there are three base tables—Doctors, Equipment, and Offices—and then there is a junction table for each possible pair: DoctorEquipment for {Doctors, Equipment}, OfficeEquipment for {Offices, Equipment}, and DoctorSchedule for {Doctors, Offices} with the Equipment implied. Therefore, if a new office opens or an existing office adds new equipment, or a doctor's training changes, all these factors are independent and do not create anomalies between each pair. However, we are at risk of creating anomalies with the DoctorSchedule table. It is possible to create a pair of doctor and office where either the doctor lacks the required training on the equipment or the office lacks the equipment. That is problematic and thus breaks the fifth normal form. To remedy this, we need to set up the data model as shown in Figure 1.12.

Note that the DoctorSchedule table has two foreign keys that partially overlap on the EquipmentID column. Those two FOREIGN KEY constraints

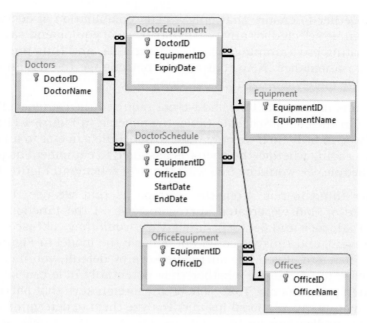

Figure 1.11 Schema diagram of a doctor/equipment/office scheduling database

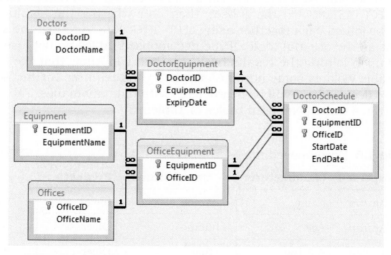

Figure 1.12 Improved schema diagram of a doctor/equipment/office scheduling database

work together to ensure that only a valid combination of doctor and office can be selected for any particular piece of equipment, saving us from writing programming logic to enforce this, and thus preventing any data anomalies. Note that we did not change the design of the tables. We merely changed the relationships.

Again, it is noteworthy that had we not required the EquipmentID as a column in the DoctorSchedule table, the schema in Figure 1.11 would already be in 5NF. So if we only want to schedule a doctor to an office, without saying whether the doctor is assigned to equipment as part of the schedule, we would be fine with the first schema in Figure 1.11.

Another thing to note from the example is that we use the composite keys. Had we created surrogate keys in the junction tables OfficeEquipment and DoctorTraining, they would have obfuscated the EquipmentID, and thus we could not achieve the model in Figure 1.12 at all. Therefore, if you use surrogate keys by default, you must take extra care to investigate whether they potentially hide crucial information in your schema. Take note of any foreign keys that participate in many-to-many relationships and analyze them to determine if they hold any implications for the relationships.

Lossless decomposition is a method you can use to analyze violations of higher normal forms. Whenever you have a large table, you should decompose a subset of columns, as though you had performed a SELECT DISTINCT on the subset, then note whether the results can then be joined back together using LEFT OUTER JOIN to return the same result as the original table. If the decomposed tables do not lose any data upon joining the results back together, you know that the original table violates some normal form and thus requires further scrutiny to decide if you will have problems with data anomalies. Table 1.5 illustrates the decomposed tables of Table 1.3.

Table 1.5 Decomposed tables from Table 1.3

Salesperson	Manufacturer
Jay Ajurap	Acme
Jay Ajurap	Ace
Sheila Nyu	A-Z Inc.

Manufacturer	Product
Acme	Slicer
Acme	Dicer
Ace	Dicer
Ace	Whomper
A-Z Inc.	Slicer
A-Z Inc.	Whomper

If you then go back to the examples we used to illustrate violations of 4NF and 5NF, you can see that if we were to take out one row from Table 1.3, the join between the `SalespeopleManufacturers` and `ManufacturerProducts` tables is now "lossy," because the join of tables in Table 1.5 won't match the modified Table 1.3. In that case the modified Table 1.3 no longer violates 4NF. Similarly, if `EquipmentID` was not a column in the `DoctorSchedule` table, we would have losses once again, and thus 5NF is not violated.[2] Note that the analysis assumes we have enough data within the tables for decomposing to properly determine if losses will occur or not.

Things to Remember

+ Higher normal forms are likely to be already achieved in most data models. Therefore, you need to watch for cases where higher normal forms are explicitly violated. It is more likely for tables that have composite keys or participate in several many-to-many relationships.

+ Fourth normal form can be violated by the special case where all possible combinations of two unrelated attributes on an entity must be enumerated for that entity.

+ Fifth normal form deals with ensuring that all join dependencies are implied by candidate keys, meaning that you should be able to constrain what are valid values for a candidate key based on the individual elements. This can happen only if the key is composite.

+ Sixth normal form deals with reducing the relations to only one non-key attribute generally, thus resulting in an explosion of tables, but enabling us to never need to define a nullable column.

+ Testing for lossless decomposition can be an effective tool for detecting if your table violates higher normal forms.

Item 9: Use Denormalization for Information Warehouses

As developers, we have the importance of normalized databases being constantly driven home to us. Normalized tables are usually smaller and have a smaller footprint than non-normalized ones. Because the data is divided among many tables, performance is usually better because the tables are small enough to fit into the buffer. Because the data is located in a single place, updates and inserts are fast.

---

2. In fact, if all fields in the schema shown in Figure 1.12 are not nullable, it is already in 6NF.

Because the data is not duplicated, there is less need for heavy-duty GROUP BY or DISTINCT queries.

However, these arguments hold because applications are usually write intensive, so the write load is more than the read load. For information warehouses, though, such is not the case: there may be no write load at all between the data loads, but even when there is, it is usually far less than the read load. A concern with fully normalized tables is that normalized data means joins between tables. The more joins there are, the more difficult it is for the optimizer to find the best possible execution plan, which can hurt the performance of reads.

Denormalized databases work well under heavy read loads, because the data is present in fewer tables and the need for joins lessens or entirely disappears, thus resulting in faster selects. A single table with all the required data also allows for much more efficient index usage. If the columns are indexed properly, results can be filtered and sorted quickly using those indexes without reading the wide table directly. Also, because writes are infrequent, there is no concern about too many indexes dramatically affecting write performance. You can, if necessary, index every column in the table to dramatically improve search and sort performance.

In order to effectively denormalize, you must have a good understanding of the data and how it will typically be accessed.

One of the easiest types of denormalization is to replicate identity fields in tables to avoid a join. For instance, a normalized database might have the EmployeeID column as a foreign key in the Customers table in order to be able to link customers to their account managers. If there is a need to report invoices together with account manager data, you need to join three tables—Invoices, Customers, and Employees. However, you can achieve the same goal if you replicate the EmployeeID column in the Invoices table. Now, you need to join only the Invoices and Employees tables. Of course, there would be no benefit to doing this if you also needed data from the Customers table.

You can take this sort of denormalization one step further. For example, if you know that many searches in the data warehouse will involve looking for invoice information by customer name, it can be beneficial to store not only the CustomerID but also the name in the Invoices table and then index the name. Yes, this violates normalization rules because you will be keeping information about multiple subjects (invoices and customers) in one table, and you will be repeating the customer name information in many rows. But the main purpose of a data warehouse is to make finding information easy and rapid. Avoiding the join to get the customer name information can save a ton of valuable resources.

Another common approach is to add indicative fields to other tables. Not only can this result in better performance, but it can also help with maintaining history. A fully normalized schema usually shows only the current state. The current customer's address is kept in the Customers table. If the customer moves, the address is changed to the new one. This can make it impossible to print exact copies of invoices at a later date unless you maintain history about the customer's address. However, if you keep a copy of the customer's address information at the time of invoicing on the Invoices table, it becomes straightforward.

Storing calculated or derived values is another common denormalization. Storing a total amount in the Invoices table, rather than totaling each relevant row in the InvoiceDetails table, not only reduces the number of tables that must be queried but eliminates the need for repeated calculations. Another advantage of storing computed values is when there are multiple possible ways of performing a given calculation. When the value is stored in the table, all queries against the database result in the same calculation.

Yet another possibility relates to the use of repeating groups. If a common requirement is to compare month-to-month performance, storing all 12 months in a single row reduces the number of rows that need to be retrieved.

Remember that there are varying requirements for how the data in an information warehouse is sliced and diced. Data warehouse expert Ralph Kimball describes the three most important themes of data warehouses as drilling down, drilling across, and handling time.[3] He talks of "fact tables" as being "the fundamental measurements of the enterprise" and "the ultimate target of most data warehouse queries" but is quick to point out that they are of little use "unless they have been chosen to reflect urgent business priorities, have been carefully quality assured and are surrounded by dimensions that provide a wealth of entry points for constraining and grouping."[4]

He describes three types of fact tables as follows:

1. Transaction fact tables, which correspond to measurements taken at a single instant

2. Periodic snapshot fact tables, which summarize activity during or at the end of a predefined span of time, such as a financial reporting period

---

3. www.kimballgroup.com/2003/03/the-soul-of-the-data-warehouse-part-one-drilling-down/
4. www.kimballgroup.com/2008/11/fact-tables/

3. Accumulating snapshot fact tables, which report predictable pro-
cesses with well-defined beginnings and ends, such as order
processing, claims processing, service call resolution, and college
admissions

Another key concept that Kimball introduced is that of slowly changing dimensions. As he put it, most of the fundamental measurements
stored in fact tables include timestamps and foreign keys connecting
to calendar date dimensions, but there are more effects of time than
just activity-based timestamps. All of the other dimensions that connect to fact tables, including fundamental entities such as customer,
product, service, terms, location, and employee, are also affected by
the passage of time. Sometimes the revised description merely cor-
rects an error in the data, but it can also represent a true change
at a point in time of the description of a particular dimension member, such as a customer or product. Because these changes occur far
less frequently than fact table measurements, they are referred to as
slowly changing dimensions (SCDs).[5] Understanding these concepts
is critical for designing efficient and effective data warehouses.

If you decide to denormalize your data, document your denormalization thoroughly. Describe, in detail, the logic behind the denormalization and the steps that you took. Then, if your organization ever
needs to normalize the data in the future, an accurate record is available for those who must do the work.

Things to Remember

✦ Decide what data to duplicate and why.

✦ Plan how to keep the data in sync.

✦ Refactor the queries to use the denormalized fields.

---

5. www.kimballgroup.com/2008/08/slowly-changing-dimensions/

Programmability and Index Design

You cannot assume that merely having a good logical data model design will allow you to write effective SQL. You must ensure that your design is physically implemented in an appropriate manner, or you may find that your ability to extract meaningful information from the data in an efficient manner using SQL will be compromised.

One of the key elements to ensure that your SQL queries perform well is proper indexing of the tables. The items in this chapter help you understand some of the often-overlooked considerations when implementing your correctly designed data model. Although creation of the tables and indexes is often left to database administrators (DBAs), it turns out that indexing is probably best done by the developers. DBAs are knowledgeable about storage system configuration and hardware setup, but creating proper indexes requires knowledge about what queries will be run against the data. That knowledge usually is not very accessible to DBAs or external consultants, but it should be readily available to the application developers. The items in this chapter help you understand the importance of indexes, and how to ensure that they have been properly implemented.

As was the case in Chapter 1, "Data Model Design," if you have control over the implementation of your database, you can review your model with regard to the items in this chapter and fix any problems you discover. If you do not have control of the design, you can use the information in the items in this chapter to provide information to the DBAs to allow them to help build your database effectively.

Item 10: Factor in Nulls When Creating Indexes

A null is a special value in a relational database that indicates "unknown" or the absence of data in a column. A null can never be equal to or not equal to another value, not even another null. To detect the presence of a null value, you must use the special IS NULL predicate.

You will typically create an index on a column or combination of columns that you reference frequently in predicates so that the performance of those queries is improved. When you index a column, you need to consider whether the column contains null values and understand how your database system treats null values in indexes.

If most of the rows in your database contain a null value in a column that is indexed, that index is probably not of much use unless you always search for something other than NULL. That index may take up an unreasonable amount of storage unless your database system offers a way to exclude null values from indexes. Some database systems treat empty strings as nulls (the system changes any empty string supplied as a column value into NULL), so that makes your decision about whether to index a column or not more difficult.

Each database system has different ways to handle null values in an index. The one feature that is common to all the major database systems is that none of them allow a null value in any column in a primary key. That is a requirement of the ISO SQL Standard, so that is a good thing. The following sections explore the issues relative to each database system and how each handles null values and zero-length strings in indexes.

IBM DB2

In all indexes other than the primary key, DB2 does index null values. You can explicitly eliminate null values in a UNIQUE index by specifying the EXCLUDE NULL KEYS option when you create the index. Listing 2.1 shows an example.

Listing 2.1 Excluding null values in a UNIQUE index in DB2

```
CREATE UNIQUE INDEX ProductUPC_IDX
  ON Products (ProductUPC ASC)
  EXCLUDE NULL KEYS;
```

For the purposes of indexing, DB2 considers all null values to be equal. Therefore, if you do not specify WHERE NOT NULL on a UNIQUE index, you will get a duplicate error if you attempt to insert more than one row that has a null value in the indexed column. The second row with a null value will be considered a duplicate of the existing entry, and duplicates are not allowed in a UNIQUE index.

For a nonunique index in DB2, you can specify to not index null values by adding the EXCLUDE NULL KEYS option. This may be particularly useful when you know a majority of the values may be NULL, so any predicate that tests for IS NULL may do a full table scan anyway instead of relying on the index. Eliminating null values requires less space in your database for the index. Listing 2.2 shows how.

Listing 2.2 Excluding null values in a standard index in DB2

```
CREATE INDEX CustPhone_IDX
  ON Customers(CustPhoneNumber)
  EXCLUDE NULL KEYS;
```

DB2 does not treat empty strings in VARCHAR and CHAR columns as though they are null values. However, if you enable the option in your DB2 installation (Linux, UNIX, and Windows, or LUW) to run with Oracle compatibility, storing an empty string in a VARCHAR column will result in a null value. See the section "Oracle" later in this item for more details.

Microsoft Access

Microsoft Access does index null values. Because a primary key cannot contain null values, you cannot store a NULL in a primary key column. You can direct Access to not store null values in an index when you set the Ignore Nulls property of the index. Figure 2.1 shows where to do that in the user interface (UI) to define indexes. The figure also shows where you can set the Unique and Primary properties.

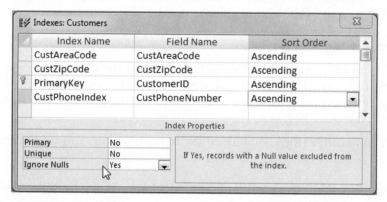

Figure 2.1 The Primary, Unique, and Ignore Nulls options on an index in the UI of Access

You can also execute a CREATE INDEX query and set the Ignore Nulls property by using WITH IGNORE NULL. Listing 2.3 on the next page shows the syntax to do this.

Listing 2.3 Setting IGNORE NULL in Access when creating an index using SQL

```
CREATE INDEX CustPhoneIndex
  ON Customers (CustPhoneNumber)
  WITH IGNORE NULL;
```

You can also specify WITH DISALLOW NULL (an option not available in the UI except by setting the Required property of the column to Yes) to forbid null values in the index.

Access treats all null values as not equal, so it is possible to store multiple rows with a NULL in a UNIQUE indexed column. One quirk in Access is that it discards all trailing blanks in any column with a data type of Text (which is the same as VARCHAR). If you attempt to store an empty string via the graphical interface, Access stores a NULL. If you try to store an empty string in a column in a primary key, you will get an error.

Likewise, you will get an error if you try to store an empty string in a column that has the Required property set to Yes. You can avoid this behavior by also setting the Allow Zero Length property of the column to Yes. When you do that, Access will not convert blank or empty strings to NULL, but you have to specifically insert the string in either SQL or the user interface with a pair of double quotes. When you insert an empty string into a column that has Allow Zero Length set to Yes, the length of the column value will be 0.

Microsoft SQL Server

Similar to DB2, SQL Server does index null values and considers null values to be equal. You cannot store a NULL in any column in a primary key, and you can store only one row with a null value in a column in a UNIQUE key.

To exclude null values from an index in SQL Server, you must create a filtered index. Listing 2.4 shows an example.

Listing 2.4 Excluding null values in a filtered index in SQL Server

```
CREATE INDEX CustPhone_IDX
  ON Customers(CustPhoneNumber)
  WHERE CustPhoneNumber IS NOT NULL;
```

Note that if you include an IS NULL predicate in a query on the CustPhoneNumber column, SQL Server will not use the filtered index to perform the search. SQL Server does not convert empty VARCHAR strings to NULL. In the example of a filtered index shown in Listing 2.4, columns containing an empty string will appear in the index.

MySQL

MySQL does not allow null values in primary key columns. It does, however, consider null values to be unequal when creating an index, so it is permissible to store multiple rows having a column with a null value and a UNIQUE index on that column.

MySQL indexes null values, and there is no option to eliminate them. MySQL uses an available index for the IS NULL and IS NOT NULL predicates.

MySQL does not turn an empty string into NULL. The length of NULL is NULL. The length of an empty string is 0.

Oracle

Oracle does not index null values, and it does not allow null values in any primary key columns. It indexes the value of a compound key (a key with multiple columns) if at least one of the columns is not NULL.

You can force Oracle to provide an index for null values by either forcing it to create a compound key with a literal constant as one of the columns or using a function-based index that can deal with NULL. Listing 2.5 shows how to force a literal value into a compound index with a column that could have null values.

Listing 2.5 Forcing Oracle to index null values with an artificial compound key

```
CREATE INDEX CustPhone_IDX
  ON Customers (CustPhoneNumber ASC, 1);
```

You can also index null values by using the NVL() function to convert all null values to something else. Listing 2.6 shows how.

Listing 2.6 Indexing null values by converting them

```
CREATE INDEX CustPhone_IDX
  ON Customers (NVL(CustPhoneNumber, 'unknown'));
```

The drawback to using NVL() to build the index is that you must use the function if you want to test for a null value, for example, WHERE NVL(CustPhoneNumber, 'unknown') = 'unknown'.

Similarly to Microsoft Access, Oracle considers zero-length VARCHAR strings to be the same as NULL. If you assign an empty string to a CHAR column, it will contain blanks and not be null. There is no option in Oracle (as there is in Access) to allow empty strings in a column that is the VARCHAR data type. Like Microsoft Access, Oracle treats null values as not equal, and it considers zero-length VARCHAR strings to be the same as NULL.

PostgreSQL

PostgreSQL does not allow nulls within a primary key. Like MySQL and Microsoft Access, it treats null values as being unequal. Therefore, you can create a UNIQUE index and insert several null values into the column covered by the UNIQUE index.

PostgreSQL includes null values in the index, but you can exclude them by defining a WHERE predicate as shown in Listing 2.7.

Listing 2.7 Excluding nulls from an index in PostgreSQL

```
CREATE INDEX CustPhone_IDX
  ON Customers(CustPhoneNumber)
  WHERE CustPhoneNumber IS NOT NULL;
```

Similarly to SQL Server, PostgreSQL does not convert a zero-length string to NULL or vice versa and considers the two things to be different.

Things to Remember

✦ Consider whether a column you want to index will contain null values.

✦ If you want to search for null values, but the majority of values in the column are likely to be NULL, it is better not to index the column. It may be also an indication that redesign of the table may be warranted.

✦ When you want to be able to search for values on a column more quickly, but the majority of the values will be NULL, build the index without null values if your database supports it.

✦ Every database system supports null values in indexes differently. Be sure you understand the options for your database system before considering building an index on a column that may contain null values.

Item 11:   Carefully Consider Creation of Indexes to Minimize Index and Data Scanning

Although throwing more hardware at the problem can be a way to improve performance, usually you can get a greater benefit for less money from tuning your queries. A common problem is the lack of indexes or having incorrect indexes, which can result in the database engine having to process more data to find the records that meet the query criteria. These issues are known as *index scans* and *table scans*.

An index scan or table scan occurs when the database engine has to scan the index or data pages to find the appropriate records, as opposed to a seek, where an index is used to pinpoint the records that are needed to satisfy the query. The more data that exists, the more time index scans can take to complete.

Consider the table given in Listing 2.8.

Listing 2.8 Table creation SQL

```
CREATE TABLE Customers (
  CustomerID int PRIMARY KEY NOT NULL,
  CustFirstName varchar(25) NULL,
  CustLastName varchar(25) NULL,
  CustStreetAddress varchar(50) NULL,
  CustCity varchar(30) NULL,
  CustState varchar(2) NULL,
  CustZipCode varchar(10) NULL,
  CustAreaCode smallint NULL,
  CustPhoneNumber varchar(8) NULL
);

CREATE INDEX CustState ON Customers(CustState);
```

Note that we created two indexes on the table. Because CustomerID is declared as PRIMARY KEY, an index is created on that column, and in addition the CREATE INDEX statement creates one on the CustPhoneNumber column.

Now, if we run the query SELECT * FROM Customers WHERE CustomerID = 1, this should do a unique index seek of the primary key, then enter the table from the index to return everything in the Customers table for CustomerID = 1.

If, instead, the query was simply SELECT CustomerID FROM Customers WHERE CustomerID = 25, because all the needed values are contained within the index, there is no need for the second stage and the query would solely do a unique index seek without consulting the table's data.

Next, let's examine the query SELECT * FROM Customers WHERE CustState = 'TX'. Although we built an index on the CustState column in Listing 2.8, it is not unique. This means it is necessary to look through the entire index to try to find all values that match the WHERE condition—an index scan. Because we are selecting columns that are not in the index, it is also necessary to go back to the table data to get those values.

Finally, if the query was SELECT CustomerID FROM Customers WHERE CustAreaCode = '905', and there is no index on CustAreaCode, it is necessary to do a table scan to find the value, because the database engine has to look at every row to find anything in the table where CustAreaCode = '905'.

There might not seem to be much difference between a table scan and an index scan in many instances, because it is necessary to search through all entries in an object to find a particular value. However, the index is usually much smaller and specially designed to be scanned, so it is generally much faster to do an index scan if you want only a small proportion of the rows in the table. If you want, say, 33% of the table, the index may not provide any benefit. Note that this is not a hard-and-fast number; some database engines might have a lower or higher threshold where scanning would be faster.

In fact, there are times when a table scan can provide better query performance. It depends, in part, on the percentage of rows returned. For the most part, though, you want to have appropriate indexes on your tables. For an in-depth discussion, refer to Item 46, "Understand how the execution plan works."

There is a risk, though, of assuming that indexes are the solution to all data retrieval problems. Many indexes do not speed up retrieval and can actually slow down updates. A problem is that whenever you update an indexed column, you force an update to one or more "index tables"—meaning more disk reads and writes. Because indexes are highly organized, making updates in them is often more expensive than the update to the table.

Operational tables typically see lots of updates, so you should justify every index on an operational table. Reporting databases (the information warehouse) typically do not see many updates, so you should not be shy about applying indexes. (Such databases are also good candidates for denormalization, as mentioned in Item 9, "Use denormalization for information warehouses.") However, simply applying indexes is not a panacea.

The most common type of index used by various DBMSs is a B-tree structure. Although various DBMSs might have additional types such as hash, spatial, or other specialized structures, B-tree is the most versatile and thus more common. A full discussion of B-tree structure is beyond the scope of the book, but as a quick recap, a B-tree structure starts with a root node that can point to a number of intermediate nodes, which in turn point to a number of leaf nodes, which then point to the actual data.

A B-tree index's contribution to query performance depends significantly on its type. There are two different index methods: clustered and nonclustered. A clustered index physically sorts the table's contents in the order of whichever columns were specified when the index was created. Because it is not possible to order the rows in a table in more than one way, you can have only one clustered index per table. In SQL Server, at least, usually a clustered index has leaf nodes that contain data directly. A nonclustered index has the same index structure as a clustered index, but with two important differences:

- Nonclustered indexes may be sorted differently from the table's physical order.

- A nonclustered index's leaf level consists of an index key plus a bookmark that points to the data, rather than containing the data.

Note

In Oracle, table data is not sorted based on the column(s) specified in an index. The optimizer maintains metadata on how well an index mirrors the table's sorting (its clustering factor), which influences its choice in the execution plan.

Whether a nonclustered index access will perform better than a table scan depends on the table size, the row's storage pattern, the row's length, and the percentage of rows the query returns. A table scan often starts to perform better than a nonclustered index access when at least 10% of the rows are selected. A clustered index usually performs better than a table scan even when the percentage of returned rows is high.

Another important consideration is how the data is usually being accessed. If a column is not typically included in the WHERE clause, there is little benefit in having it indexed. As illustrated earlier, if a column has low cardinality (a large percentage of the index entries all have the same value), there is little benefit in having it indexed. If an index will not result in the database engine reading less than a minimum percentage of the table, the engine will not use the index.

In addition, an index makes sense only if the table is large. Most database engines load small tables into memory. Once a table is in memory, searching it goes quickly, no matter what you do or do not do. What "small" means depends on the number of rows, the size of each row, how it fits into a page, and how much memory your database server has available.

The combination of columns is important as well. If certain columns are typically included together in most queries, an index containing all of those columns should be created. The fact that each of the columns is indexed individually does not necessarily mean that an efficient access plan can be created. When creating an index of multiple columns, the order in which the columns are specified in the index is important. If some queries look for a specific value of CustLastName, but other queries look for specific values of both CustFirstName and CustLastName, the index should be on CustLastName, then CustFirstName (as shown in Listing 2.9), not the reverse (as shown in Listing 2.10).

Listing 2.9 Appropriate index creation SQL

```
CREATE INDEX CustName
   ON Customers(CustLastName, CustFirstName);
```

Listing 2.10 Less appropriate index creation SQL

```
CREATE INDEX CustName
   ON Customers(CustFirstName, CustLastName);
```

Things to Remember

✦ Analyze your data so that the appropriate indexes are created to improve performance.

✦ Ensure that the indexes you have created are, in fact, going to be used.

Item 12: Use Indexes for More than Just Filtering

Database indexes are distinct data structures in the database. Each index requires its own disk space, and because it holds a copy of the indexed table data, it is pure redundancy. However, this redundancy is acceptable, because indexes improve the speed of data retrieval operations on a table by quickly locating data without having to search every row in the table with each access. Note, though, that indexes are useful in many other ways as well.

The WHERE clause defines the search condition of an SQL statement. As such, it uses the core functional purpose of an index, which is to find data quickly. A poorly written WHERE clause is the first ingredient of a slow query.

Whether or not a column is indexed can affect how efficiently joins between tables get executed. In essence, the JOIN operation allows the data from a normalized data model to be transformed into a denormalized form for a specific processing purpose. Because JOIN operations combine data that is scattered through many tables, thus needing more reads from different pages, they are particularly sensitive to disk seek latencies, so proper indexing can have a great impact on response times.

Three common join algorithms are used when querying (nested loops, hash join, and sort-merge join), but all are similar in that they process only two tables at a time. An SQL query involving more tables requires multiple steps. First, an intermediate result set is built by joining two tables, then that result set is joined with the next table, and so forth.

The nested loops join is the most fundamental join algorithm. Think of it as two nested queries: the outer (driving) query fetches the results from one table, and the second query fetches the corresponding data from the other table for each row of the driving query. Nested loops joins, therefore, work best with indexes on the columns being joined. Nested loops joins deliver good performance if the driving query returns a small result set. Otherwise, the optimizer will likely choose a different join algorithm.

Hash joins load the candidate records from one side of the join into a hash table that can be probed very quickly for each row from the other side of the join. Tuning a hash join requires an entirely different indexing approach from the nested loops join. Because the join is done using the hash table, there is no need to index the columns that are being joined. The only indexes that can improve the performance of a hash join are on columns in the WHERE predicate or the ON predicate of joins; in fact, that is the only time when a hash join uses an index. Realistically, the performance of hash joins is achieved by reducing the size of the hash table either horizontally (fewer rows) or vertically (fewer columns).

A sort-merge join requires that both sides of the join be sorted by the join predicates. It then combines the two sorted lists like a zipper. In many ways, a sort-merge join is similar to a hash join. Indexing the join predicates alone is useless, but there should be an index for the independent conditions to read all candidate records in one shot. There is one aspect, however, that is unique to the sort-merge join: the join order does not make any difference, not even for performance. For the other algorithms, the direction of the outer joins (left or right) implies the join order. However, that is not the case for sort-merge joins. The sort-merge join can even do a left and right outer join (a so-called full outer join) at the same time. Although the sort-merge join performs well once the inputs are sorted, it is seldom used because sorting both sides is very expensive. However, if there is an index corresponding to the sort order, the sort operations can be avoided entirely, and the sort-merge join shines. Otherwise, because the hash join needs to preprocess only one side of the join, it is superior in many cases.

To some extent, the preceding discussion of join algorithms is somewhat theoretical. Although it is possible (at least in SQL Server and Oracle, using query hints) to force the use of a specific join type, it is far better to allow the query optimizer to select the algorithm it feels is most appropriate given the data as it currently exists, and ensure that your indexing is appropriate.

Note

It should be pointed out that MySQL does not support either hash joins or sort-merge joins.

Another way indexes can be used is through data clustering. Clustering data means that data that will be accessed consecutively is stored close together so that accessing it requires fewer I/O operations. Consider the query shown in Listing 2.11.

Listing 2.11 Sample query SQL using LIKE in the WHERE clause

```
SELECT EmployeeID, EmpFirstName, EmpLastName
FROM Employees
WHERE EmpState = 'WA'
  AND EmpCity LIKE '%ELLE%';
```

The use of the LIKE expression with a leading wildcard for EmpCity means that a table scan is necessary, because an index cannot be used. However, the condition on EmpState is well suited for indexing. If the accessed rows are stored in a single table block, the table access should not be that significant an issue because the database can fetch all rows with a single read operation. However, if the same rows are spread across many different blocks, the table access can become a serious issue because the database has to fetch many blocks in order to retrieve all the rows. In other words, the performance depends on the physical distribution of the accessed rows.

It is possible to improve query performance by reordering the rows in the table so that they correspond to the index order. Doing so, however, is rarely applicable because you can store the table rows in only one sequence, meaning that you can optimize the table for one index only.

An index like that shown in Listing 2.12, where the first column corresponds to the equality in the WHERE clause, will prove useful.

Listing 2.12 Sample index creation SQL

```
CREATE INDEX EmpStateName
  ON Employees (EmpState, EmpCity);
```

If you can eliminate the need to go to the table at all to retrieve data, the query can be made even more efficient. Consider the table illustrated in Listing 2.13.

Listing 2.13 Sample table creation SQL

```
CREATE TABLE Orders (
  OrderNumber int IDENTITY (1, 1) NOT NULL,
  OrderDate date NULL,
  ShipDate date NULL,
  CustomerID int NULL,
  EmployeeID int NULL,
  OrderTotal decimal NULL
);
```

If there is a need to produce order totals per customer, as shown in Listing 2.14, the index shown in Listing 2.15 includes all the needed columns, so the table would not even be accessed.

Listing 2.14 Sample query SQL for a totals query

```
SELECT CustomerID, Sum(OrderTotal) AS SumOrderTotal
FROM Orders
GROUP BY CustomerID;
```

Listing 2.15 Sample index creation SQL

```
CREATE INDEX CustOrder
  ON Orders (CustomerID, OrderTotal);
```

> **Note**
>
> On some DBMSs, a table scan may still be preferred over the index created in Listing 2.15 if there is only a small amount of data.

One thing to be aware of, though, is that while you would expect the query in Listing 2.16 on the next page to run faster than the query in Listing 2.14 because it involves fewer rows, the fact that the OrderDate is not in the index means that the likely choice is a table scan.

Listing 2.16 Sample query SQL with a WHERE clause

```
SELECT CustomerID, Sum(OrderTotal) AS SumOrderTotal
FROM Orders
WHERE OrderDate > '2015-12-01'
GROUP BY CustomerID;
```

Indexes also have an impact on the efficiency of ORDER BY clauses. Sorting is resource intensive. Although it typically is CPU intensive, the main problem is that the database must temporarily buffer the results: all the input must be read before the first output can be produced. An index provides an ordered representation of the indexed data. In fact, an index stores the data in a presorted fashion. This allows us to use indexes to avoid the sort operation to satisfy an ORDER BY clause.

Unlike joins, which can use "pipelining" (each row from the intermediate result can be immediately pipelined to the next JOIN operation, so as not to require storing the intermediate result set) to reduce memory usage, the complete sort operation must be completed before it can produce the first output.

Because an index, particularly a B-tree index, provides an ordered representation of the indexed data, we can think of the index as storing the data in a presorted fashion. This means that indexes can be used to avoid the sort operation required to satisfy an ORDER BY clause. In fact, not only can an ordered index save the sorting effort, but it is also possible to return the first results without processing all input data, providing a pipelined effect. Note that in order for this to happen, though, the same index that is used for the WHERE clause must also cover the ORDER BY clause.

Be aware that databases can read indexes in both directions. That means that a pipelined ORDER BY is possible even if the scanned index range is in the exact opposite order specified by the ORDER BY clause. This does not affect the index's usability for the WHERE clause. However, sort direction can be significant in an index containing more than one column.

> **Note**
>
> MySQL ignores ASC and DESC modifiers in index declarations.

Things to Remember

+ Whether or not columns in WHERE clauses are included in indexes has an impact on the performance of the query.

+ Whether or not columns in SELECT clauses are indexed can also affect the efficiency of the query.

✦ Whether or not a column is indexed can affect how efficiently joins between tables get executed.

✦ Indexes can also have an impact on the efficiency of ORDER BY clauses.

✦ The existence of multiple indexes can have an impact on write operations.

Item 13: Don't Go Overboard with Triggers

Most RDBMSs include the ability to run triggers (stored procedures) automatically whenever a DELETE, INSERT, or UPDATE is performed on a table. Although many developers use triggers in order to prevent orphaned records, using the built-in DRI shown in Item 6, "Define foreign keys to protect referential integrity," is easier, and it executes faster and more efficiently. Triggers can also be used to update calculated values, but (as was pointed out in Item 5, "Understand why storing calculated data is usually a bad idea") there are better ways to achieve that.

You achieve DRI through the use of constraints. Constraints let you define the way the database engine automatically enforces the integrity of a database. They define rules regarding the values allowed in columns and are the standard mechanism for enforcing integrity. Using constraints is preferred to using DML (Data Manipulation Language) triggers, rules, and defaults. The query optimizer also uses constraint definitions to build high-performance query execution plans.

When you have declared DRI for INSERT, the RDBMS checks when inserting a new row into the child table whether the entered key value exists in the parent table. If it does not, no insert is possible. It is also possible to specify DRI actions on UPDATE and DELETE, such as CASCADE (forwards a change/delete in the parent table to the child tables), NO ACTION (if the specific row is referenced, changing the key is not allowed), or SET NULL/ SET DEFAULT (a changed/deleted key in the parent table results in setting the child values to NULL or to the default value if one is specified).

The code in Listing 2.17 illustrates how to use DRI to prevent orphan records in the child table if the corresponding entry in the parent table is deleted. (In this case, the relevant entries in the Order_Details table will be deleted when an entry is deleted from the Orders table.)

Listing 2.17 Using DRI to prevent orphan records in the child table

```
ALTER TABLE Order_Details
  ADD CONSTRAINT fkOrder FOREIGN KEY (OrderNumber)
    REFERENCES Orders (OrderNumber) ON DELETE CASCADE;
```

The code in Listing 2.18 shows how to create a trigger to do the same thing.

Listing 2.18 Creating a trigger to prevent orphan records in the child table

```
CREATE TRIGGER DelCascadeTrig
  ON Orders
  FOR DELETE
AS
  DELETE Order_Details
  FROM Order_Details, deleted
  WHERE Order_Details.OrderNumber = deleted.OrderNumber;
```

As mentioned previously, the DRI approach executes faster and more efficiently than the trigger approach.

As was implied in Item 5, triggers can also be used to calculate values. For instance, Listing 2.19 (for SQL Server) shows how the Order-Totals column in the Orders table from Item 5 could be updated by a trigger that runs anytime the Order_Details table is changed.

> **Note**
>
> Listing 2.19 is for SQL Server. See https://github.com/TexanInParis/Effective-SQL for the equivalent for other DBMSs.

Listing 2.19 SQL for a sample trigger to maintain a computed value

```
CREATE TRIGGER updateOrdersOrderTotals
  ON Orders
  AFTER INSERT, DELETE, UPDATE
AS
BEGIN UPDATE Orders
  SET OrderTotal = (
      SELECT SUM(QuantityOrdered * QuotedPrice)
      FROM Order_Details OD
      WHERE OD.OrderNumber = Orders.OrderNumber
  )
  WHERE Orders.OrderNumber IN(
    SELECT OrderNumber FROM deleted
    UNION
    SELECT OrderNumber FROM inserted
  );
END;
```

Compare the complexity of writing that code to the simplicity of using a calculated column defined for the Orders table (as illustrated in Item 5), and couple that with the fact that the solutions shown in Item 5 are more efficient to run.

As with many things in database design, there are several ways of achieving the same result. Although triggers are one approach to maintaining the data, they may not be the best. There are times, of course, when triggers are appropriate. Some of those times include the following:

- **Maintenance of duplicate or derived data**: Denormalized databases generally introduce data redundancy. You can keep the data synchronized through triggers.

- **Complex column constraints**: If a column constraint depends on other rows within the same table, or rows in other tables, a trigger is the best method for that column constraint.

- **Complex defaults**: You can use a trigger to generate default values based on data in other columns, rows, or tables.

- **Inter-database referential integrity**: When related tables are found in two different databases, you can use triggers to ensure referential integrity across the databases.

Note

In those cases where triggers are used, it might be preferable to create the triggers on views, not on the table. This can make things easier, because you may not want triggers fired during bulk import/export operations, but need them to fire when used in an application.

Note

DBMSs have different restrictions on what is possible with constraints or defaults. For example, some DBMSs do not permit you to create a CHECK constraint with subqueries, necessitating using triggers as an alternative. Check your DBMS documentation to determine if you are able to accomplish what you need without a trigger.

Upsizing from Microsoft Access

A common question is how to decide whether to use DRI or triggers to enforce table relationships when upsizing from Microsoft Access. When converting to Microsoft SQL Server, the Upsizing Wizard's Export Table Attributes screen lets you choose between the two options in order to enforce referential integrity. Which one to use depends on how you created the table relationships in Access.

---

continues

DRI causes SQL Server to create its own tables with the Access relationships and references. Unfortunately, SQL Server's DRI does not support cascade update or cascade delete, so if you choose DRI, you lose any update or delete cascading functionality you have in Access.

In Access, open the Relationships window (Tools, Relationships), click on the line that connects two tables, right-click to open the shortcut menu, then choose Edit Relationship to open the Edit Relationships dialog box. As shown in Figure 2.2, the grid at the top of this box shows the two tables in the relationship and the related fields in each table. Beneath the grid are three check boxes:

- Enforce Referential Integrity

- Cascade Update Related Fields

- Cascade Delete Related Records

If only Enforce Referential Integrity has been enabled, you can use the DRI option on the wizard. If either (or both) of Cascade Update Related Fields or Cascade Delete Related Records has been selected for any relationship, you must choose the wizard's trigger option.

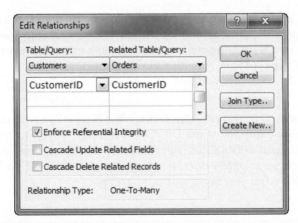

Figure 2.2 Microsoft Access Edit Relationships dialog box

One issue is that while Access allows cascade update and cascade delete on self-references (the same table can be at both ends of the relationship), SQL Server does not. That means that although the code depicted in Listing 2.20 is valid for Access, it will raise an error in SQL Server.

> **Listing 2.20** Table creation SQL with DRI for a self-referencing relationship
>
> ```
> CREATE TABLE OrgChart (
>   employeeID INTEGER NOT NULL PRIMARY KEY,
>   manager_employeeID INTEGER
> CONSTRAINT SelfReference FOREIGN KEY (manager_employeeID)
> REFERENCES OrgChart (employeeID)
> ON DELETE SET NULL
> ON UPDATE CASCADE
> );
> ```
>
> Note that since Access 2010, it has been possible to have data macros, which are the equivalent of triggers in SQL Server. Should your Access database use data macros, conversion to SQL Server triggers may be the best alternative.

Things to Remember

✦ Because performance is usually better with DRI provided through the use of constraints and with calculated columns using built-in features when you create a table, we recommend that constraints or the built-in features for calculated columns be the default approach.

✦ Triggers are generally not portable: it is difficult to create a trigger for one DBMS and expect it to run without modifications on another DBMS.

✦ Use triggers only when absolutely necessary. If possible, ensure that the triggers are idempotent.

Item 14: Consider Using a Filtered Index to Include or Exclude a Subset of Data

You seldom want to return all the rows from the table(s) involved in your query, so you add a WHERE clause. Although this ensures that fewer rows are returned, it does not necessarily reduce the amount of I/O done to get the results.

A filtered index (SQL Server) or partial index (PostgreSQL) is a non-clustered index that contains only a subset of the number of rows contained in a table. They are typically much smaller than traditional nonclustered indexes which have a 1:1 ratio between the number of rows in the table and the number of rows in the index. So, a filtered index can provide both performance and storage advantages because there are fewer rows in the index, and therefore less I/O is required. Where a DBMS supports it, partitioning of a table can also be used in a similar manner to the filtered index.

Note

Access (at least as of 2016) and MySQL (at least as of version 5.6) do not support filtered indexes.

Note

Although neither Oracle nor DB2 supports filtered indexes directly, there are ways to emulate them.[1]

Filtered indexes are created by adding a WHERE clause when you create an index. The performance boost over a traditional index can be significant if you have a value that is frequently used in a WHERE clause but accounts for only a small percentage of the total values for that table.

Filtered indexes are created by adding a WHERE clause. You can define them as restricted to only those values that are not NULL or only those values that are NULL. (See Item 10, "Factor in nulls when creating indexes," for more about using null values in indexes.) It is only possible to use deterministic functions in the WHERE clause, and you cannot use the OR operator. (See the sidebar "Deterministic versus Nondeterministic" in Chapter 1, "Data Model Design.") SQL Server has some additional restrictions: the filter predicate cannot reference a computed column, a UDT (user-defined type) column, a spatial data type column, or a hierarchyID data type column, and you cannot use BETWEEN, NOT IN, or a CASE statement.

Note that the column being filtered need not be included in the index. Consider a Products table with a QuantityOnHand column. To be able to query only those products that are running low on stock, you could create a filtered index as shown in Listing 2.21.

Listing 2.21 Sample SQL to create a filtered index on QuantityOnHand

```
CREATE NONCLUSTERED INDEX LowProducts
  ON Products (ProductNumber)
  WHERE QuantityOnHand < 10;
```

Another possible scenario is a document management system. Typically, you would have a DocumentStatus table with a Status column that contains values such as Draft, Reviewed, Pending publication,

---

1. http://use-the-index-luke.com/sql/where-clause/null/partial-index

Published, Pending expiration, and Expired. You may have a requirement to follow up on documents that are in Pending publication or Pending expiration status. Listing 2.22 shows an index that could be created for that purpose.

Listing 2.22 Sample SQL to create a filtered index

```
CREATE NONCLUSTERED INDEX PendingDocuments
  ON DocumentStatus (DocumentNumber, Status)
  WHERE Status IN ('Pending publication', 'Pending expiration');
```

Note that it is possible to create multiple filtered indexes on the same column, as shown in Listing 2.23.

Listing 2.23 Sample SQL to create multiple filtered indexes on the same column

```
CREATE NONCLUSTERED INDEX PendPubDocuments
  ON DocumentStatus (DocumentNumber, Status)
  WHERE Status = 'Pending publication';
CREATE NONCLUSTERED INDEX PendExpDocuments
  ON DocumentStatus (DocumentNumber, Status)
  WHERE Status = 'Pending expiration';
```

In Item 12, "Use indexes for more than just filtering," we mentioned that indexes can be used to avoid the sort operation required to satisfy an ORDER BY clause. Using a filtered index can extend this concept. Consider a query like the one in Listing 2.24. The index in Listing 2.25 can be used to avoid a sort operation.

Listing 2.24 Sample query that requires a sort operation

```
SELECT ProductNumber, ProductName
FROM Products
WHERE CategoryID IN (1, 5, 9)
ORDER BY ProductName;
```

Listing 2.25 Sample SQL to create filtered indexes to eliminate a sort

```
CREATE INDEX SelectProducts
  ON Products(ProductName, ProductNumber)
  WHERE CategoryID IN (1, 5, 9);
```

There are, of course, limits to what you can do with a filtered or partial index. For instance, because it is not possible to use date functions such as GETDATE(), you cannot create a rolling date range; values in the WHERE clause must be exact.

Things to Remember

✦ Filtered indexes are useful to preserve space when the index is useful for only a small fraction of the rows.

✦ Filtered indexes can be used to implement unique constraints on a subset of rows (i.e., only those WHERE active = 'Y').

✦ Filtered indexes can be used to avoid a sort operation.

✦ Consider whether partitioning your table can offer benefits similar to a filtered index without the overhead of maintaining another index.

Item 15: Use Declarative Constraints Instead of Programming Checks

We cannot overstate the importance of enforcing data integrity in your database. It is necessary to identify valid values for each field and to decide how to enforce the integrity of the data in those fields in order to have a properly functioning database. Fortunately, SQL provides a number of different constraints that can help in this area.

SQL constraints provide a way to specify rules for the data in a table. For any data action (INSERT, DELETE, UPDATE), all constraints are checked. If there are any violations of those constraints, the action is aborted.

The following six constraints exist:

1. **NOT NULL**: By default, a table column can hold null values. A NOT NULL constraint ensures that a field must always contain a value by not allowing it to accept null values.

2. **UNIQUE**: A UNIQUE constraint ensures that no duplicate values can be entered in the specified field. You can use UNIQUE constraints to make sure that no duplicate values are entered in specific columns that do not participate in a primary key. Unlike PRIMARY KEY constraints, UNIQUE constraints allow null values.

3. **PRIMARY KEY**: Similar to the UNIQUE constraint, a PRIMARY KEY constraint uniquely identifies each record in a database table. In addition to containing unique values, a PRIMARY KEY cannot contain null values. Multiple UNIQUE constraints can be defined on a table, whereas only one PRIMARY KEY constraint can be defined on a table. (See Item 1, "Verify that all tables have a primary key.")

4. **FOREIGN KEY**: A foreign key in one table points to a primary key in another table. (See Item 6, "Define foreign keys to protect referential integrity.")

5. **CHECK:** CHECK constraints can be defined on a single field or on a table. When a CHECK constraint is defined on a single field, only specified values can be stored in that field. When it is defined on a table, the values in certain fields can be limited based on values in other fields in the same row.

6. **DEFAULT:** A DEFAULT clause is used to define a default value for a field. If no other value is specified when adding a new record, the database system uses the default value.

Note

Technically, a DEFAULT clause is not a constraint according to the definitions in the SQL Standard. However, it can be used as a means to enforce business rules, often in conjunction with the NOT NULL constraint.

Note

SQL Server allows only one null value per column in UNIQUE index constraints. DB2 allows one null value per column in UNIQUE index constraints unless you include a WHERE NOT NULL filter.

Constraints can be specified when the table is created (as part of a CREATE TABLE statement) or after the table is created (as part of an ALTER TABLE statement).

To be sure, there are other methods of enforcing referential integrity than the DRI provided through the use of constraints. It can be enforced through procedural referential integrity, where rules are checked using procedural code. There are several mechanisms that implement procedural referential integrity:

- Code in the client application

- Stored procedures

- Triggers

When developing computer systems to work with the data, it is certainly possible to include program code that will ensure that all of the rules associated with the database are enforced. However, this is not a good idea. Enforcing and maintaining business rules and relationships in the data is part of the data model, and the responsibility belongs to the database, not the application program. Data rules should be separated from the applications in order to ensure that everyone is working with the same data and that updates are done one way. This eliminates the need to write and maintain thousands of lines of the same code over and over. Sure, it is possible to subvert data integrity, but when it is defined as part of the database itself, you have to try very hard to do it!

The inclusion of stored procedures to enforce integrity at least keeps the rules in the database, but it can be a much more difficult approach, especially for updates. Also, although the stored procedures can enforce the rules, it is necessary to ensure that users modify the data only through the stored procedures. This can be accomplished by granting users permission to execute the stored procedures but not allowing them to update the underlying tables directly, but that is an additional level of work that must be done.

Triggers can be used to enforce referential integrity and cascading actions, and it is a self-contained solution that can use the same INSERT, UPDATE, and DELETE statements to modify the base tables as you would normally use. However, Item 13, "Don't go overboard with triggers," has already discussed some of the liabilities of using triggers.

Things to Remember

✦ Consider using constraints to enforce data integrity.

✦ The query optimizer can use constraint definitions to build high-performance query execution plans.

Item 16: Know Which SQL Dialect Your Product Uses and Write Accordingly

SQL is generally considered to be the standard language for accessing databases. But even though SQL became a standard of the American National Standards Institute (ANSI) in 1986, and of the International Organization for Standardization (ISO) in 1987, specific SQL implementations do not necessarily completely follow standards and are generally incompatible between vendors. Such details as date and time syntax, string concatenation, the handling of nulls, and comparison case sensitivity vary from vendor to vendor. It is important that you understand what specific dialect of SQL your DBMS uses in order to write effective SQL statements.

We will attempt to list some examples of differences in implementation in this item. For more information, Troels Arvin, a Danish database administrator, maintains a page comparing different SQL implementations at http://troels.arvin.dk/db/rdbms/ that does a good job of highlighting differences.

Ordering Result Sets

The SQL Standard does not actually specify how nulls should be ordered in comparison with non-null values, except

- Any two nulls are to be considered equally ordered.

- Nulls should sort either above or below all non-null values.

It should come as no surprise, then, that there is no consistency among the DBMSs!

- **IBM DB2**: Nulls are considered higher than any non-null value.

- **Microsoft Access**: Nulls are considered lower than any non-null value.

- **Microsoft SQL Server**: Nulls are considered lower than any non-null value.

- **MySQL**: Nulls are considered lower than any non-null value, although Troels Arvin says there is an undocumented feature in MySQL whereby this is not the case if a – (minus) character is added before the column name and ASC is changed to DESC, or DESC to ASC.

- **Oracle**: By default, nulls are considered higher than any non-null value; however, this sorting behavior may be changed by adding NULLS FIRST or NULLS LAST to the ORDER BY expression.

- **PostgreSQL**: By default, nulls are considered higher than any non-null value; however (since version 8.3), this sorting behavior may be changed by adding NULLS FIRST or NULLS LAST to the ORDER BY expression.

Limiting Result Sets

The SQL Standard provides three ways of limiting the number of rows returned:

- Using FETCH FIRST

- Using a window function, one of which is ROW_NUMBER() OVER

- Using a cursor

Note

What is being referred to here is a "simple limit," getting only *n* rows in the result set. This is not the same as a top-*n* query.

Here is how this is implemented in various DBMSs:

- **IBM DB2**: Supports all standards-based approaches.

- **Microsoft Access**: Does not support any standards-based approaches.

- **Microsoft SQL Server**: Supports ROW_NUMBER() and cursor standards-based approaches.

- **MySQL**: Provides the LIMIT operator as an alternative solution and cursor standards-based approaches.

- **Oracle**: Supports ROW_NUMBER() and cursor standards-based approaches as well as the ROWNUM pseudo column.

- **PostgreSQL**: Supports all standards-based approaches.

The BOOLEAN Data Type

The SQL Standard treats the BOOLEAN data type as optional but says that a BOOLEAN may be one of the following literals:

- TRUE

- FALSE

- UNKNOWN or NULL (unless prohibited by a NOT NULL constraint)

The DBMS may interpret NULL as equivalent to UNKNOWN. (It is unclear from the specification if the DBMS must support UNKNOWN, NULL, or both as Boolean literals.) It is defined that TRUE > FALSE (true is larger than false).

Here is how this is implemented in various DBMSs:

- **IBM DB2**: Does not support the BOOLEAN type.

- **Microsoft Access**: Offers a non-nullable Yes/No type.

- **Microsoft SQL Server**: Does not support the BOOLEAN type. The BIT type (which may have 0, 1, or NULL as a value) is a possible alternative.

- **MySQL**: Offers a nonconforming BOOLEAN type (it is one of many aliases to its TINYINT(1) type).

- **Oracle**: Does not support the BOOLEAN type.

- **PostgreSQL**: Follows the standard. Accepts NULL as a Boolean literal; does not accept UNKNOWN as a Boolean literal.

SQL Functions

This is one of the biggest areas for differences. Space does not permit an adequate discussion of which functions the SQL Standard specifies and which functions are actually implemented. (Note that many DBMSs have functions that are not part of the standard in addition to whether or not they implement specified functions!) Troels Arvin's site discusses some of the standard functions and their implementation, but you are best off reading the documentation for whatever you use. Note that we do provide an overview of the functions related to the date and time data types in the Appendix, "Date and Time Types, Operations, and Functions."

The UNIQUE Constraint

The SQL Standard states that a column (or set of columns) that is subject to a UNIQUE constraint must also be subject to a NOT NULL constraint, unless the DBMS implements an optional "nulls allowed" feature. The optional feature adds some characteristics to the UNIQUE constraint:

- Columns involved in a UNIQUE constraint may also have NOT NULL constraints, but they do not have to.

- If columns with UNIQUE constraints do not also have NOT NULL constraints, the columns may contain any number of null values (a logical consequence of the fact that NULL<>NULL).

Here is how this is implemented in various DBMSs:

- **IBM DB2**: Follows the nonoptional parts of the UNIQUE constraint. It does not implement the optional "nulls allowed" feature.

- **Microsoft Access**: Follows the standard.

- **Microsoft SQL Server**: Offers the "nulls allowed" feature, but allows at most one instance of a null value (i.e., breaks the second characteristic of the standard).

- **MySQL**: Follows the standard, including the optional "nulls allowed" feature.

- **Oracle**: Offers the "nulls allowed" feature. If the UNIQUE constraint is imposed on a single column, the column may contain any number of nulls (as expected from the second characteristic of the standard). However, if the UNIQUE constraint is specified for multiple columns, Oracle sees the constraint as violated if any two rows contain at least one NULL in a column and identical, non-null values in the rest of the columns.

- **PostgreSQL**: Follows the standard, including the optional "nulls allowed" feature.

Things to Remember

- Even though a statement may be compliant with the SQL Standards, it may not work with your DBMS.

- Because different DBMSs implement things differently, they have different performance trade-offs for the same SQL statements.

✦ Always consult the documentation for your DBMS.

✦ Check http://troels.arvin.dk/db/rdbms/ to see additional differences that may exist.

Item 17: Know When to Use Calculated Results in Indexes

We wrote about using functions rather than storing calculated columns in Item 11, "Carefully consider creation of indexes to minimize index and data scanning." It turns out that it is possible to index function-based calculated columns, so you may not be penalized as much as you might have thought.

DB2 has supported function-based indexes in zOS versions since version 9, but only since version 10.5 on LUW. However, user-defined functions cannot be used in indexes. One solution is to create a real column in the table to hold the result of the function or expression (which must be maintained via a trigger or by the application layer) and index that column. That new column can be indexed, and the WHERE clause can use the new column (without the expression).

MySQL has been able to create indexes on generated columns since version 5.7. Older versions must use the same approach as outlined for DB2.

Oracle has supported function-based indexes since release 8i, and virtual columns were added in release 11g.

PostgreSQL has fully supported indexes on expressions since release 7.4 and partially supported them since release 7.2.

SQL Server has allowed computed columns to be indexed since release 2000. It is possible to index a calculated column as long as the following conditions are met:

- **Ownership requirements**: All function references in the computed column must have the same owner as the table.

- **Determinism requirements**: The computed column must be deterministic. (See the sidebar "Deterministic versus Nondeterministic" in Chapter 1, "Data Model Design.")

- **Precision requirements**: The function cannot be an expression of the float or real data types and cannot use a float or real data type in its definition.

- **Data type requirements**: The function cannot resolve to text, ntext, or image.

- **SET option requirements**: The ANSI_NULLS connection-level option must be set to ON when the CREATE TABLE or ALTER TABLE statement that defines the computed column is executed.

One very common reason for wanting to have an index based on a function is to allow case-insensitive queries. SQL Server, MySQL, and Microsoft Access are case insensitive by default. (MySQL is also accent insensitive by default.) Consider the query shown in Listing 2.26.

Listing 2.26 Sample SQL for case-insensitive RDBMSs

```
SELECT EmployeeID, EmpFirstName, EmpLastName
FROM Employees
WHERE EmpLastName = 'Viescas';
```

Regardless of whether the name has been stored as viescas, VIESCAS, Viescas, or even ViEsCaS, SQL Server, MySQL, and Access will find the employee(s). Other DBMSs, though, will find the employee only if the name has been stored exactly as Viescas. To retrieve the other variations requires a query like that shown in Listing 2.27.

Listing 2.27 Sample SQL for case-sensitive RDBMSs

```
SELECT EmployeeID, EmpFirstName, EmpLastName
FROM Employees
WHERE UPPER(EmpLastName) = 'VIESCAS';
```

The fact that there is a function in the WHERE clause working on a column in the table means that the query is not sargable (see Item 28, "Write sargable queries to ensure that the engine will use indexes"), and so a table scan will be performed, because the function needs to be applied to every row in the table.

If, however, we create the index illustrated in Listing 2.28, the query shown in Listing 2.27 will, in fact, use that index.

Listing 2.28 SQL to create an index for case-sensitive RDBMSs

```
CREATE INDEX EmpLastNameUpper
  ON Employees (UPPER(EmpLastName));
```

With DB2, Oracle, PostregSQL, and SQL Server, function-based indexing is not limited to built-in functions like UPPER(). It is possible to use expressions such as Column1 + Column2 and even user-defined functions in the index definition.

Note

In SQL Server, you cannot simply create an index based on a function. You must add a computed field to the table, then index that computed field.

There is an important limitation with user-defined functions, though. The function must be deterministic. (See the sidebar "Deterministic versus Nondeterministic" in Chapter 1, "Data Model Design.") For instance, it is not possible to refer to the current time (either directly or indirectly) in the function and then use that function to create an index. Let's assume that you want to be able to extract employees based on their age, so you create a function like that shown in Listing 2.29 which uses the current date (SYSDATE()) to calculate the age based on the supplied date of birth.

Listing 2.29 Nondeterministic function

```
CREATE FUNCTION CalculateAge(Date_of_Birth DATE)
  RETURNS NUMBER
AS
BEGIN
  RETURN
    TRUNC((SYSDATE() - Date_of_Birth) / 365);
END
```

Note

The CalculateAge() function in Listing 2.29 is valid for Oracle. SQL Server would use DATEDIFF("d", Date_Of_Birth, Date) / 365. DB2 would require something like TRUNC((DAYS(CURRENT_DATE) - DAYS(date_of_birth)) / 365, 0), and MySQL would require TRUNCATE(DATEDIFF(SYSDATE, date_of_birth) / 365). Access does not allow the creation of functions using SQL. You need to use VBA instead. Note that the function does not calculate age correctly. You can find an example that calculates age correctly using CASE in Item 24, "Know when to use CASE to solve a problem."

Listing 2.30 illustrates how it is possible to use the CalculateAge() function to find those employees who are over 50 years of age.

Listing 2.30 SQL statement using the CalculateAge() function

```
SELECT EmployeeID, EmpFirstName, EmpLastName,
  CalculateAge(EmpDOB) AS EmpAge
FROM Employees
WHERE CalculateAge(EmpDOB) > 50;
```

Because the function is used in the WHERE clause and will cause a table scan as is, it would seem obvious that you should create a function-based index in order to optimize the query. Unfortunately, CalculateAge() is nondeterministic, because the result of the function call is not fully determined by its parameters: the result of the CalculateAge() function depends on the value returned by the SYSDATE() function. Only deterministic functions can be indexed.

PostgreSQL and Oracle require that the keyword DETERMINISTIC (Oracle) or IMMUTABLE (PostgreSQL) be used when defining the function. Both trust the developer to have declared the function correctly, so you could declare the CalculateAge() function to be deterministic and use it in an index definition. However, it will not work as intended because the age stored in the index is calculated when the index is created and does not change as the date changes.

Because function-based indexing would appear to provide much benefit for query optimization, there is a tendency to go overboard and index everything. This is not a good idea! Every index requires ongoing maintenance. The more indexes on a table, the slower updates to that table will be. Function-based indexes are particularly troublesome because they make it very easy to create redundant indexes.

Things to Remember

✦ Do not go overboard with your indexes.

✦ Analyze the expected database usage to ensure that filtered indexes are used only where they truly make sense.

When You Can't Change the Design

You have spent considerable time ensuring that you have a proper logical data model for your situation. You have worked hard to ensure that it has been implemented as an appropriate physical model. Unfortunately, you find that some of your data must come from a source outside your control.

This does not mean that you are doomed to have SQL queries that will not perform well. The items in this chapter are intended to help you understand some options you have to be able to work with that inappropriately designed data from other sources. We will consider both the case when you can create objects to hold the transformations and the case when you must perform the transformation as part of the query itself.

Because you do not have control over the external data, there is nothing you can do to change the design. However, you can use the information in the items in this chapter to work with the DBAs and still end up with effective SQL.

Item 18: Use Views to Simplify What Cannot Be Changed

Views are simply a composition of a table in the form of a predefined SQL query on one or many tables or other views. Although they are simple, there is much merit to their use.

Note

Microsoft Access does not actually have an object called a view, but saved queries in Access can be thought of as views.

You can use views to ameliorate some denormalization issues. You have already seen the denormalized CustomerSales table in Item 2,

"Eliminate redundant storage of data items," and how it should have been modeled as four separate tables (Customers, AutomobileModels, SalesTransactions, and Employees). You've also seen the Assignments table with repeating groups in Item 3, "Get rid of repeating groups," that should have been modeled as two separate tables (Drawings and Predecessors). While working to fix such problems, you could use views to represent how the data should appear.

You can create different views of CustomerSales as shown in Listing 3.1.

Listing 3.1 Views to normalize a denormalized table

```
CREATE VIEW vCustomers AS
SELECT DISTINCT cs.CustFirstName, cs.CustLastName, cs.Address,
  cs.City, cs.Phone
FROM CustomerSales AS cs;

CREATE VIEW vAutomobileModels AS
SELECT DISTINCT cs.ModelYear, cs.Model
FROM CustomerSales AS cs;

CREATE VIEW vEmployees AS
SELECT DISTINCT cs.SalesPerson
FROM CustomerSales AS cs;
```

As Figure 3.1 shows, vCustomers would still include two entries for Tom Frank because two different addresses were listed in the original table. However, you have a smaller set of data to work with. By sorting the data on CustFirstName and CustLastName, you should be able to see the duplicate entry, and you can correct the data in the CustomerSales table.

CustFirstName ▾	CustLastName ▾	Address ▾	City ▾	Phone ▾
Amy	Bacock	111 Dover Lane	Chicago	312-222-1111
Barney	Killjoy	4655 Rainier Ave.	Auburn	253-111-2222
Debra	Smith	3223 SE 12th Pl.	Seattle	206-333-4444
Homer	Tyler	1287 Grady Way	Renton	425-777-8888
Tom	Frank	7435 NE 20th St.	Bellevue	425-888-9999
Tom	Frank	7453 NE 20th St.	Bellevue	425-888-9999

Figure 3.1 Data for view vCustomers

You saw in Item 3 how to use a UNION query to "normalize" a table that contains repeating groups. You can use views to do the same thing, as shown in Listing 3.2.

Listing 3.2 Views to normalize a table with repeating groups

```
CREATE VIEW vDrawings AS
SELECT a.ID AS DrawingID, a.DrawingNumber
FROM Assignments AS a;

CREATE VIEW vPredecessors AS
SELECT 1 AS PredecessorID, a.ID AS DrawingID,
  a.Predecessor_1 AS Predecessor
FROM Assignments AS a
WHERE a.Predecessor_1 IS NOT NULL
UNION
SELECT 2, a.ID, a.Predecessor_2
FROM Assignments AS a
WHERE a.Predecessor_2 IS NOT NULL
UNION
SELECT 3, a.ID, a.Predecessor_3
FROM Assignments AS a
WHERE a.Predecessor_3 IS NOT NULL
UNION
SELECT 4, a.ID, a.Predecessor_4
FROM Assignments AS a
WHERE a.Predecessor_4 IS NOT NULL
UNION
SELECT 5, a.ID, a.Predecessor_5
FROM Assignments AS a
WHERE a.Predecessor_5 IS NOT NULL;
```

One point that needs to be mentioned is that although all the views shown previously mimic what the proper table design should be, they can be used only for reporting purposes. Because of the use of SELECT DISTINCT in the views in Listing 3.1, and the use of UNION in Listing 3.2, the views are not updatable. Some vendors allow you to work around this limitation by defining triggers on views (also known as INSTEAD OF triggers) so that you can write the logic for applying modifications made via the view to the underlying base table yourself.

Note

DB2, Oracle, PostgreSQL, and SQL Server allow triggers on views. MySQL does not.

Some other reasons to use views include the following:

- **To focus on specific data**: You can use views to focus on specific data and on specific tasks. The view can return all rows of a table or tables, or a WHERE clause can be included to limit the rows returned. The view can also return only a subset of the columns in one or more tables.

- **To simplify or clarify column names**: You can use views to provide aliases on column names so that they are more meaningful.

- **To bring data together from different tables**: You can use views to combine multiple tables into a single logical record.

- **To simplify data manipulation**: Views can simplify how users work with data. For example, assume you have a complex query that is used for reporting purposes. Rather than make each user define the subqueries, outer joins, and aggregation to retrieve data from a group of tables, create a view. Not only does the view simplify access to the data (because the underlying query does not have to be written each time a report is being produced), but it ensures consistency by not forcing each user to create the query. You can also create inline user-defined functions that logically operate as parameterized views, or views that have parameters in WHERE clause search conditions or other parts of the query. Note that inline table-valued functions are not the same as scalar functions!

- **To protect sensitive data**: When the table contains sensitive data, that data can be left out of the view. For instance, rather than reveal customer credit card information, you can create a view that uses a function to "munge" the credit card numbers so that users are not aware of the actual numbers. Depending on the DBMS, only the view would be made accessible to users, and the underlying tables need not be directly accessible. Views can be used to provide both column-level and row-level security. Note that a WITH CHECK OPTION clause is necessary to protect the data integrity by preventing users from performing updates or deletes that go beyond the constraints imposed by the view.

- **To provide backward compatibility**: Should changes be required to the schemas for one or more of the tables, you can create views that are the same as the old table schemas. Applications that used to query the old tables can now use the views, so that the application does not have to be changed, especially if it is only reading data. Even applications that update data can sometimes still use a view if INSTEAD OF triggers are added to the new view to map INSERT, DELETE, and UPDATE operations on the view to the underlying tables.

- **To customize data**: You can create views so that different users can see the same data in different ways, even when they are using the same data at the same time. For example, you can create a view that retrieves only the data for those customers of interest to a specific user based on that user's login ID.

- **To provide summarizations**: Views can use aggregate functions (SUM(), AVERAGE(), etc.) and present the calculated results as part of the data.

- **To export and import data**: You can use views to export data to other applications. You can create a view that gives you only the desired data, and then use an appropriate data utility to export just that data. You can also use views for import purposes when the source data does not contain all columns in the underlying table.

Do Not Create Views on Views

It is permissible to create a view that references another view(s). Those coming from a programming background might be tempted to treat a view the way they would treat a procedure in an imperative programming language. That is actually a big mistake and will cause more performance and maintenance problems, likely offsetting any savings gained from having a generic view that is then used as a base for other views. Listing 3.3 demonstrates an example of creating views on other views.

Listing 3.3 Three view definitions

```
CREATE VIEW vActiveCustomers AS
SELECT c.CustomerID, c.CustFirstName, c.CustLastName,
   c.CustFirstName + ' ' + c.CustLastName AS CustFullName
FROM Customers AS c
WHERE EXISTS
  (SELECT NULL
   FROM Orders AS o
   WHERE o.CustomerID = c.CustomerID
     AND o.OrderDate > DATEADD(MONTH, -6, GETDATE()));

CREATE VIEW vCustomerStatistics AS
SELECT o.CustomerID, COUNT(o.OrderNumber) AS OrderCount,
   SUM(o.OrderTotal) AS GrandOrderTotal,
   MAX(o.OrderDate) AS LastOrderDate
FROM Orders AS o
GROUP BY o.CustomerID;
```

---

continues

```
CREATE VIEW vActiveCustomerStatistics AS
SELECT a.CustomerID, a.CustFirstName, a.CustLastName,
  s.LastOrderDate, s.GrandOrderTotal
FROM vActiveCustomers AS a
  INNER JOIN vCustomerStatistics AS s
    ON a.CustomerID = s.CustomerID;
```

There are several potential issues, not all of which might be manifested the same way on different vendors' products. However, generally speaking, giving the optimizer the view as the source means that the optimizer has to first decompose the view. If there are other view references, those must also be decomposed. In an ideal implementation, the optimizer would efficiently "inline" the three view definitions into the equivalent statement in Listing 3.4.

Listing 3.4 Equivalent statement of combined views

```
SELECT c.CustomerID, c.CustFirstName, c.CustLastName,
  s.LastOrderDate, s.GrandOrderTotal
FROM Customers AS c
  INNER JOIN
    (SELECT o.CustomerID,
        SUM(o.OrderTotal) AS GrandOrderTotal,
        MAX(o.OrderDate) AS LastOrderDate
    FROM Orders AS o
    GROUP BY o.CustomerID) AS s
    ON c.CustomerID = s.CustomerID
WHERE EXISTS
  (SELECT NULL
    FROM Orders AS o
    WHERE o.CustomerID = c.CustomerID
      AND o.OrderDate > DATEADD(MONTH, -6, GETDATE()));
```

Note that certain columns or expressions are already pruned from Listing 3.4 where they are actually not used. In particular, OrderCount and CustFullName were not present anywhere within the main query and subquery. However, in practice the optimizer might be forced to preprocess the views completely, including evaluating all expressions in order to create intermediate results for joining to other intermediate results. Because the final view did not use them all, some expressions were discarded in spite of all the hard work put into calculating them.

The same concerns apply to the rows that could be filtered. For example, inactive customers were included in vCustomerStatistics but ultimately were not in the final view because vActiveCustomers excluded those customers. This can potentially result in far more I/Os than you anticipated. You can learn more about those considerations in Item 46, "Understand how the execution plan works." Although this is a somewhat oversimplified example, it is fairly easy to create a view that the optimizer simply cannot inline when it is referenced in other views. Worse, there would be more than one way to create such views that would prevent inlining. Finally, the optimizer generally does a better job when it is given a simpler query expression that asks for exactly the data it actually needs.

For those reasons, it is best to avoid creating views on views. If you need a different presentation of the view, create a new view that directly references the base tables with the appropriate filters or groupings applied. You can also embed subqueries in a view, which can be useful in making the aggregated calculations "private" to the view. This approach helps to prevent proliferation of several views that are not directly usable, making the database solution much more maintainable. Refer to Item 42, "If possible, use common table expressions instead of subqueries," for additional techniques.

Things to Remember

+ Use views to structure data in a way that users will find natural or intuitive.

+ Use views to restrict access to the data such that users can see (and sometimes modify) exactly what they need and no more. Remember to use WITH CHECK OPTION when necessary.

+ Use views to hide and reuse complex queries.

+ Use views to summarize data from various tables that can be used to generate reports.

+ Use views to implement and enforce naming and coding standards, especially when working with legacy database designs that need to be updated.

Item 19: Use ETL to Turn Nonrelational Data into Information

Extract, Transform, Load (ETL) is a set of procedures or tools you can use to **E**xtract data from an external source, **T**ransform it to conform to relational design rules or to conform to other requirements, then **L**oad it into your database for further use or analysis. Nearly all database systems provide various utilities to aid in this process. These utilities are, quite simply, a means to convert raw data into information.

To get an idea of what these utilities can do, let's take a look at some of the tools in Microsoft Access—one of the first Windows-era database systems to provide built-in ways to load and transform data into something useful. Assume you work as the marketing manager for a company that produces breakfast cereals. You need not only to analyze competitive sales from another manufacturer but also to break down this analysis by individual brands.

You can certainly glean total sales information from publicly available documents, but you really want to try to break down competitive sales by individual brand. To do this, you might strike up an agreement with a major grocery store chain to get them to provide their sales information by brand in return for a small discount on your products. The grocery chain promises to send you a spreadsheet containing sales data from all its stores broken down by competitive brand for the previous year. The data you receive might look like Table 3.1.

Table 3.1 Sample competitive sales data

Product		Jan		Feb		Mar
Alpha-Bits		57775.87		40649.37		. . .
Golden Crisp		33985.68		17469.97		. . .
Good Morenings		40375.07		36010.81		. . .
Grape-Nuts		55859.51		38189.64		. . .
Great Grains		37198.23		41444.41		. . .
Honey Bunches of Oats		63283.28		35261.46		. . .
. . . *additional rows* . . .						

It is clear that some blank columns that you do not need were added for readability. You also need to transform the data to end up with one row per product per month, and you have a separate table listing competitive products that has its own primary key, so you need to match on product name to get the key value to use as a foreign key.

Let's start by extracting the data from the spreadsheet into a more usable form. Microsoft Access can import data in many different formats, so let's fire up the Import tool to import a spreadsheet. In the first step, you identify the file and tell Access what you want to do with the output (import into a new table, append the data to an existing table, or link as a read-only table).

When you go to the next step, Access shows you a grid with a sample of the data it found, as shown in Figure 3.2. Because it determined that the first row might very well be usable as column names, it has used the names it found and has assigned generated names to the blank columns.

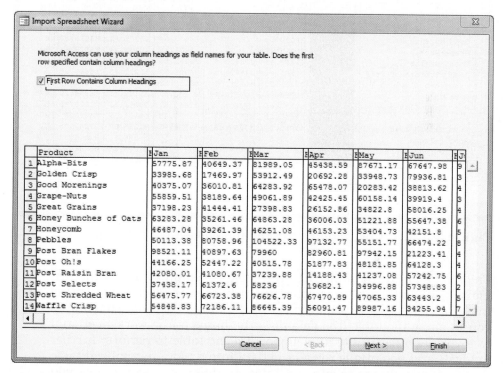

Figure 3.2 The Import Spreadsheet utility performing an initial analysis of the data

In the following step, Access shows you a display where you can select columns one at a time, tell Access to skip unimportant columns, and fix the data type that the utility has assumed. Figure 3.3 on the next page shows one of the data columns selected. The utility has assumed that the numbers, because they contain decimal points, should be imported as the very flexible Double data type. We know that these are all dollar sales figures, so it makes sense to change the data type to Currency to make it easier to work with the data. You can also see the "Do not import" check box (behind the drop-down) that you can select for columns that you want to ignore.

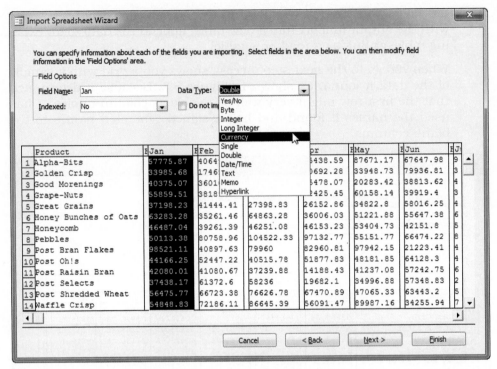

Figure 3.3 Selecting columns to skip and choosing a data type

The next step in the utility lets you pick a column to act as the primary key, ask the utility to generate an ID column with incrementing integers, or assign no primary key to the table. The final step allows you to name the table (the default is the name of the worksheet) and to invoke another utility after importing the table to perform further analysis and potentially reload the data into a more normalized table design. If you choose to run the Table Analyzer, Access presents you with a design tableau as shown in Figure 3.4. In the figure, we have already dragged and dropped the Product column into a separate table and named both tables. As you can see, the utility automatically generates a primary key in the product table and provides a matching foreign key in the sales data table.

Even after using the Table Analyzer, you can see that there is still plenty of work to do to further normalize the sales data into one row per month. You can "unpivot" the sales data by using a UNION query to turn the columns into rows, as shown in Listing 3.5. (See also Item 21, "Use UNION statements to 'unpivot' non-normalized data.")

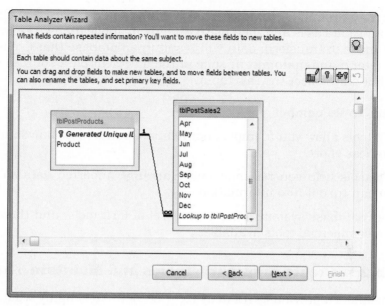

Figure 3.4 Using the Table Analyzer to break out products into a separate table

Listing 3.5 Using a UNION query to "unpivot" a repeating group

```
SELECT '2015-01-01' AS SalesMonth, Product, Jan AS SalesAmt
FROM tblPostSales
UNION ALL
SELECT '2015-02-01' AS SalesMonth, Product, Feb AS SalesAmt
FROM tblPostSales
UNION ALL
  ... etc. for all 12 months.
```

The tools in Microsoft Access are fairly simple (for example, they cannot handle totals rows), but they give you an idea of the amount of work that can be saved when trying to perform ETL to load external data into your database. As noted earlier, most database systems provide similar—and in some cases more powerful—tools that you can use. Examples include Microsoft SQL Server Integration Services (SSIS), Oracle Data Integrator (ODI), and IBM InfoSphere DataStage. Commercial tools are available from vendors such as Informatica, SAP, and SAS, and you can also find a number of open-source tools available on the Web.

The main point here is that you should use those tools so that your data conforms to the data model that your business needs, not the other way around. A common mistake is to build tables that fit the incoming data as is and then use it directly in applications. The investment made to transform data will result in a database that is easy to understand and maintain in spite of the divergent data sources from which it may collect the raw input.

Things to Remember

+ ETL tools allow you to import nonrelational data into your database with less effort.

+ ETL tools help you reformat and rearrange imported data so that you can turn it into information.

+ Most database systems offer some level of ETL tools, and there are also commercial tools available.

Item 20: Create Summary Tables and Maintain Them

We mentioned previously (in Item 18, "Use views to simplify what cannot be changed") that views can be used to simplify complex queries, and we even suggested that views can be used to provide summarizations. Depending on the volume of data, there are times when it may be more appropriate to create summary tables.

When you have a summary table, you can be sure that everything is in one place, making it easier to understand the data structure and quicker to return information.

One approach is to create a table that summarizes your data in your details table, and write triggers to update the summary table every time something changes in the details table. However, if your details table is frequently modified, this can be processor intensive.

Another approach is to use a stored procedure to refresh the summary table on a regular basis: delete all existing data rows and reinsert the summarized information.

DB2 has the concept of summary tables built into it. DB2 summary tables can maintain a summary of data in one or multiple tables. You have the option to have the summary refreshed every time the data in underlying table(s) changes, or you can refresh it manually. DB2 summary tables not only allow users to obtain results faster, but the optimizer can use the summary tables when user queries indirectly request information already summarized in the summary tables if ENABLE QUERY OPTIMIZATION is specified when you create the summary table. Although there may still be "costs" associated with all that activity, at least you did not have to write triggers or stored procedures to maintain the data for you.

Listing 3.6 shows how to create a summary table named SalesSummary that summarizes data from six different tables in DB2. Note that the SQL is not much different from that for creating a view. In fact, a summary table is a specific type of materialized query table, identified by the inclusion of a GROUP BY clause in the CREATE SQL. Note that we had to use Cartesian joins with filters, because of the restriction against using INNER JOIN in a materialized query table, and additionally provide COUNT(*) in the SELECT list to enable the use of the REFRESH IMMEDIATE clause. Those are necessary to permit the optimizer to use it.

Listing 3.6 Creating a summary table based on six tables (DB2)

```
CREATE SUMMARY TABLE SalesSummary AS (
SELECT
  t5.RegionName AS RegionName,
  t5.CountryCode AS CountryCode,
  t6.ProductTypeCode AS ProductTypeCode,
  t4.CurrentYear AS CurrentYear,
  t4.CurrentQuarter AS CurrentQuarter,
  t4.CurrentMonth AS CurrentMonth,
  COUNT(*) AS RowCount,
  SUM(t1.Sales) AS Sales,
  SUM(t1.Cost * t1.Quantity) AS Cost,
  SUM(t1.Quantity) AS Quantity,
  SUM(t1.GrossProfit) AS GrossProfit
FROM Sales AS t1, Retailer AS t2, Product AS t3,
  datTime AS t4, Region AS t5, ProductType AS t6
WHERE t1.RetailerId = t2.RetailerId
  AND t1.ProductId = t3.ProductId
  AND t1.OrderDay = t4.DayKey
  AND t2.RetailerCountryCode = t5.CountryCode
  AND t3.ProductTypeId = t6.ProductTypeId
GROUP BY t5.RegionName, t5.CountryCode, t6.ProductTypeCode,
  t4.CurrentYear, t4.CurrentQuarter, t4.CurrentMonth
)
DATA INITIALLY DEFERRED
REFRESH IMMEDIATE
ENABLE QUERY OPTIMIZATION
MAINTAINED BY SYSTEM
NOT LOGGED INITIALLY;
```

Listing 3.7 on the next page shows how to provide a similar capability in Oracle through the use of a materialized view.

Listing 3.7 Creating a materialized view based on six tables (Oracle)

```
CREATE MATERIALIZED VIEW SalesSummary
  TABLESPACE TABLESPACE1
  BUILD IMMEDIATE
  REFRESH FAST ON DEMAND
AS
SELECT SUM(t1.Sales) AS Sales,
  SUM(t1.Cost * t1.Quantity) AS Cost,
  SUM(t1.Quantity) AS Quantity,
  SUM(t1.GrossProfit) AS GrossProfit,
  t5.RegionName AS RegionName,
  t5.CountryCode AS CountryCode,
  t6.ProductTypeCode AS ProductTypeCode,
  t4.CurrentYear AS CurrentYear,
  t4.CurrentQuarter AS CurrentQuarter,
  t4.CurrentMonth AS CurrentMonth
FROM Sales AS t1
  INNER JOIN Retailer AS t2
    ON t1.RetailerId = t2.RetailerId
  INNER JOIN Product AS t3
    ON t1.ProductId = t3.ProductId
  INNER JOIN datTime AS t4
    ON t1.OrderDay = t4.DayKey
  INNER JOIN Region AS t5
    ON t2.RetailerCountryCode = t5.CountryCode
  INNER JOIN ProductType AS t6
    ON t3.ProductTypeId = t6.ProductTypeId
GROUP BY t5.RegionName, t5.CountryCode, t6.ProductTypeCode,
  t4.CurrentYear, t4.CurrentQuarter, t4.CurrentMonth;
```

Although SQL Server does not directly support materialized views, the fact that you can create indexes on views has a similar effect, and thus you can use indexed views in a similar manner.

Note

Various vendors implement additional restrictions. We advise first consulting your documentation to determine what is actually supported before creating a summary table/materialized view/indexed view.

Note that there can be some negative aspects to summary tables as well, such as the following:

- Each summary table occupies storage.

- The administrative work (triggers, constraints, stored procedures) may need to exist on both the original table and any summary tables.

- You need to know in advance what users want to query in order to precompute the required aggregations and include them in the summary tables.

- You may need multiple summary tables if you need different groupings or filters applied.

- You may need to set up a schedule to manage the refresh of the summary tables.

- You may need to manage the periodicity of the summary tables via SQL. For example, if the summary table is supposed to show the past 12 months, you need a way to remove data that is more than a year old from the table.

One possible suggestion to avoid some of the increased administrative costs of having redundant triggers, constraints, and stored procedures is to use what Ken Henderson referred to as inline summarization in his book *The Guru's Guide to Transact-SQL* (Addison-Wesley, 2000). This involves adding aggregation columns to the existing table. You would use an INSERT INTO SQL statement to aggregate data and store those aggregations in the same table. Columns that are not part of the aggregated data would be set to a known value (such as NULL or some fixed date). An advantage of doing inline summarization is that the summary and the detail data can be easily queried together or separately. The summarized records are easily identified by the known values in certain columns, but other than that, they are indistinguishable from the detail records. However, this approach necessitates that all queries on the table containing both detail and summary data be written appropriately.

Things to Remember

- Storing summarized data can help minimize the processing required for aggregation.

- Using tables to store the summarized data allows you to index fields containing the aggregated data for more efficient queries on aggregates.

- Summarization works best on tables that are more or less static. If the source tables change too often, the overhead of summarization may be too great.

- Triggers can be used to perform summarization, but a stored procedure to rebuild the summary table is usually better.

Item 21: Use UNION Statements to "Unpivot" Non-normalized Data

You saw in Item 3, "Get rid of repeating groups," how UNION queries can be used to deal with repeating groups. We explore UNION queries a little bit more in this item. As you will learn in Item 22, "Understand relational algebra and how it is implemented in SQL," the Union operation is one of the eight relational algebra operations that can be performed within the relational model defined by Dr. Edgar F. Codd. It is used to merge data sets created by two (or more) SELECT statements.

Assume that the only way you are able to get some data for analysis is in the form of the Excel spreadsheet pictured in Figure 3.5, which is obviously not normalized.

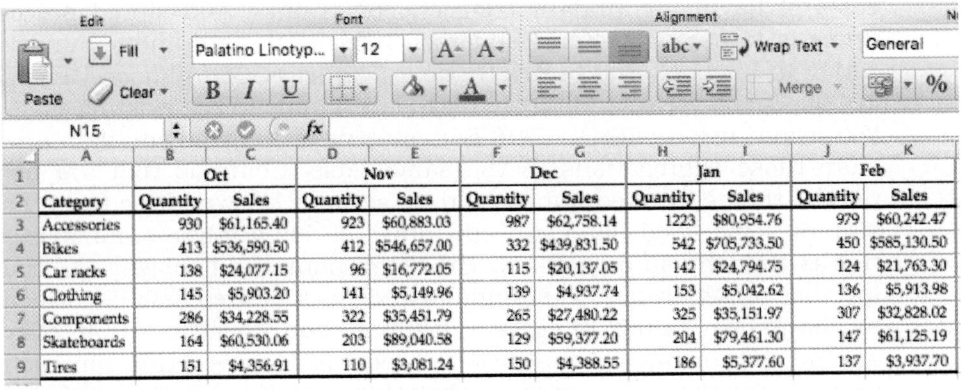

| | Oct | | Nov | | Dec | | Jan | | Feb | |
Category	Quantity	Sales	Quantity	Sales	Quantity	Sales	Quantity	Sales	Quantity	Sales
Accessories	930	$61,165.40	923	$60,883.03	987	$62,758.14	1223	$80,954.76	979	$60,242.47
Bikes	413	$536,590.50	412	$546,657.00	332	$439,831.50	542	$705,733.50	450	$585,130.50
Car racks	138	$24,077.15	96	$16,772.05	115	$20,137.05	142	$24,794.75	124	$21,763.30
Clothing	145	$5,903.20	141	$5,149.96	139	$4,937.74	153	$5,042.62	136	$5,913.98
Components	286	$34,228.55	322	$35,451.79	265	$27,480.22	325	$35,151.97	307	$32,828.02
Skateboards	164	$60,530.06	203	$89,040.58	129	$59,377.20	204	$79,461.30	147	$61,125.19
Tires	151	$4,356.91	110	$3,081.24	150	$4,388.55	186	$5,377.60	137	$3,937.70

Figure 3.5 Non-normalized data from Excel

Assuming you can import that data into your DBMS, at best you will end up with a table (SalesSummary) that has five pairs of repeating groups, which we will call OctQuantity, OctSales, NovQuantity, NovSales, and so on to FebQuantity and FebSales.

Listing 3.8 shows a query that would let you look at the October data.

Listing 3.8 SQL to extract October data

```
SELECT Category, OctQuantity, OctSales
FROM SalesSummary;
```

Of course, to look at the data for a different month, you need a different query. And let's not forget that data that is not normalized can be more difficult to use for analysis purposes. This is where a UNION query can help.

There are three basic rules that apply when using UNION queries:

1. There must be the same number of columns in each of the queries making up the UNION query.

2. The order of the columns in each of the queries making up the UNION query must be the same.

3. The data types of the columns in each of the queries must be compatible.

Note that there is nothing in those rules about the names of the columns in the queries that make up the UNION query.

Listing 3.9 shows how to combine all of the data into a normalized view.

Listing 3.9 Using UNION to normalize the data

```
SELECT Category, OctQuantity, OctSales
FROM SalesSummary
UNION
SELECT Category, NovQuantity, NovSales
FROM SalesSummary
UNION
SELECT Category, DecQuantity, DecSales
FROM SalesSummary
UNION
SELECT Category, JanQuantity, JanSales
FROM SalesSummary
UNION
SELECT Category, FebQuantity, FebSales
FROM SalesSummary;
```

Table 3.2 shows a partial extract of the data returned.

Table 3.2 Partial extract of data returned by the UNION query in Listing 3.9

Category	OctQuantity	OctSales
Accessories	923	60883.03
Accessories	930	61165.40
. . .	. . .	. . .
Bikes	450	585130.50
Bikes	542	705733.50

continues

Table 3.2 Partial extract of data returned by
the UNION query in Listing 3.9 (*continued*)

Category	OctQuantity	OctSales
Car racks	96	16772.05
Car racks	115	20137.05
Car racks	124	21763.30
. . .	. . .	. . .
Skateboards	203	89040.58
Skateboards	204	79461.30
Tires	110	3081.24
Tires	137	3937.70
Tires	150	4388.55
Tires	151	4356.91
Tires	186	5377.60

Two things should stand out. First, there is no way to distinguish
to which month the data applies. The first two rows, for instance,
represent the quantity and sales amount for Accessories for October
and November, but there is no way to tell that from the data. As well,
despite the fact that the data represents five months of sales, the columns are named OctQuantity and OctSales. That is because UNION
queries get their column names from the names of the columns in the
first SELECT statement.

Listing 3.10 shows a query that remedies both of those issues.

Listing 3.10 Tidying up the UNION query used to normalize the data

```
SELECT Category, 'Oct' AS SalesMonth, OctQuantity AS Quantity,
   OctSales AS SalesAmt
FROM SalesSummary
UNION
SELECT Category, 'Nov', NovQuantity, NovSales
FROM SalesSummary
UNION
SELECT Category, 'Dec', DecQuantity, DecSales
FROM SalesSummary
```

```
UNION
SELECT Category, 'Jan', JanQuantity, JanSales
FROM SalesSummary
UNION
SELECT Category, 'Feb', FebQuantity, FebSales
FROM SalesSummary;
```

Table 3.3 shows the same partial extract returned by the query in Listing 3.10.

Table 3.3 Partial extract of data returned by the UNION query in Listing 3.10

Category	SalesMonth	Quantity	SalesAmount
Accessories	Dec	987	62758.14
Accessories	Feb	979	60242.47
. . .	. . .	. . .	. . .
Bikes	Nov	412	546657.00
Bikes	Oct	413	536590.50
Car racks	Dec	115	20137.05
Car racks	Feb	124	21763.30
Car racks	Jan	142	24794.75
. . .	. . .	. . .	. . .
Skateboards	Nov	203	89040.58
Skateboards	Oct	164	60530.06
Tires	Dec	150	4388.55
Tires	Feb	137	3937.70
Tires	Jan	186	5377.60
Tires	Nov	110	3081.24
Tires	Oct	151	4356.91

Should you want the data presented in a different sequence, the ORDER BY clause must appear after the last SELECT in the UNION query, as shown in Listing 3.11 on the next page.

Listing 3.11 Specifying the sort order of the UNION query

```
SELECT Category, 'Oct' AS SalesMonth, OctQuantity AS Quantity,
  OctSales AS SalesAmt
FROM SalesSummary
UNION
SELECT Category, 'Nov', NovQuantity, NovSales
FROM SalesSummary
UNION
SELECT Category, 'Dec', DecQuantity, DecSales
FROM SalesSummary
UNION
SELECT Category, 'Jan', JanQuantity, JanSales
FROM SalesSummary
UNION
SELECT Category, 'Feb', FebQuantity, FebSales
FROM SalesSummary
ORDER BY SalesMonth, Category;
```

Table 3.4 shows a partial extract returned by the query in Listing 3.11.

Table 3.4 Partial extract of data returned by the UNION query in Listing 3.11

Category	SalesMonth	Quantity	SalesAmount
Accessories	Dec	987	62758.14
Bikes	Dec	332	439831.50
Car racks	Dec	115	20137.05
Clothing	Dec	139	4937.74
Components	Dec	265	27480.22
Skateboards	Dec	129	59377.20
Tires	Dec	150	4388.55
Accessories	Feb	979	60242.47
Bikes	Feb	450	585130.50
Car racks	Feb	124	21763.30
. . .	. . .	. . .	. . .

Note

Some DBMSs (such as Microsoft Access) allow you to put ORDER BY clauses other than at the end, but they do not actually cause the order to change.

When specifying the columns in the ORDER BY clause, usually you have the option of referring to them by name (remembering that the column names are specified in the first SELECT) or by position number. In other words, Listing 3.11 could use ORDER BY 2, 1 instead of ORDER BY SalesMonth, Category. Oracle, however, insists on using ordinal references.

Another consideration is that UNION queries eliminate any duplicate rows. Should this not be what you want, you can specify UNION ALL instead of UNION, and duplicates will not be eliminated. On the other hand, UNION ALL can provide performance improvements as it skips the step of deduplicating the result set, so if you know that the sources will not overlap, it can be advantageous to specify UNION ALL for those queries.

Things to Remember

+ Each of the SELECT statements in the UNION query must have the same number of columns.

+ Although the names of the columns in the various SELECT statements do not matter, the data types of each column must be compatible.

+ To control the order in which the data appears, you can use an ORDER BY clause after the last SELECT statement.

+ Use UNION ALL rather than UNION if you do not wish to eliminate duplicate rows or pay the performance penalty of deduplicating rows.

Filtering and Finding Data

Perhaps the most important task you can do in SQL when attempting to turn the data found in one or more tables into useful information is look for data of interest or filter out data not of interest. Sometimes filtering involves matching an entire set of data with another entire set. Other times you accomplish filtering by testing for specific values in one or more columns. This chapter explores all the techniques you can use to find exactly the information you need from your database.

Item 22: Understand Relational Algebra and How It Is Implemented in SQL

Dr. Edgar F. Codd is widely recognized as the "father" of the relational model of database management. He introduced terms such as *relation* (a table or view), *tuple* (a row), and *attribute* (a column). He also described a set of operations—relational algebra—that can be performed within the model. These operations are

1. Select (also known as Restrict)
2. Project
3. Join
4. Intersect
5. Cartesian Product
6. Union
7. Divide
8. Difference

You can perform any of the operations using modern SQL, but the names of the keywords are often different. In the case of Divide (see also Item 26, "Divide your data if you need a perfect match"), you need a combination of SQL operations to achieve the result.

Select (Restrict)

Select or Restrict is the selection and filtering of rows to obtain a sub-set. In SQL, you define the source set of data you want in the FROM clause and then filter the rows returned using the WHERE or HAVING clause. Picturing a set of data as a set of columns and rows, the Select (Restrict) operation returns the light green shaded rows shown in Figure 4.1.

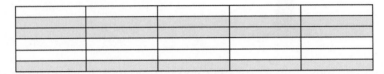

Figure 4.1 Performing a Select operation

Project

Project is the selection of columns or expressions that you want the database system to return. In SQL, you use the SELECT clause, includ-ing aggregate functions, and the GROUP BY clause to define what col-umns the database system returns. Imagining a Selected set as a set of columns and rows, the Project operation returns the yellow shaded columns shown in Figure 4.2.

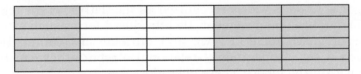

Figure 4.2 Performing a Project operation

Note that it is perfectly valid to Select (Restrict) the rows returned using values in columns that are not ultimately chosen by the Project operation.

Join

Join is the linking of related tables or sets of data on key values. A critical component of the relational model is that all relations (tables) must have a unique identifier (primary key), and that any related tables must contain a copy of the unique identifier (foreign key) from the related table. As you might suspect, you use the JOIN keyword in a FROM clause to perform a Join. SQL expands the concept by allowing you to specify INNER JOIN, NATURAL JOIN, or OUTER JOIN. Figure 4.3 shows two tables and the result of performing both INNER JOIN and OUTER JOIN on two related tables, using the PKey in Table One matched with the FKey in Table Two.

Table One

PKey	ColA	ColB
1	A	q
2	B	r
3	C	s
4	D	t
5	E	u
6	F	v

Table Two

PKey	FKey	ColX	ColY
90	1	55	ABC
91	6	62	GHI
92	3	77	PQR
93	5	50	KLM
94	2	32	STU
95	3	84	DEF
96	6	48	XYZ

Table One INNER JOIN Table Two

PKey	ColA	ColB	PKey	ColX	ColY
1	A	q	90	55	ABC
2	B	r	94	32	STU
3	C	s	92	77	PQR
3	C	s	95	84	DEF
5	E	u	93	50	KLM
6	F	v	91	62	GHI
6	F	v	96	48	XYZ

Table One LEFT OUTER JOIN Table Two

PKey	ColA	ColB	PKey	ColX	ColY
1	A	q	90	55	ABC
2	B	r	94	32	STU
3	C	s	92	77	PQR
3	C	s	95	84	DEF
4	D	t	Null	Null	Null
5	E	u	93	50	KLM
6	F	x	91	62	GHI
6	F	x	96	48	XYZ

Figure 4.3 The result of performing INNER JOIN and OUTER JOIN on two related tables

Notice that the result of INNER JOIN includes only the rows from the two tables that match in both tables. OUTER JOIN includes all rows from Table One and any matching rows from Table Two. For the row in Table One that has no matching value in Table Two, the result returns null values in the Table Two columns.

Note

NATURAL JOIN is similar to INNER JOIN, but it matches rows on columns from the two tables with the same name. You do not specify an ON clause. Of the major implementations, only MySQL, PostgreSQL, and Oracle support NATURAL JOIN.

Intersect

The Intersect operation must be performed on two sets with identical columns. The result of an Intersect is the set of rows from the two sets where all the values match in the respective columns. A number of major database systems support the Intersect operation directly: DB2, Microsoft SQL Server, Oracle, and PostgreSQL. When the database supports Intersect directly, you create one set with a Select (Restrict) and Project and then INTERSECT the first set with a second set.

If your database does not support the Intersect operation (Microsoft Access and MySQL do not), you can achieve the same result by performing an inner join on all the columns from both sets. Listing 4.1 shows how to find customers who have purchased both a bike and a skateboard using INTERSECT.

> **Note**
>
> The actual product names in the Sales Orders sample database are not simply Skateboard and Bike, so the example queries in Listing 4.1, Listing 4.2, and Listing 4.3 in this item actually return no rows. To solve these using the sample database, you would need to use LIKE '%Bike%' and LIKE '%Skateboard%' to see results. We used the simple values in the example queries to make them easier to understand, with the caveat that those are not the most efficient methods for searching.

Listing 4.1 Solving a problem using an Intersect operation

```
SELECT c.CustFirstName, c.CustLastName
FROM Customers AS c
WHERE c.CustomerID IN
  (SELECT o.CustomerID
   FROM Orders AS o
     INNER JOIN Order_Details AS od
       ON o.OrderNumber = od.OrderNumber
     INNER JOIN Products AS p
       ON p.ProductNumber = od.ProductNumber
   WHERE p.ProductName = 'Bike')
INTERSECT
SELECT c2.CustFirstName, c2.CustLastName
FROM Customers AS c2
WHERE c2.CustomerID IN
  (SELECT o.CustomerID
   FROM Orders AS o
     INNER JOIN Order_Details AS od
       ON o.OrderNumber = od.OrderNumber
     INNER JOIN Products AS p
       ON p.ProductNumber = od.ProductNumber
   WHERE p.ProductName = 'Skateboard');
```

Listing 4.2 shows how to solve the same problem using INNER JOIN.

Listing 4.2 Solving a problem using INNER JOIN to emulate an Intersect operation

```
SELECT c.CustFirstName, c.CustLastName
FROM
  (SELECT DISTINCT c.CustomerFirstName,
     c.CustomerLastName
   FROM Customers AS c
     INNER JOIN Orders AS o
       ON c.CustomerID = o.CustomerID
     INNER JOIN Order_Details AS od
       ON o.OrderNumber = od.OrderNumber
     INNER JOIN Products AS p
       ON p.ProductNumber = od.ProductNumber
   WHERE p.ProductName = 'Bike') AS c
INNER JOIN
  (SELECT DISTINCT c.CustomerFirstName,
     c.CustomerLastName
   FROM Customers AS c
     INNER JOIN Orders AS o
       ON c.CustomerID = o.CustomerID
     INNER JOIN Order_Details AS od
       ON o.OrderNumber = od.OrderNumber
     INNER JOIN Products AS p
       ON p.ProductNumber = od.ProductNumber
   WHERE p.ProductName = 'Skateboard'
   ) AS c2
     ON c.CustFirstName = c2.CustFirstName
       AND c.CustLastName = c2.CustLastName;
```

When you use INTERSECT, your database system eliminates any duplicate rows produced by the operation. Some database systems, such as DB2 and PostgreSQL, support INTERSECT ALL, which returns all rows, including duplicates.

Cartesian Product

A Cartesian Product is the result of combining all rows in one set with all rows in the second set. It is called a product because the resulting number of rows is the number of rows in the first set times the number of rows in the second set. For example, if the first set contains eight rows, and the second set contains three rows, the resulting set contains 24 rows (8 * 3 = 24).

To produce a Cartesian Product, simply list your tables or sets in your FROM clause with no JOIN clause. All major database systems support this syntax, but some insert the keywords CROSS JOIN after you save your work. See Chapter 8, "Cartesian Products," and Chapter 9, "Tally Tables," for examples using Cartesian Products.

Union

The Union operation merges two sets that have identical columns. All major implementations of SQL support the UNION keyword. Similarly to Intersect, your SQL should Select and Project one set, add the UNION keyword, and then Select and Project the second set.

One twist to UNION as implemented in SQL is that you can specify UNION ALL. When you do that, your database system does not remove any duplicate rows found in the two sets, so you may find some rows repeated if they appear in both sets.

The Union operation can be useful, for example, to assemble a mailing list to both customers and suppliers by extracting the name, address, city, and state from the two unrelated tables. As we have already discussed in Chapter 3, "When You Can't Change the Design," UNION can be useful to create a "normalized" set of data from a table badly designed with repeating groups.

Divide

Divide in relational algebra is not quite as simple as dividing one number by another to achieve a quotient and a remainder. When you divide one set with another, you are asking your database system to return all the rows in the dividend set that contain all the members of the divisor set. This can be useful, for example, to find all applicants (with a set of qualifications) who meet all the requirements (with another set of qualifications) for a particular job. The result of dividing applicants by qualifications yields the set of applicants who meet all the requirements.

No commercial implementation of SQL provides a Divide operation. You can, however, gain the equivalent of a Divide operation using standard SQL. See Item 26 for examples.

Difference

The Difference operation is basically subtracting one set from another. As for Union and Intersect, you should be working with two sets that contain identical columns. DB2, PostgreSQL, and Microsoft SQL Server all support Difference, but using the EXCEPT keyword. (DB2 also supports EXCEPT ALL, which does not eliminate duplicate rows.) Oracle supports the operation using the MINUS keyword. MySQL and Microsoft Access do not support Difference directly, but you can emulate the operation using OUTER JOIN and a test for null values in the set you are subtracting.

Let's say you want to find all customers who ordered a skateboard but did not order a helmet. Listing 4.3 shows how to do that using both EXCEPT and OUTER JOIN.

Listing 4.3 Solving a problem using a Difference operation

```
SELECT c.CustFirstName, c.CustLastName
FROM Customers AS c
WHERE c.CustomerID IN
  (SELECT o.CustomerID
   FROM Orders AS o
     INNER JOIN Order_Details AS od
       ON o.OrderNumber = od.OrderNumber
     INNER JOIN Products AS p
       ON p.ProductNumber = od.ProductNumber
   WHERE p.ProductName = 'Skateboard')
EXCEPT
SELECT c2.CustFirstName, c2.CustLastName
FROM Customers AS c2
WHERE c2.CustomerID IN
  (SELECT o.CustomerID
   FROM Orders AS o
     INNER JOIN Order_Details AS od
       ON o.OrderNumber = od.OrderNumber
     INNER JOIN Products AS p
       ON p.ProductNumber = od.ProductNumber
   WHERE p.ProductName = 'Helmet');
```

To learn how to solve a Difference problem using OUTER JOIN and a test for IS NULL, see Item 29, "Correctly filter the 'right' side of a 'left' join."

Although SQL does not exactly correspond one to one with the relational algebra operations, all major database engines do use relational algebra as part of optimizing SQL queries, so being familiar with relational algebra is helpful in understanding how your database engine transforms an SQL query into an execution plan. The rest of the items in this chapter mention the relational operation being performed where there is no direct operation in SQL. Also, understanding the material covered in this item will be helpful for reading Item 46, "Understand how the execution plan works," where engines will expose the internal working and, therefore, the relational algebra.

Things to Remember

✦ The relational model defines eight operations that you can perform on sets.

✦ All major implementations of SQL support Select, Project, Join, Cartesian Product, and Union.

✦ Some implementations support Intersect and Difference using the INTERSECT and EXCEPT or MINUS keywords.

✦ No major implementation directly supports Divide, but you can achieve the same result using other parts of SQL.

Item 23: Find Non-matches or Missing Records

Although it is common to use SQL statements to retrieve details of what has occurred from a database, sometimes you need to retrieve details of what has not occurred.

Imagine that you are in charge of inventory for your company. You know that your company sells a variety of products, and you know how to retrieve details from your Sales Orders database to tell you how well a particular product is selling. What about those that are not selling? How can you identify them?

Perhaps the approach that is easiest to understand involves making a list of those products that have been purchased and seeing which ones are not in that list, as illustrated in Listing 4.4. You can see the subquery against the Order_Details table which determines those products that have been purchased, and the use of the NOT IN operator to determine which items in Products are not in that list.

Listing 4.4 Using NOT IN

```
SELECT p.ProductNumber, p.ProductName
FROM Products AS p
WHERE p.ProductNumber
  NOT IN (SELECT ProductNumber FROM Order_Details);
```

Running the query in Listing 4.4 returns the results shown in Table 4.1.

Table 4.1 Products that have not been purchased

ProductNumber	ProductName
4	Victoria Pro All Weather Tires
23	Ultra-Pro Rain Jacket

Although that query may be easy to understand, it turns out that it is very expensive to run. The subquery must go through the entire Order_Details table to build the list of products that have been purchased, sifting through duplicate values, and then each ProductNumber in the Products table must be compared to that list.

There must be more efficient ways to achieve those results, and there are. One approach is to use the EXISTS operator, which checks whether a subquery returns at least one row, as shown in Listing 4.5. You can see that the subquery against Order_Details is now limited to checking for a specific product. In theory, the use of EXISTS should be faster than using NOT IN, especially when the subquery returns a large result set, because once the query engine has found the first record, it can stop processing the subquery.

Listing 4.5 Using an existence check

```
SELECT p.ProductNumber, p.ProductName
FROM Products AS p
WHERE NOT EXISTS
  (SELECT *
   FROM Order_Details AS od
   WHERE od.ProductNumber = p.ProductNumber);
```

> ### Note
>
> See Item 41, "Know the difference between correlated and non-correlated subqueries," for a discussion about the appropriateness of using a correlated subquery.

Another approach is to use the LEFT JOIN operator, combined with a WHERE clause looking for null values, as shown in Listing 4.6. This is sometimes referred to as a "frustrated join": LEFT JOIN would normally return all records from the "left" table, but the WHERE clause "frustrates" that by limiting the results to only those rows where there is no matching record in the "right" table.

Listing 4.6 Using a "frustrated join"

```
SELECT p.ProductNumber, p.ProductName
FROM Products AS p LEFT JOIN Order_Details AS od
  ON p.ProductNumber = od.ProductNumber
WHERE od.ProductNumber IS NULL;
```

Unfortunately, there is no clear-cut answer as to which approach is best. Each DBMS engine tends to have a different bias: some (such as Microsoft Access and older versions of MySQL) seem to favor frustrated joins, but others (such as Microsoft SQL Server) seem to prefer existence checks. You will learn in Item 44, "Learn to use your system's query analyzer," how to test which method works best for the data you have. And even though each DBMS engine seems to have its own preference, you will always find cases where the engine prefers a different method because of the specific distribution of the data.

One more factor to consider is the fact that sometimes a DBMS's optimizer is smart enough to convert a query as written in Listing 4.4 to one like Listing 4.5 or Listing 4.6. However, for more complex queries, automatic transformation might not be possible, so it is beneficial to pay attention to what is a good default for your DBMS and test where performance is critical.

Things to Remember

+ Although easy to understand, using the NOT IN operator is usually not the most efficient approach.

+ Using the NOT EXISTS operator should be faster than using the NOT IN operator.

+ Using a "frustrated join" is often very efficient, but it depends on how the DBMS handles nulls.

+ Use your DBMS query analyzer to determine which approach is best for your specific situation.

Item 24: Know When to Use CASE to Solve a Problem

Use CASE when you need to test some value or expression to determine the correct output. It is literally an IF . . . THEN . . . ELSE for SQL. You can use CASE anywhere you can use a value expression—as a column to be returned in a SELECT clause, or as a search condition in a WHERE or HAVING clause.

Let's say your customers receive a discount based on their customer rating at the time they place an order. "A" customers get 10% off, "B" customers get 5% off, and "C" customers pay full price. You could perhaps use a lookup table that has the three rating values and the related discount that you would link to each customer row, but you can also use CASE to directly test the rating value and apply the correct discount. Using a lookup table gives you a bit more flexibility over time because it is easy to modify the percentages in a table, but that would always require an additional JOIN in your queries.

Perhaps several of your tables use code values (such as M or F for gender), but you want to output the full word in a report. Maybe you have international customers who want to be billed in their local currency, so you need to supply the appropriate currency symbol when you display money values. In a database containing international weather data, you use a C or F symbol to denote temperatures recorded in Centigrade or Fahrenheit, but you want to display both values in a report, so you test the code and apply the appropriate conversion formula.

Term Definitions

- **Value expression:** A literal, a column reference, a function call, a CASE expression, or a subquery that returns a scalar value. Value expressions can be combined with operators such as +, –, *, /, or || depending on data type.

- **Search condition:** One or more predicates optionally preceded by NOT and combined using AND or OR.

- **Predicate:** A test that returns true or false. A predicate can be a comparison, a range, a set membership, a pattern match, a null, quantified, or existence. Comparison is two value expressions compared using =, <>, <, >, <=, or >=. A range is a value expression, optionally NOT, between a value expression and another value expression. Set membership is a value expression, optionally NOT, in a list returned by a subquery or a list of value expressions. A pattern match is a value expression, optionally NOT, like a pattern string. A null is a value expression, optionally NOT, the keyword NULL. Quantified is a value expression followed by a comparison operator, the keywords ALL, SOME, or ANY, and a subquery. Exists is the keyword EXISTS followed by a subquery that typically filters on a value returned by the outer query.

The CASE statement comes in two forms: simple and searched. A simple CASE statement tests one value expression for equality with another value expression and returns one value expression if they match and another value expression if they do not. Listing 4.7 shows some examples of a simple CASE expression.

Note

The ISO Standard states that you can specify WHEN IS NULL, but most major implementations do not support that syntax. If you need to test for NULL, use NULLIF or <expression> IS NULL in the WHEN clause in a searched CASE.

Listing 4.7 Examples using a simple CASE expression

```
-- (Replace a code with a word - two examples.)
CASE Students.Gender
  WHEN 'M'
    THEN 'Male'
    ELSE 'Female' END

CASE Students.Gender
  WHEN 'M' THEN 'Male'
  WHEN 'F' THEN 'Female'
  ELSE 'Unknown' END
```

```
-- (Convert a Centigrade reading to Fahrenheit.)
CASE Readings.Measure
  WHEN 'C'
    THEN (Temperature * 9 / 5) + 32
    ELSE Temperature
END

-- (Return the discount amount based on customer rating.)
CASE (SELECT Customers.Rating FROM Customers
    WHERE Customers.CustomerID = Orders.CustomerID)
  WHEN 'A' THEN 0.10
  WHEN 'B' THEN 0.05
  ELSE 0.00 END
```

When you need to perform something other than an equality test, or you need to test the values in more than one value expression, use searched CASE. Instead of using a value expression immediately after the CASE keyword, you can code one or more WHEN clauses that use a search condition. The search condition can be as simple as a comparison operator between two value expressions but can be as complex as a range, a set membership, a pattern match, a null, a quantified test, or an existence test. Listing 4.8 shows some examples of a searched CASE expression. Note that the database system stops evaluating the rest of the expression as soon as it encounters a true result.

Listing 4.8 Examples using a searched CASE expression

```
-- (Generate a salutation based on gender and marital status.)
CASE WHEN Students.Gender = 'M' THEN 'Mr.'
  WHEN Students.MaritalStatus = 'S' THEN 'Ms.'
  ELSE 'Mrs.' END

-- (Rate sales based by Product on quantity sold.)
SELECT Products.ProductNumber, Products.ProductName,
CASE WHEN
    (SELECT SUM(QuantityOrdered)
     FROM Order_Details
     WHERE Order_Details.ProductNumber =
       Products.ProductNumber) <= 200
  THEN 'Poor'
  WHEN
    (SELECT SUM(QuantityOrdered)
     FROM Order_Details
     WHERE Order_Details.ProductNumber =
       Products.ProductNumber) <= 500
  THEN 'Average'
  WHEN
```

```
    (SELECT SUM(QuantityOrdered)
     FROM Order_Details
     WHERE Order_Details.ProductNumber =
        Products.ProductNumber) <= 1000
  THEN 'Good'
  ELSE 'Excellent' END
FROM Products;

-- (Calculate raises based on position.)
CASE Staff.Title
  WHEN 'Instructor'
  THEN ROUND(Salary * 1.05, 0)
  WHEN 'Associate Professor'
  THEN ROUND(Salary * 1.04, 0)
  WHEN 'Professor' THEN ROUND(Salary * 1.035, 0)
  ELSE Salary END
```

As you might imagine, the possibilities are endless, particularly when you use searched CASE. To help cement the uses for CASE, let's look at a few examples in context in a complete SQL statement. The first example, shown in Listing 4.9, correctly calculates a person's age based on birth date. (The sample code in this listing first appeared in John Viescas and Michael J. Hernandez, *SQL Queries for Mere Mortals, Third Edition* [Addison-Wesley, 2014].)

Listing 4.9 Calculating a person's age using CASE

```
SELECT S.StudentID, S.LastName, S.FirstName,
   YEAR(SYSDATE) - YEAR(S.BirthDate) -
    CASE WHEN MONTH(S.BirthDate) < MONTH(SYSDATE)
       THEN 0
    WHEN MONTH(S.BirthDate) > MONTH(SYSDATE)
       THEN 1
    WHEN DAY(S.BirthDate) > DAY(SYSDATE())
       THEN 1
       ELSE 0 END AS Age
  FROM Students AS S;
```

Note

In DB2, use the CURRENT DATE special register rather than SYSDATE(). In Oracle, use EXTRACT rather than YEAR. In SQL Server, use SYSDATETIME() or GETDATE(). Microsoft Access does not support CASE, but you can get similar results using its IIf() and Date() functions.

You certainly can use CASE as part of a predicate in a WHERE or HAVING clause, but it might not be as efficient as some alternatives. Problems that involve multiple "if this and not that" criteria can often be challenging to solve. One such problem is "Display all customers who purchased skateboards but not helmets." Listing 4.10 shows one way to solve that problem using CASE in the WHERE clause.

Note

The actual product names in the Sales Orders sample database are not simply Skateboard and Helmet, so the example query in Listing 4.10 actually returns no rows. To solve this using the sample database, you would need to use LIKE '%Skateboard%' and LIKE '%Helmet%' to see results. We used the simple values in the example queries to make them easier to understand.

Listing 4.10 Finding customers who bought skateboards but not helmets

```
SELECT CustomerID, CustFirstName, CustLastName
FROM Customers
WHERE (1 =
  (CASE WHEN CustomerID NOT IN
    (SELECT Orders.CustomerID
     FROM Orders
       INNER JOIN Order_Details
         ON Orders.OrderNumber = Order_Details.OrderNumber
       INNER JOIN Products
         ON Order_Details.ProductNumber
            = Products.ProductNumber
     WHERE Products.ProductName = 'Skateboard')
    THEN 0
  WHEN CustomerID IN
    (SELECT Orders.CustomerID
     FROM Orders
       INNER JOIN Order_Details
         ON Orders.OrderNumber = Order_Details.OrderNumber
       INNER JOIN Products
         ON Order_Details.ProductNumber
            = Products.ProductNumber
     WHERE Products.ProductName = 'Helmet')
    THEN 0
    ELSE 1 END));
```

Note that we first eliminated customers who did not buy a skateboard and then eliminated customers who bought a helmet. In Item 25, "Know techniques to solve multiple-criteria problems," we will show you how to solve that problem using IN and NOT IN directly.

Things to Remember

✦ CASE is a powerful tool whenever you need to solve an IF . . . THEN . . . ELSE problem.

✦ You can use simple CASE to perform equals tests and searched CASE to use complex predicates.

✦ You can use CASE wherever you can use a value expression, including as a column definition in a SELECT clause or as part of a predicate in a WHERE or HAVING clause.

Item 25: Know Techniques to Solve Multiple-Criteria Problems

Solving problems using criteria on one table—even compound criteria—is relatively straightforward. When you want to return rows from one table based on criteria applied to a related table, it can get a bit tricky, particularly when you need to apply compound criteria. An example might be "Find all orders for skateboards that also include helmets or knee pads." To solve that, you want to return rows from the Orders table, but you must apply criteria to the Order_Details table.

It gets even more complicated if you go up one level: "List all customers who have ordered a skateboard and who have also ordered a helmet and knee pads and gloves." Solving this requires that you fetch rows from the Customers table while applying criteria through the related Orders and Order_Details tables.

Some of the techniques you can use to solve this sort of problem include the following:

- INNER JOIN or OUTER JOIN with an IS NULL test
- IN or NOT IN using subqueries
- EXISTS or NOT EXISTS using subqueries

Let's find all the really conscientious customers. We want to display all the customers who ordered not only a skateboard but also a helmet, knee pads, and gloves. Assume we have a "typical" Sales Orders database that includes tables as shown in Figure 4.4 on the next page.

Note

For simplicity, we assume that an equal match on the product name will suffice. In reality, you might also need to join to a product categories table to match on the category name because a realistic sales database is likely to offer more than one brand or model of skateboards, gloves, knee pads, and helmets. The actual product names in the Sales Orders sample database are not simply Skateboard, Helmet, Knee Pads, and Gloves, so the example queries in the listings in this item actually return no rows. To solve this using the sample database, you would need to use LIKE '%Skateboard%', LIKE '%Helmet%', and so on to see results.

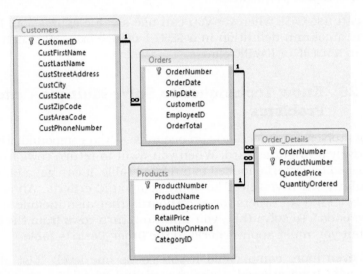

Figure 4.4 Design for a typical Sales Orders database

You might be tempted to solve this all-inclusive problem by writing a query as shown in Listing 4.11.

Listing 4.11 Solving compound inclusive criteria the wrong way

```
SELECT c.CustomerID, c.CustFirstName, c.CustLastName
FROM Customers AS c
WHERE c.CustomerID IN
  (SELECT o.CustomerID
   FROM Orders AS o
     INNER JOIN Order_Details AS od
       ON o.OrderNumber = od.OrderNumber
     INNER JOIN Products AS p
       ON p.ProductNumber = od.ProductNumber
   WHERE p.ProductName
     IN ('Skateboard', 'Helmet', 'Knee Pads', 'Gloves'));
```

That will not get you what you want because it will list any customer who ever ordered a skateboard *or* a helmet *or* knee pads *or* gloves. The correct way involves using SQL that is much more complex. First, we will solve it using INNER JOIN as shown in Listing 4.12.

Listing 4.12 Solving compound inclusive criteria correctly

```
SELECT c.CustomerID, c.CustFirstName, c.CustLastName
FROM Customers AS c
  INNER JOIN
    (SELECT DISTINCT Orders.CustomerID
     FROM Orders AS o
       INNER JOIN Order_Details AS od
         ON o.OrderNumber = oc.OrderNumber
       INNER JOIN Products AS p
         ON p.ProductNumber = od.ProductNumber
     WHERE p.ProductName = 'Skateboard') AS OSk
    ON c.CustomerID = OSk.CustomerID
  INNER JOIN
    (SELECT DISTINCT Orders.CustomerID
     FROM Orders AS o
       INNER JOIN Order_Details AS od
         ON o.OrderNumber = od.OrderNumber
       INNER JOIN Products AS p
         ON p.ProductNumber = od.ProductNumber
     WHERE p.ProductName = 'Helmet') AS OHel
    ON c.CustomerID = OHel.CustomerID
  INNER JOIN
    (SELECT DISTINCT Orders.CustomerID
     FROM Orders AS o
       INNER JOIN Order_Details AS od
         ON o.OrderNumber = od.OrderNumber
       INNER JOIN Products AS p
         ON p.ProductNumber = od.ProductNumber
     WHERE p.ProductName = 'Knee Pads') AS OKn
    ON c.CustomerID = OKn.CustomerID
  INNER JOIN
    (SELECT DISTINCT Orders.CustomerID
     FROM Orders AS o
       INNER JOIN Order_Details AS od
         ON o.OrderNumber = od.OrderNumber
       INNER JOIN Products AS p
         ON p.ProductNumber = od.ProductNumber
     WHERE p.ProductName = 'Gloves') AS OGl
    ON c.CustomerID = OGl.CustomerID;
```

Although much more complex, the second query returns the correct answer because it finds only the customers who match on all four subqueries embedded in the outer FROM clause. Note that we used DISTINCT in the subqueries to ensure that we ended up with only one row per customer. You can also solve this type of problem using four subqueries and the IN predicate in a WHERE clause applied to the Customers table, as shown in Listing 4.13. To make the final SQL easier to read, we first create a function to handle the subqueries.

Listing 4.13 Using a function to solve compound inclusive criteria correctly

```
CREATE FUNCTION CustProd(@ProdName varchar(50)) RETURNS Table
AS
RETURN
  (SELECT Orders.CustomerID AS CustID
   FROM Orders
     INNER JOIN Order_Details
       ON Orders.OrderNumber
          = Order_Details.OrderNumber
   INNER JOIN Products
     ON Products.ProductNumber
        = Order_Details.ProductNumber
   WHERE ProductName = @ProdName);

SELECT C.CustomerID, C.CustFirstName, C.CustLastName
FROM Customers AS C
WHERE C.CustomerID IN
  (SELECT CustID FROM CustProd('Skateboard'))
AND C.CustomerID IN
  (SELECT CustID FROM CustProd('Helmet'))
AND C.CustomerID IN
  (SELECT CustID FROM CustProd('Knee Pads'))
AND C.CustomerID IN
  (SELECT CustID FROM CustProd('Gloves'));
```

Finally, you could solve this problem similarly to using IN and subqueries with EXISTS and correlated subqueries. (See also Item 41, "Know the difference between correlated and non-correlated subqueries.") Listing 4.14 gives you an idea of how you might begin to construct your WHERE clause using EXISTS.

Listing 4.14 Solving compound inclusive criteria using EXISTS

```
SELECT c.CustomerID, c.CustFirstName, c.CustLastName
FROM Customers AS c
WHERE EXISTS
  (SELECT o.CustomerID
   FROM Orders AS o
     INNER JOIN Order_Details AS od
       ON o.OrderNumber = od.OrderNumber
     INNER JOIN Products AS p
```

```
      ON p.ProductNumber = od.ProductNumber
    WHERE p.ProductName = 'Skateboard'
      AND o.CustomerID = C.CustomerID)
  AND EXISTS ...
```

You will run into the same challenges when you need to find a row using multiple positive and negative criteria on a related table. It has been interesting up to this point to find all the customers who did buy protective gear with their skateboards, but from a marketing standpoint store owners might be more interested in those who bought just the skateboard so that they can send out a mailer or e-mails to remind those folks that they should also get the protective gear.

So, let's search for all customers who purchased a skateboard but did not buy a helmet, gloves, and knee pads. You might be tempted to solve the problem as shown in Listing 4.15.

Listing 4.15 Looking for customers who did not buy protective gear

```
SELECT c.CustomerID, c.CustFirstName, c.CustLastName
FROM Customers AS c
WHERE c.CustomerID IN
  (SELECT o.CustomerID
   FROM Orders AS o
     INNER JOIN Order_Details AS od
       ON o.OrderNumber = od.OrderNumber
     INNER JOIN Products AS p
       ON p.ProductNumber = od.ProductNumber
   WHERE p.ProductName = 'Skateboard')
  AND c.CustomerID NOT IN
  (SELECT o.CustomerID
   FROM Orders AS o
     INNER JOIN Order_Details AS od
       ON o.OrderNumber = od.OrderNumber
     INNER JOIN Products AS p
       ON p.ProductNumber = od.ProductNumber
   WHERE p.ProductName
     IN ('Helmet', 'Gloves', 'Knee Pads'));
```

Do you understand why that will not work? As long as customers have purchased a helmet *or* gloves *or* knee pads, you will not find them in the query results. Let's refine that query and take advantage of the function we created earlier. The correct solution is in Listing 4.16.

Listing 4.16 Finding customers who did not purchase all the protective gear

```
SELECT c.CustomerID, c.CustFirstName, c.CustLastName
FROM Customers AS c
```

```
WHERE c.CustomerID IN
    (SELECT CustID FROM CustProd('Skateboard'))
  AND (c.CustomerID NOT IN
    (SELECT CustID FROM CustProd('Helmet'))
  OR c.CustomerID NOT IN
    (SELECT CustID FROM CustProd('Gloves'))
  OR c.CustomerID NOT IN
    (SELECT CustID FROM CustProd('Knee Pads')));
```

Notice that the first predicate in the WHERE clause finds customers who purchased skateboards, and the remaining predicates find customers who did not purchase helmets *or* did not purchase gloves *or* did not purchase knee pads. As you can see, when you require something, you use AND, and when you include possibilities, you use OR.

Things to Remember

✦ Correctly solving problems requiring tests for multiple criteria via a related table or tables is not simple or straightforward.

✦ When you want rows from a parent table that qualifies for more than one criterion applied to one or more related child tables, you must use INNER JOIN or OUTER JOIN with a null test (aka frustrated join) on table subqueries or IN and AND or NOT IN and OR on table subqueries to achieve the correct answer.

Item 26: Divide Your Data If You Need a Perfect Match

Division is one of the eight set operations defined by Dr. E. F. Codd in his classic book *The Relational Model for Database Management* published by Addison-Wesley. (The others are Select, Project, Join, Intersect, Cartesian Product, Union, and Difference. See Item 22, "Understand relational algebra and how it is implemented in SQL," for details about the other operations.) The operation involves "dividing" one large set (the dividend) by a smaller set (the divisor) to obtain the quotient—all the members of the dividend set that completely match the divisor set.

Common problems you can solve with division include these:

- Find all job candidates who meet all the requirements for a given job.

- List all suppliers who can provide all the parts to build a component.

- Display all customers who ordered a certain set of products.

To help you visualize a division operation, consider Figure 4.5.

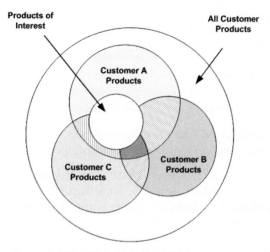

Figure 4.5 Dividing all customer products by a set of products of interest

In the figure, the outer circle represents all products that customers have purchased. The three shaded circles represent the products that specific customers have purchased, and you can see that there are some products that all of them have purchased. The small white circle represents a subset of products for which we want to determine the customers who purchased them.

In this simple example, all three customers purchased some of the items in the set of products of interest, but only Customer A purchased all of them. If you divide the set of all customer products by the set of products of interest, the answer should be Customer A—the only customer who purchased them all.

Unfortunately, there is no single operation in SQL to perform a division, so you must use a combination of the supported operations to achieve the result. We actually showed you one way to solve a Divide in Item 25, "Know techniques to solve multiple-criteria problems," which involved using IN and a subquery for each member of the divisor set. That is an acceptable way to do it when the divisor contains just a few entries, but it becomes nearly unworkable when the divisor set is large.

Let's begin by defining views for the two sets—the dividend and the divisor. Listing 4.17 creates the dividend set—the set of all customers and the products that they have purchased.

Listing 4.17 Creating a view for all customers and their products

```
CREATE VIEW CustomerProducts AS
SELECT DISTINCT c.CustomerID, c.CustFirstName,
  c.CustLastName, p.ProductName
```

```
FROM Customers AS c
  INNER JOIN Orders AS o
    ON c.CustomerID = o.CustomerID
  INNER JOIN Order_Details AS od
    ON o.OrderNumber = od.OrderNumber
  INNER JOIN Products AS p
    ON p.ProductNumber = od.ProductNumber;
```

Note that we use DISTINCT to produce one row per customer and product just in case a customer ordered the same product more than once.

Now let's create a view on the divisor set—the set of all products of interest. Just as we did in Item 25, let's find all customers who purchased a skateboard, a helmet, knee pads, and gloves. Listing 4.18 shows the code to create the view.

Listing 4.18 Creating a view to list the products of interest

```
CREATE VIEW ProdsOfInterest AS
SELECT Products.ProductName
FROM Products
WHERE ProductName IN
  ('Skateboard', 'Helmet', 'Knee Pads', 'Gloves');
```

> **Note**
>
> In the Sales Orders sample database, there are actually no simple products named Skateboard, Helmet, Knee Pads, and Gloves, so the simple solutions presented for Listings 4.17, 4.18, 4.19, and 4.20 will not work. We provided the simpler versions in the text to help you understand the process. In the sample files, you will find both the versions presented here and slightly more complex versions that use LIKE to convert the product name to a category name for the division to produce a true result.

Now let's take a look at one way to do a Divide to achieve the result. This technique was described by Chris Date, a partner of Dr. Codd, in his books. Listing 4.19 shows a solution.

Listing 4.19 Dividing customer products by products of interest using subqueries

```
SELECT DISTINCT CP1.CustomerID, CP1.CustFirstName,
  CP1.CustLastName
FROM CustomerProducts AS CP1
WHERE NOT EXISTS
  (SELECT ProductName
   FROM ProdsOfInterest AS PofI
```

```
WHERE NOT EXISTS
  (SELECT CustomerID
   FROM CustomerProducts AS CP2
   WHERE CP2.CustomerID = CP1.CustomerID
     AND CP2.ProductName = PofI.ProductName));
```

Simply stated, we want all customer product rows where there is not a product where there is not a row in customer products that matches the product and customer ID. That is a confusing double negative in English, but the logic is sound. An interesting side effect of this technique is that when the divisor set (the products of interest in this case) is empty, the query returns all customer product rows.

Now let's look at another technique using GROUP BY and HAVING—a technique made popular by Joe Celko in his books. For this technique, it is critical that we use DISTINCT in the first view to create unique customer product rows because we are going to count to get the solution, and we do not want duplicate purchases to mess up the count. For example, if a customer buys a skateboard, a helmet, and two pairs of gloves (in separate orders), the count of rows is four, which matches the count of products of interest. Without DISTINCT, the customer would be selected in error even though he or she did not purchase knee pads. Rows selected from the Products table by product name in the second view are unique, so we do not need DISTINCT there. Listing 4.20 shows the answer.

Listing 4.20 Dividing the two sets using GROUP BY and HAVING

```
SELECT CP.CustomerID, CP.CustFirstName, CP.CustLastName
FROM CustomerProducts AS CP
  CROSS JOIN ProdsOfInterest AS PofI
WHERE CP.ProductName = PofI.ProductName
GROUP BY CP.CustomerID, CP.CustFIrstName, CP.CustLastName
HAVING COUNT(CP.ProductName) =
  (SELECT COUNT(ProductName) FROM ProdsOfInterest);
```

Basically, we have found all customers' product rows that match any row in the products of interest, but we keep only those rows where we get a match on all the rows in products of interest by comparing the count. Note that when the divisor set is empty, this query returns no rows, which is different from the first technique.

Things to Remember

✦ Divide is one of the eight recognized relational set operations, but neither the SQL Standard nor any major database systems implement a DIVIDE keyword.

✦ You can use Divide to discover the rows in one set that match all the rows in a second set.

✦ You can perform a Divide by testing for each row in the divisor set (IN with subqueries shown in Item 25), NOT EXISTS, and GROUP BY/HAVING.

Item 27: Know How to Correctly Filter a Range of Dates on a Column Containing Both Date and Time

Using the WHERE clause to limit what your query returns should be second nature to you by now. However, we find that many developers do not filter date ranges as effectively as they could.

As the Appendix, "Date and Time Types, Operations, and Functions," describes, there are a number of different data types that can be used to store dates and times. We are specifically concerned with data stored using the data types listed in Table 4.2.

Table 4.2 Date and time data types

DBMS	Data Type
IBM DB2	TIMESTAMP
Microsoft Access	Date/Time
Microsoft SQL Server	smalldatetime, datetime, datetime2, datetimeoffset
MySQL	datetime, timestamp
Oracle	TIMESTAMP
PostgreSQL	TIMESTAMP

Consider the table created in Listing 4.21.

Listing 4.21 Table creation Data Definition Language (DDL) for a log table

```
CREATE TABLE ProgramLogs (
  LogID int PRIMARY KEY,
  LogUserID varchar(20) NOT NULL,
  LogDate timestamp NOT NULL,
  Logger varchar(50) NOT NULL,
  LogLevel varchar(10) NOT NULL,
  LogMessage varchar(1000)  NOT NULL
);
```

Should you want to see the log messages for a particular day, you might be tempted to use a statement such as is shown in Listing 4.22.

Listing 4.22 First attempt to list log messages for a specific day

```
SELECT L.LogUserID, L.Logger, L.LogLevel, L.LogMessage
FROM ProgramLogs AS L
WHERE L.LogDate = CAST('7/4/2016' AS timestamp);
```

However, there is a subtle issue at play here. Although you wrote the query and knew that you intended to get data for July 4, what happens if the system has British regional settings or the language is set to French? That date could very well be interpreted as April 7! Much better to use an unambiguous date format, such as yyyy-mm-dd, yyyymmdd, or yyyy-mm-dd hh:mm:ss[.nnn].

Note

Although the ISO 8601 format yyyy-mm-ddThh:mm:ss[.nnn] is often listed as a valid option, it is not actually part of the SQL Standard. The ANSI SQL Standard for date and time is yyyy-mm-dd hh:mm:ss, which does not actually conform to the ISO 8601 Standard that requires a "T" separator. Not all DBMSs support ISO 8601 specifications.

However, even that may not be sufficient. For example, Microsoft has chosen a nonstandard implementation for dates in nnnn-nn-nn format. If the general date format is dmy, SQL Server interprets dates as being in ydm format when the year is first. Because the default format for date depends on the setting of each individual login, it is conceivable that 2016-07-04 could be interpreted as 07 April 2016 depending on the user's language settings. To avoid issues like this, you should use an explicit date conversion function rather than relying on implicit date conversion. For instance, Listing 4.22 should be rewritten as shown in Listing 4.23.

Listing 4.23 Second attempt to list log messages for a specific day

```
SELECT L.LogUserID, L.Logger, L.LogLevel, L.LogMessage
FROM ProgramLogs AS L
WHERE L.LogDate = CONVERT(datetime, '2016-07-04', 120);
```

Note

The SQL in this item is for SQL Server. Consult your database documentation for alternatives if, for example, your database does not support the CONVERT() function. Though SQL Server supports CAST(), which is a part of the SQL Standard, it does not allow for explicitly specifying the date style; 120 indicates that the format is given in a yyyy-mm-dd hh:nn:ss format.

When you run the query, odds are you will not actually get any data returned. Remember that the LogDate column is defined as a time-stamp, meaning that it contains both date and time. Because the date literal provided has no time component, the database system will convert the value to 2016-07-04 00:00:00, and unless there was an entry logged at exactly that time, the system will return no rows.

You could try removing the time component from the column by using CAST(L.LogDate AS date), but that would make the query non-sargable, so the system will not use any indexes. (See Item 28, "Write sargable queries to ensure that the engine will use indexes," for more details.)

Listing 4.24 shows a sargable query that could work.

Listing 4.24 Third attempt to list log messages for a specific day

```
SELECT L.LogUserID, L.Logger, L.LogLevel, L.LogMessage
FROM ProgramLogs AS L
WHERE L.LogDate BETWEEN CONVERT(datetime, '2016-07-04', 120)
  AND CONVERT(datetime, '2016-07-05', 120);
```

A potential issue is that BETWEEN is inclusive: if there are any records in the table for 2016-07-05 00:00:00, they will be included as well. To avoid that, you could try to formulate a more exact final datetime, as shown in Listing 4.25.

Listing 4.25 Fourth attempt to list log messages for a specific day

```
SELECT L.LogUserID, L.Logger, L.LogLevel, L.LogMessage
FROM ProgramLogs AS L
WHERE L.LogDate BETWEEN CONVERT(datetime, '2016-07-04', 120)
  AND CONVERT(datetime, '2016-07-04 23:59:59.999', 120);
```

The problem with that, however, is that (at least in SQL Server) the resolution for the datetime type is 3.33 ms. That means that SQL Server will actually round up 2016-07-04 23:59:59.999 to 2016-07-05 00:00:00.000, so it buys you nothing. Although you could change the precision to 2016-07-04 23:59:59.997 to get around the rounding problem, not all datetime fields have the same precision, and it turns out that would still be rounded up for smalldatetime fields. There is also the possibility that the precision could change in a new release, or vary from DBMS to DBMS. A far more stable solution is to avoid the inclusivity of the BETWEEN statement as shown in Listing 4.26.

Listing 4.26 Recommended approach to list log messages for a specific day

```
SELECT L.LogUserID, L.Logger, L.LogLevel, L.LogMessage
FROM ProgramLogs AS L
```

```
WHERE L.LogDate >= CONVERT(datetime, '2016-07-04', 120)
  AND L.LogDate < CONVERT(datetime, '2016-07-05', 120);
```

There is one more consideration to think about. If the query would contain input from users (e.g., as a part of a stored procedure with parameters for dates), users might often enter something like 2016-07-04 for start and 2016-07-05 for end. But they really want >= '2016-07-04' and < '2016-07-06'. Therefore, it is a good habit to write the query to use a DATEADD function to advance the date as illustrated in Listing 4.27.

Listing 4.27 Advancing the end date provided by user input

```
WHERE L.LogDate >=
    CONVERT(datetime, @startDate, 120)
  AND L.LogDate <
    CONVERT(datetime, DATEADD(DAY, 1, @endDate) 120);
```

The key point is that you should use DATEADD or an equivalent function in your DBMS to ensure that a date is incremented in a well-defined manner rather than relying on the DBMS's implementation and to account for the difference between how users and software programs interpret what is the "end."

Things to Remember

✦ Do not rely on implicit date conversion; use explicit conversion functions to date literals.

✦ Do not apply functions to datetime columns or the query will not be sargable.

✦ Remember that rounding errors can cause datetime values to be inexact; use >= and < rather than BETWEEN.

Item 28: Write Sargable Queries to Ensure That the Engine Will Use Indexes

We wrote about the importance of appropriate indexes to improve query performance in Item 11, "Carefully consider creation of indexes to minimize index and data scanning." Having indexes alone is not sufficient, though. In order for the DBMS engine to take advantage of an index, the predicate of the query (i.e., the WHERE, ORDER BY, GROUP BY, or HAVING clause) needs to be "sargable" (the term is derived from a contraction of **S**earch **ARG**ument **ABLE**). It is important, therefore, to understand what prevents a query from being sargable.

Note

DB2 used to refer to sargable and non-sargable predicates in v1 and v2, but those terms are no longer used. Instead, DB2 now refers to Stage 1 and Stage 2 predicates, where Stage 1 predicates outperform Stage 2. Specific predicates tend to migrate from Stage 2 to Stage 1 depending on DB2 version.

Depending on the value that is being checked, the following operators can usually be considered sargable:

- =

- >

- <

- >=

- <=

- BETWEEN

- LIKE (without leading wildcards)

- IS [NOT] NULL

Although the following operators may be sargable, their use rarely improves performance:

- <>

- IN

- OR

- NOT IN

- NOT EXISTS

- NOT LIKE

The following all result in non-sargable queries:[1]

- Using a function that operates on one or more fields in the WHERE clause conditions. (Because the function has to be evaluated against each row, the query optimizer will not use the index unless the index itself contains the same function.)

- Performing arithmetic calculation on a field in a WHERE clause.

- Using a wildcard search query such as LIKE '%something%'.

---

1. The SELECT clause can contain non-sargable expressions without adversely affecting performance.

Consider the Employees table shown in Listing 4.28. Note that the SQL creates indexes for each field in the table.

Listing 4.28 Table and index creation DDL

```
CREATE TABLE Employees (
  EmployeeID int IDENTITY (1, 1) PRIMARY KEY,
  EmpFirstName varchar(25) NULL,
  EmpLastName varchar(25) NULL,
  EmpDOB date NULL,
  EmpSalary decimal(15,2) NULL
);
CREATE INDEX [EmpFirstName]
  ON [Employees]([EmpFirstName] ASC);
CREATE INDEX [EmpLastName]
  ON [Employees]([EmpLastName] ASC);
CREATE INDEX [EmpDOB]
  ON [Employees]([EmpDOB] ASC);
CREATE INDEX [EmpSalary]
  ON [Employees]([EmpSalary] ASC);
```

Listing 4.29 shows a non-sargable way to limit the data to only those employees born in a particular year. This is because it is necessary to perform the Year function call on every row in the table in order to determine which rows match, meaning that the index on EmpDOB will not be used.

Listing 4.29 Non-sargable query to limit data to a particular year

```
SELECT EmployeeID, EmpFirstName, EmpLastName
FROM Employees
WHERE YEAR(EmpDOB) = 1950;
```

> **Note**
>
> Oracle does not have a Year() function. You need to use EXTRACT(year FROM EmpDOB).

Listing 4.30 shows how to retrieve the same data in a sargable way.

Listing 4.30 Sargable query to limit data to a particular year

```
SELECT EmployeeID, EmpFirstName, EmpLastName
FROM Employees
WHERE EmpDOB >= CAST('1950-01-01' AS Date)
  AND EmpDOB < CAST('1951-01-01' AS Date);
```

Listing 4.31 shows a non-sargable query attempting to find all employees whose surnames start with a specific letter.

Listing 4.31 Non-sargable query to limit data to a particular initial

```
SELECT EmployeeID, EmpFirstName, EmpLastName
FROM Employees
WHERE LEFT(EmpLastName, 1) = 'S';
```

Note

Oracle does not have a Left() function. You need to use the function SUBSTR(EmpLastName, 1, 1).

Listing 4.32 shows how to do the same thing in a sargable manner. Note that the use of the LIKE operator does not make the query non-sargable, because the wildcard character is only at the end of the string. Note that this by itself does not guarantee that indexes will be used.

Listing 4.32 Sargable query to limit data to a particular initial

```
SELECT EmployeeID, EmpFirstName, EmpLastName
FROM Employees
WHERE EmpLastName LIKE 'S%';
```

Listing 4.33 shows another non-sargable query with the use of the IsNull() function.

Listing 4.33 Non-sargable query to find a particular name in a field that can be null

```
SELECT EmployeeID, EmpFirstName, EmpLastName
FROM Employees
WHERE IsNull(EmpLastName, 'Viescas') = 'Viescas';
```

Note

IsNull() is an SQL Server function. Oracle uses NVL(), and DB2 and MySQL use IFNULL(). Another possibility is to use the COALESCE() function.

Listing 4.34 shows how to perform that same query in a sargable manner.

Listing 4.34 Sargable query to find a particular name in a field that can be null

```
SELECT EmployeeID, EmpFirstName, EmpLastName
FROM Employees
```

```
WHERE EmpLastName = 'Viescas'
  OR EmpLastName IS NULL;
```

In fact, the use of the OR may well prevent the index on EmpLastName from being used, so the query in Listing 4.35 may be safer. This is particularly true when you have separate filtered indexes for values and nulls.

Listing 4.35 Improved sargable query to find a particular name in a field that can be null

```
SELECT EmployeeID, EmpFirstName, EmpLastName
FROM Employees
WHERE EmpLastName = 'Viescas'
UNION ALL
SELECT EmployeeID, EmpFirstName, EmpLastName
FROM Employees
WHERE EmpLastName IS NULL;
```

The query in Listing 4.36 is non-sargable because of the calculation on the field. The index on EmpSalary will not be used, and the calculation will be done for every row in the table.

Listing 4.36 Non-sargable query to find a calculated value

```
SELECT EmployeeID, EmpFirstName, EmpLastName
FROM Employees
WHERE EmpSalary*1.10 > 100000;
```

If, however, the calculation does not involve the field, as in Listing 4.37, the query becomes sargable.

Listing 4.37 Sargable query to find a calculated value

```
SELECT EmployeeID, EmpFirstName, EmpLastName
FROM Employees
WHERE EmpSalary > 100000/1.10;
```

Unfortunately, there is no way to make LIKE '%something%' sargable.

Things to Remember

✦ Avoid using non-sargable operators.

✦ Do not use functions that operate on one or more fields in a WHERE clause.

✦ Do not perform arithmetic calculations on fields in a WHERE clause.

✦ When using the LIKE operator, only use a wildcard at the end of the string (not '%something' or 'some%thing').

Item 29: Correctly Filter the "Right" Side of a "Left" Join

Suppose you are asked to find all customers who never placed an order. To do that, you need to perform a Difference relational operation in SQL (in other words, return the data that is in set 1 but not in set 2), and you use OUTER JOIN with an IS NULL test. For example, to find all customers who have never placed an order, you use Customers LEFT OUTER JOIN Orders and test for a null value in the primary key of the Orders table (sometimes called a "frustrated" outer join). You are subtracting all the customer orders from the set of all customers to find the customers who are not in the set of customers who placed orders.

Note

See Item 22, "Understand relational algebra and how it is implemented in SQL," for details about the other relational operations.

When you need to apply a filter to the set that you are subtracting from a larger set (basically, the table or set on the "right" side of a "left" join or vice versa), it is easy to make a mistake. In a query that does Customers LEFT JOIN Orders, Customers is on the "left" side of the join, and Orders is on the "right" side. For example, consider this problem:

Show me all customers and, if some exist, any orders that they placed during the last quarter of 2015.

You might be tempted to solve the problem using SQL as shown in Listing 4.38.

Listing 4.38 First attempt to show all customers and a subset of orders

```
SELECT c.CustomerID, c.CustFirstName, c.CustLastName,
  o.OrderNumber, o.OrderDate, o.OrderTotal
FROM Customers AS c
  LEFT JOIN Orders AS o
    ON c.CustomerID = o.CustomerID
WHERE o.OrderDate BETWEEN CAST('2015-10-01' AS DATE)
  AND CAST('2015-12-31' AS DATE);
```

Note

The SQL in this item uses ISO Standard SQL. Consult your database documentation for alternatives if, for example, your database does not support the CAST() function.

When you run the query, you find order data in every row, and it seems that many of the customers are missing. Then you remember that you have to test for NULL if you want the "missing" rows to show up, so next you try the SQL shown in Listing 4.39.

Listing 4.39 Second attempt to show all customers and a subset of orders

```
SELECT c.CustomerID, c.CustFirstName, c.CustLastName,
  o.OrderNumber, o.OrderDate, o.OrderTotal
FROM Customers AS c
  LEFT JOIN Orders AS o
    ON c.CustomerID = o.CustomerID
WHERE (o.OrderDate BETWEEN CAST('2015-10-01' AS DATE)
    AND CAST('2015-12-31' AS DATE))
  OR o.OrderNumber IS NULL;
```

The output of the second query looks a bit better, but you still might not see all the customer rows.

A database engine first resolves the FROM clause, then applies the WHERE clause, and finally returns the columns requested in the SELECT clause. In the first query, Customers LEFT JOIN Orders certainly does return all customer rows and any matching rows from the Orders table. Applying the WHERE clause automatically eliminates any customers who have not placed orders because those rows contain a null in the columns from the Orders table. NULL can never compare to any value, so filtering by a range of dates eliminates those rows. So with the query in Listing 4.38, all you get are the customers who placed an order in the specified date range—the same result you would get with INNER JOIN.

In the query in Listing 4.39, we asked for not only the orders within the date range but also any rows containing a null in the OrderNumber column in the hope that we would thus get all customer rows. The set returned by the FROM clause does indeed include all customers. When a customer has placed any order, the columns from the Orders table will not be null. When a customer has never placed an order at all, the query returns exactly one row for that customer with null values in the columns from the Orders table.

So, the query in Listing 4.39 does return all customers who have never placed an order and any customers who did place an order in the last quarter of 2015. If there is a customer who placed an order earlier, but not in the last quarter, that customer will not show up at all because the date filter removes that row.

The correct solution is to filter the "subtraction" set before it is joined with the set from which you are subtracting. You do that by using a SELECT statement in the FROM clause (also called a derived table in the SQL Standard) to provide the filtered set. Listing 4.40 shows how.

Listing 4.40 Correctly fetching all customers and a subset of orders

```
SELECT c.CustomerID, c.CustFirstName, c.CustLastName,
  OFil.OrderNumber, OFil.OrderDate, OFil.OrderTotal
FROM Customers AS c
  LEFT JOIN
    (SELECT o.OrderNumber, o.CustomerID,
        o.OrderDate, o.OrderTotal
     FROM Orders AS o
     WHERE o.OrderDate BETWEEN CAST('2015-10-01' AS DATE)
        AND CAST('2015-12-31' AS DATE)) AS OFil
    ON c.CustomerID = OFil.CustomerID;
```

Logically, the query in Listing 4.40 first fetches the subset of orders placed between the two dates and then performs the join with the Customers table. This query does return all customers. When a customer did not place an order in the specified time frame, the columns from the OFiltered subquery are null. If you want to list just the customers who did not place an order in the last quarter of 2015, simply add a test for NULL in a WHERE clause after the ON join specification.

Things to Remember

✦ Use OUTER JOIN to perform a Difference operation in SQL.

✦ You won't achieve the result you want when you apply a filter in an outer WHERE clause to the "right" side of a "left" join or vice versa.

✦ To correctly subtract a filtered subset, you must apply any filter before the database system performs the outer join.

5

Aggregation

From its inception, the SQL Standard has supported aggregating data, which can be useful for generating reports. However, when you start aggregating something, it is no longer enough just to say, "I want data from this and that, and only if it's x, y, or z." To ask for totals over "this and that" is usually insufficient; typically, we want to see "totals per customer," "count of orders by day," or "average sales of each category by month." It is the part after the "per," "by," and "of each" that requires additional attention. In this chapter we discuss GROUP BY and HAVING clauses that deal with those classes of questions. You will also learn about techniques to get the best performance from your aggregation and avoid common mistakes made with aggregated queries. Finally, the SQL standards committee has been expanding the standard in response to increased demand for more complex aggregations, and their answer is window functions. This is a change from the past when they would have said, "Just take data out of the database and dump it in a spreadsheet, then slice and dice the data." Nowadays, with the explosive increase in data volume, this might not be desirable or practical. For those reasons, it behooves you to know the ins and outs of aggregating in SQL.

Item 30: Understand How GROUP BY Works

You often need to be able to partition your data into groups (where a group is a set of rows with the same values for all of the grouping columns) in order to be able to apply some type of aggregation to your data. You can do this using a GROUP BY clause (often accompanied by a HAVING clause). Although that sounds simple, there does seem to be confusion about how to create queries that group correctly.

The general syntax for an SQL SELECT statement is shown in Listing 5.1 on the next page.

Listing 5.1 Syntax for SQL SELECT statements

```
SELECT select_list
FROM table_source
[WHERE search_condition ]
[GROUP BY group_by_expression ]
[HAVING search_condition ]
[ORDER BY order_expression [ ASC | DESC ] ]
```

> **Note**
>
> Although the ISO SQL Standard states that a SELECT without FROM is not standards-conforming SQL, many DBMSs do allow the FROM clause to be optional.

Here is how a query works:

1. The FROM clause generates the data set.

2. The WHERE clause filters the data set generated by the FROM clause.

3. The GROUP BY clause aggregates the data set that was filtered by the WHERE clause.

4. The HAVING clause filters the data set that was aggregated by the GROUP BY clause.

5. The SELECT clause transforms the filtered aggregated data set (usually through the use of aggregate functions).

6. The ORDER BY clause sorts the transformed data set.

Those columns included in the GROUP BY clause are referred to as the grouping columns. It is not actually necessary that columns included in the GROUP BY clause be included in the SELECT clause (although not showing the values being grouped can lead to odd-looking results!). You cannot use aliases in a GROUP BY clause.

Columns that are in the SELECT clause and do not appear in the GROUP BY clause must have aggregate functions applied to them (although computations can be done on the results of the aggregation or constants). Aggregate functions are deterministic functions that perform a calculation on a set of values and return a single value. (See the sidebar "Deterministic versus Nondeterministic" in Chapter 1, "Data Model Design.") In this case, the sets of values are the result of the GROUP BY clause. For each group, there can be one or more aggregations, which act upon every row in the group. (If you do not provide any aggregations, GROUP BY acts similarly to SELECT DISTINCT.)

The ISO SQL Standard defines a large number of aggregate functions. These are the most commonly used functions:

- COUNT() counts the rows in the set or group.
- SUM() totals the values in the set or group.
- AVG() calculates the average of numerical values in the set or group.
- MIN() finds the smallest value in the set or group.
- MAX() finds the largest value in the set or group.
- VAR_POP() and VAR_SAMP() return the population variance or the sample variance of the specified column within the set or group.
- STDDEV_POP() and STDDEV_SAMP() return the population standard deviation or the sample standard deviation of the specified column within the set or group.

How the columns appear in the SELECT clause impacts how they must appear in the GROUP BY clause because any column appearing in the clause that is not used in an aggregate function must appear in the GROUP BY clause. Listing 5.2 gives examples of groupings that are consistent with how the columns appear in the SELECT clause.

Listing 5.2 Valid GROUP BY clauses

```
SELECT ColumnA, ColumnB
FROM Table1 GROUP BY ColumnA, ColumnB;

SELECT ColumnA + ColumnB
FROM Table1 GROUP BY ColumnA, ColumnB;

SELECT ColumnA + ColumnB
FROM Table1 GROUP BY ColumnA + ColumnB;

SELECT ColumnA + ColumnB + constant
FROM Table1 GROUP BY ColumnA, ColumnB;

SELECT ColumnA + ColumnB + constant
FROM Table1 GROUP BY ColumnA + ColumnB;

SELECT ColumnA + constant + ColumnB
FROM Table1 GROUP BY ColumnA, ColumnB;
```

However, if the grouping is inconsistent with how the columns appear in the SELECT clause, the grouping is not allowed, as shown in Listing 5.3 on the next page.

Listing 5.3 Invalid GROUP BY clauses

```
SELECT ColumnA, ColumnB
FROM Table1 GROUP BY ColumnA + ColumnB;

SELECT ColumnA + constant + ColumnB
FROM Table1 GROUP BY ColumnA + ColumnB;
```

According to the ISO SQL Standard, the GROUP BY clause does not order the result set. You must use an ORDER BY clause to order the result set. In practice, though, most DBMSs build a temporary working index on the GROUP BY, so the results end up sorted by the columns in the GROUP BY clause in the absence of any other directive. If the order of your results is important, always include an ORDER BY clause to ensure the order you want.

You should filter the data in the WHERE clause as much as possible, because that will reduce the amount of data that needs to be aggregated. You should use a HAVING clause only when the filtering depends on the results of the aggregation, such as HAVING Count(*) > 5 or HAVING Sum(Price) < 100.

More complex grouping operations are possible using the features of ROLLUP, CUBE, and GROUPING SETS, which allow you to group the data selected by the FROM and WHERE clauses separately by each specified grouping set and compute aggregates for each group. You do this by listing a series of one or more columns to be used for grouping. An empty grouping set means that all rows are aggregated down to a single group, similar to when you do not include a GROUP BY clause on an aggregated query.

Note

Some SQL products, including Access and MySQL, do not support grouping with ROLLUP and CUBE.

Consider the data shown in Table 5.1 that we will use as the base for sample queries.

Table 5.1 Sample inventory data

Color	Dimension	Quantity
Red	L	10
Blue	M	20
Red	M	15
Blue	L	5

With ROLLUP, you gain additional aggregates for each set of columns in a group. You would use the query shown in Listing 5.4 to get the results shown in Table 5.2.

Listing 5.4 ROLLUP sample query

```
SELECT Color, Dimension, SUM(Quantity)
FROM Inventory
GROUP BY ROLLUP (Color, Dimension);
```

Table 5.2 Aggregated inventory with ROLLUP data

Color	Dimension	Quantity
Blue	L	5
Blue	M	20
Blue	NULL	25
Red	L	10
Red	M	15
Red	NULL	25
NULL	NULL	50

We obtain a total quantity for each color and the overall quantity. However, we do not have any data on the total quantity by dimension, not considering color, because the ROLLUP works from right to left. To get that additional data, we can use CUBE instead. Listing 5.5 demonstrates the statement to obtain the results shown in Table 5.3.

Listing 5.5 CUBE sample query

```
SELECT Color, Dimension, SUM(Quantity)
FROM Inventory
GROUP BY CUBE (Color, Dimension);
```

Table 5.3 Aggregated inventory with CUBE data

Color	Dimension	Quantity
Red	M	15
Red	L	10
Red	NULL	25
Blue	M	20
Blue	L	5
Blue	NULL	25
NULL	M	35
NULL	L	15
NULL	NULL	50

Finally, if you wish to have more control over the aggregates and what additional grouping you wish to include, you can use GROUPING SETS. You can use the SQL statement in Listing 5.6 to produce the results shown in Table 5.4. Note that the SQL statement contains three separate grouping sets: color, dimension, and an empty set (which results in a grand total being produced).

Listing 5.6 GROUPING SETS sample query

```
SELECT Color, Dimension, SUM(Quantity)
FROM Inventory
GROUP BY GROUPING SETS ((Color), (Dimension), ());
```

Table 5.4 Data results from the GROUPING SETS sample query

Color	Dimension	Quantity
Red	NULL	25
Blue	NULL	25
NULL	L	15
NULL	M	35
NULL	NULL	50

Observe that we were able to specify exactly which aggregates we wanted in the results, unlike with ROLLUP and CUBE, which give you all combinations whether you want them or not. In essence, GROUPING SETS, as well as ROLLUP and CUBE, allow you to do in one query what would have taken several queries UNIONed together. Listing 5.7 shows how you would have to code a query using a simple GROUP BY to get the same results as the query in Listing 5.5.

Listing 5.7 Using simple GROUP BY instead of GROUPING SETS

```
SELECT Color, NULL AS Dimension, SUM(Quantity)
FROM Inventory
GROUP BY Color
UNION
SELECT NULL, Dimension, SUM(Quantity)
FROM Inventory
GROUP BY Size
UNION
SELECT NULL, NULL, SUM(Quantity)
FROM Inventory;
```

None of ROLLUP, CUBE, or GROUPING SETS is available in Microsoft Access. As well, Access users should be aware that the query builder defaults to using a HAVING clause whenever you add criteria to the grid. The query shown in Figure 5.1 results in the SQL shown in Listing 5.8.

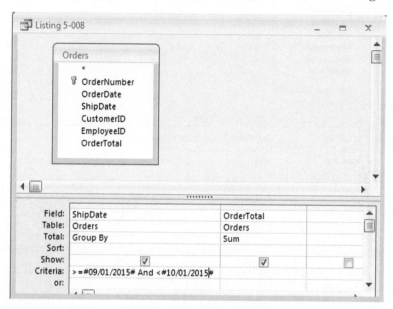

Figure 5.1 Building a totals query in Access

Listing 5.8 SQL generated for the query in Figure 5.1

```
SELECT O.ShipDate, Sum(O.OrderTotal) AS SumOfOrderTotal
FROM Orders AS O
GROUP BY O.ShipDate
HAVING (((O.ShipDate) >= #9/1/2015#
  AND (O.ShipDate) < #10/1/2015#));
```

You need to separate the criteria explicitly, as shown in Figure 5.2 on the next page, in order to produce the more desirable SQL statement shown in Listing 5.9.

Listing 5.9 SQL generated for the query in Figure 5.2

```
SELECT o.ShipDate, Sum(o.OrderTotal) AS SumOfOrderTotal
FROM Orders AS o
WHERE o.ShipDate >= #9/1/2015#
  AND o.ShipDate < #10/1/2015#
GROUP BY o.ShipDate;
```

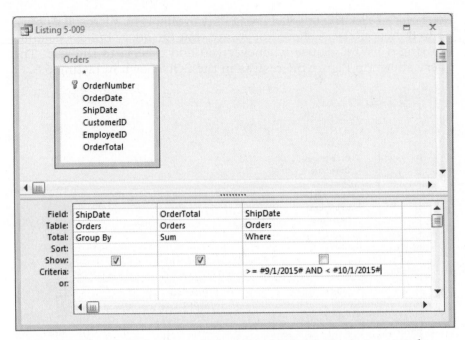

Figure 5.2 Preferred approach for introducing criteria to a totals query in Access

Things to Remember

+ The WHERE clause is applied before aggregation is done.

+ The GROUP BY clause aggregates the filtered data set.

+ The HAVING clause filters the aggregated data set.

+ The ORDER BY clause sorts the transformed data set.

+ Any field in the SELECT clause that is not involved in an aggregate function or calculation must appear in the GROUP BY clause.

+ Using ROLLUP, CUBE, and GROUPING SETS gives you more possible combinations in a single query in lieu of creating multiple aggregated queries and UNIONing them.

Item 31: Keep the GROUP BY Clause Small

Up to the SQL-92 Standard, it was mandatory that all columns that are not aggregated appear in the GROUP BY clause, and many vendors have complied with this stipulation. Listing 5.10 demonstrates a possible query that has several columns added to the GROUP BY clause.

Listing 5.10 An aggregated query with several columns in the GROUP BY clause, compliant with the SQL-92 Standard

```
SELECT c.CustomerID, c.CustFirstName,
  c.CustLastName, c.CustState,
  MAX(o.OrderDate) AS LastOrderDate,
  COUNT(o.OrderNumber) AS OrderCount,
  SUM(o.OrderTotal) AS TotalAmount
FROM Customers AS c
  LEFT JOIN Orders AS o
    ON c.CustomerID = o.CustomerID
GROUP BY c.CustomerID, c.CustFirstName,
  c.CustLastName, c.CustState;
```

This query will run on any DBMS. However, note that we included four columns in the GROUP BY. Consider the fact that we grouped on CustomerID, which is a primary key of the Customers table. Because a primary key by definition must be unique, it would not matter what values the other three columns contained. They could be identical and it would not change the result of the aggregations.

This is called *functional dependency*. The CustFirstName, CustLastName, and CustState columns are functionally dependent on the CustomerID. This was recognized in SQL-99 and onward. So the query in Listing 5.11 actually would be sufficient to satisfy the current SQL Standard.

Listing 5.11 Modified version of Listing 5.10 that complies with the current SQL Standard

```
SELECT c.CustomerID, c.CustFirstName,
  c.CustLastName, c.CustState,
  MAX(o.OrderDate) AS LastOrderDate,
  COUNT(o.OrderNumber) AS OrderCount,
  SUM(o.OrderTotal) AS TotalAmount
FROM Customers AS c
  LEFT JOIN Orders AS o
    ON c.CustomerID = o.CustomerID
GROUP BY c.CustomerID;
```

However, at the time of writing, only MySQL and PostgreSQL permit this version. Other DBMS products reject it, returning an error about a column reference that is not aggregated or a part of an expression. However, we can rewrite the same query to minimize the number of columns in the GROUP BY by using subqueries, as Listing 5.12 on the next page illustrates.

Listing 5.12 Modified version of Listing 5.10 that is portable

```
SELECT c.CustomerID, c.CustFirstName, c.CustLastName,
  c.CustState, o.LastOrderDate, o.OrderCount, o.TotalAmount
FROM Customers AS c
  LEFT JOIN (
    SELECT t.CustomerID, MAX(t.OrderDate) AS LastOrderDate,
      COUNT(t.OrderNumber) AS OrderCount,
      SUM(t.OrderTotal) AS TotalAmount
    FROM Orders AS t
    GROUP BY t.CustomerID
    ) AS o
    ON c.CustomerID = o.CustomerID;
```

> ### Note
> Refer to Item 42, "If possible, use common table expressions instead of subqueries," to make a more readable version of the query shown in Listing 5.12.

The rewritten query in Listing 5.12 has another important benefit: it is now easy to understand what we are actually aggregating. In the examples, we used CustomerID, a primary key, but we do not necessarily always do aggregation grouping on primary keys. Consider the GROUP BY clause shown in Listing 5.13.

Listing 5.13 A complex GROUP BY clause

```
...
GROUP BY CustCity, CustState, CustZip, YEAR(OrderDate),
  MONTH(OrderDate), EmployeeID
...
```

Can you see if there are any functionally dependent columns in this GROUP BY that could be removed? Are we doing aggregations by customers' area? Or are we doing aggregations by year/month and the employee who took the orders? Or something else? Likely, you cannot; you would need to analyze the entire query and study the results to determine what is essential for grouping. The end result is that the query's intention is now obfuscated with many columns that were included only for details. It would be hard to analyze, understand, and therefore rewrite the query if you needed to optimize it or determine what indices you need to apply to the underlying tables.

For this reason, it is a very good habit to write your aggregating queries in such a way that only columns that you actually need for aggregating data correctly are present in the GROUP BY clause. If you need additional columns for detail, push them out to an outer query instead of adding them to the GROUP BY clause.

Things to Remember

✦ Several DBMSs require that you add nonaggregated columns to GROUP BY even though the current SQL Standard no longer requires this.

✦ Excessive columns in GROUP BY can negatively impact the query's performance and also make it hard to read, understand, and rewrite.

✦ For queries that need both aggregations and details, do all aggregations in subqueries first, then join those to the tables to retrieve the details.

Item 32: Leverage GROUP BY/HAVING to Solve Complex Problems

Aggregate functions give you a powerful way to calculate a value across an entire set or across groups of rows within the set. You learned in Item 30, "Understand how GROUP BY works," how that clause defines the sets of data to be aggregated. In this item, we discuss how to use HAVING to further refine your results.

Whereas the WHERE clause filters rows before they are aggregated, HAVING lets you filter the aggregates themselves. You may want only the aggregate values that are greater than or less than some literal value. But the real power of HAVING is the ability to compare an aggregate result for a group with another aggregate value. You can use this to solve problems like these:

- Find the vendors whose average delivery time exceeds the average delivery time for all vendors. (Pick out slow vendors.)

- List the products whose total sales for a given period of time are greater than the average sales of all products in the same category. (Find best sellers by category.)

- Display customers who on any day have placed orders totaling more than $1,000. (List big spenders each day.)

- Calculate what percentage of orders in the last quarter are for a single item.

Let's solve the first two problems so that you can get an idea of how to leverage the HAVING clause. Figure 5.3 on the next page shows the tables we need to use.

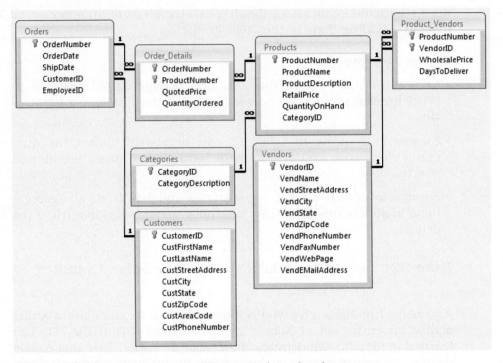

Figure 5.3 Tables in a typical Sales Orders database

First, let's find the slow vendors. We assume we are working in a sales database that has Vendors and PurchaseOrders tables. In the PurchaseOrders table, there is a foreign key (VendorID) to the Vendors table and OrderDate and DeliveryDate columns to calculate how long it took for the vendor to deliver a particular order. Listing 5.14 shows the SQL to find the answer to our question for the last quarter of 2015.

Note

We use Microsoft SQL Server functions to perform datetime arithmetic. Consult the Appendix, "Date and Time Types, Operations, and Functions," or your database documentation for equivalent functions.

Listing 5.14 Find vendors whose delivery time is longer than the average for Q4 2015

```
SELECT v.VendName, AVG(DATEDIFF(DAY, p.OrderDate,
    p.DeliveryDate)) AS DeliveryDays
FROM Vendors AS v
  INNER JOIN PurchaseOrders AS p
    ON v.VendorID = p.VendorID
```

```
WHERE p.DeliveryDate IS NOT NULL
  AND p.OrderDate BETWEEN '2015-10-01' AND '2015-12-31'
GROUP BY v.VendName
HAVING AVG(DATEDIFF(DAY, p.OrderDate, p.DeliveryDate)) > (
  SELECT AVG(DATEDIFF(DAY, p2.OrderDate, p2.DeliveryDate))
  FROM PurchaseOrders AS p2
  WHERE p2.DeliveryDate IS NOT NULL
    AND p2.OrderDate BETWEEN '2015-10-01' AND '2015-12-31'
  );
```

After running a query to display the average delivery time in that quarter as 14 days, we are not surprised to see the results shown in Table 5.5. Of course, slow delivery times in the last quarter are expected in the United States because of the Thanksgiving and Christmas holidays. That is why most retailers order stock well in advance of those holidays. But a report like this helps identify the least-favored vendors during that time period if we need to place an urgent order.

Table 5.5 Vendors with slow delivery times in Q4 2015

VendName	DeliveryDays
Armadillo Brand	15
Big Sky Mountain Bikes	17
Nikoma of America	22
ProFormance	15

Note

The results for DeliveryDays may vary among DBMSs. They also implement the ROUND() function differently, so if you do not want partial dates, you need to format the average results.

Note that in most implementations (and in the ISO SQL Standard) it is illegal to reference the column DeliveryDays, calculated in the SELECT clause, in the HAVING clause, even though the expression is exactly the same. You must repeat the expression.

Next, let's list the products whose total sales for a given period of time are greater than the average sales of all products in the same category. Listing 5.15 on the next page shows how.

Listing 5.15 Finding best sellers by category in the last quarter of 2015

```
SELECT c.CategoryDescription, p.ProductName,
  SUM(od.QuotedPrice * od.QuantityOrdered) AS TotalSales
FROM Products AS p
  INNER JOIN Order_Details AS od
    ON p.ProductNumber = od.ProductNumber
  INNER JOIN Categories AS c
    ON c.CategoryID = p.CategoryID
  INNER JOIN Orders AS o
    ON o.OrderNumber = od.OrderNumber
WHERE o.OrderDate BETWEEN '2015-10-01' AND '2015-12-31'
GROUP BY p.CategoryID, c.CategoryDescription, p.ProductName
HAVING SUM(od.QuotedPrice * od.QuantityOrdered) > (
  SELECT AVG(SumCategory)
  FROM (
    SELECT p2.CategoryID,
      SUM(od2.QuotedPrice * od2.QuantityOrdered)
        AS SumCategory
    FROM Products AS p2
      INNER JOIN Order_Details AS od2
        ON p2.ProductNumber = od2.ProductNumber
      INNER JOIN Orders AS o2
        ON o2.OrderNumber = od2.OrderNumber
    WHERE p2.CategoryID = p.CategoryID
      AND o2.OrderDate BETWEEN '2015-10-01' AND '2015-12-31'
    GROUP BY p2.CategoryID, p2.ProductNumber
    ) AS s
  GROUP BY CategoryID
  )
ORDER BY c.CategoryDescription, p.ProductName;
```

The problem is complicated because in the HAVING clause, you first must calculate the sum of the sales by product within the category of the current group and then calculate the average of those sums—while filtering the category by the category in the current group in the outer query. It is further complicated because we also want to limit the data to a specific date range, so we must include a join to the Orders table to get the date. The end result might look something like Table 5.6.

If you skip forward to Item 42, "If possible, use common table expressions instead of subqueries," you will find that you could further simplify this query by using a common table expression (CTE). To whet your appetite, Listing 5.16 shows the query again using a CTE.

Table 5.6 Products that sold more than the category average in the fourth quarter of 2015

CategoryDescription	ProductName	TotalSales
Accessories	Cycle-Doc Pro Repair Stand	32595.76
Accessories	Dog Ear Aero-Flow Floor Pump	15539.15
Accessories	Glide-O-Matic Cycling Helmet	23640.00
Accessories	King Cobra Helmet	27847.26
Accessories	Viscount CardioSport Sport Watch	16469.79
Bikes	GT RTS-2 Mountain Bike	527703.00
Bikes	Trek 9000 Mountain Bike	954516.00
Clothing	StaDry Cycling Pants	8641.56
Components	AeroFlo ATB Wheels	37709.28
Components	Cosmic Elite Road Warrior Wheels	32064.45
Components	Eagle SA-120 Clipless Pedals	17003.85
Car racks	Ultimate Export 2G Car Rack	31014.00
Tires	Ultra-2K Competition Tire	5216.28
Skateboards	Viscount Skateboard	196964.30

Listing 5.16 Simplifying Listing 5.15 using a CTE

```
WITH CatProdData AS (
  SELECT c.CategoryID, c.CategoryDescription,
    p.ProductName, od.QuotedPrice, od.QuantityOrdered
  FROM Products AS p
    INNER JOIN Order_Details AS od
      ON p.ProductNumber = od.ProductNumber
    INNER JOIN Categories AS c
      ON c.CategoryID = p.CategoryID
    INNER JOIN Orders AS o
      ON o.OrderNumber = od.OrderNumber
  WHERE o.OrderDate BETWEEN '2015-10-01' AND '2015-12-31'
  )
SELECT d.CategoryDescription, d.ProductName,
  SUM(d.QuotedPrice * d.QuantityOrdered) AS TotalSales
FROM CatProdData AS d
GROUP BY d.CategoryID, d.CategoryDescription, d.ProductName
```

```
HAVING SUM(d.QuotedPrice * d.QuantityOrdered) > (
  SELECT AVG(SumCategory)
  FROM (
    SELECT d2.CategoryID,
      SUM(d2.QuotedPrice * d2.QuantityOrdered)
        AS SumCategory
    FROM CatProdData AS d2
    WHERE d2.CategoryID = d.CategoryID
    GROUP BY d2.CategoryID, d2.ProductName
    ) AS s
  GROUP BY CategoryID
  )
ORDER BY d.CategoryDescription, d.ProductName;
```

The CTE lets you define the complex join and filter on dates just once, then reuse it in both the outer query and the subquery.

Things to Remember

+ Use the WHERE clause to filter rows before grouping; use HAVING to filter rows after grouping.

+ The HAVING clause gives you the ability to filter aggregate expressions.

+ Even though you have given a name to an aggregate expression in the SELECT clause, you must repeat the expression if you want to use it in the HAVING clause. You cannot use the name you assigned in SELECT.

+ You can compare an aggregate to either a simple literal value or a value returned by a complex aggregate value subquery.

Item 33: Find Maximum or Minimum Values Without Using GROUP BY

You can solve many questions using GROUP BY, but sometimes too much data gets aggregated, and you cannot get some of the details you desired. If you are using a DBMS that does not support window functions (see Item 37, "Know how to use window functions"), having alternatives that allow you to get additional columns without aggregating those columns would be useful. This item expands on the ideas introduced in Item 23, "Find non-matches or missing records," to make it possible to find maximum or minimum values without aggregating.

Consider the data presented in Table 5.7.

Table 5.7 BeerStyles table

Category	Country	Style	MaxABV
American Beers	United States	American Barley Wine	12
American Beers	United States	American Lager	4.2
American Beers	United States	American Malt Liquor	9
American Beers	United States	American Stout	11.5
American Beers	United States	American Style Wheat	5.5
American Beers	United States	American Wild Ale	10
American Beers	United States	Double/Imperial IPA	10
American Beers	United States	Pale Lager	5
British or Irish Ales	England	English Barley Wine	12
British or Irish Ales	England	India Pale Ale	7.5
British or Irish Ales	England	Ordinary Bitter	3.9
British or Irish Ales	Ireland	Irish Red Ale	6
British or Irish Ales	Scotland	Strong Scotch Ale	10
European Ales	Belgium	Belgian Black Ale	6.2
European Ales	Belgium	Belgian Pale Ale	5.6
European Ales	Belgium	Flanders Red	6.5
European Ales	France	Bière de Garde	8.5
European Ales	Germany	Berliner Weisse	3.5
European Ales	Germany	Dunkelweizen	6
European Ales	Germany	Roggenbier	6
European Lagers	Austria	Vienna Lager	5.9
European Lagers	Germany	Maibock	7.5
European Lagers	Germany	Rauchbier	6
European Lagers	Germany	Schwarzbier	3.9
European Lagers	Germany	Traditional Bock	7.2

If you wanted to know the highest alcohol level for each category, you would use the SQL statement shown in Listing 5.17.

Listing 5.17 SQL statement to determine the highest alcohol level per category

```
SELECT Category, MAX(MaxABV) AS MaxAlcohol
FROM BeerStyles
GROUP BY Category;
```

You would get the results shown in Table 5.8.

Table 5.8 Highest alcohol level per category

Category	MaxAlcohol
American Beers	12
British or Irish Ales	12
European Ales	8.5
European Lagers	7.5

Note

As was mentioned in Item 30, "Understand how GROUP BY works," depending on your DBMS, you may get your results in a slightly different order, because no ORDER BY clause was included.

However, if you wanted to know not only the highest alcohol level but also in which country the style of beer that has that level originated, you cannot just extend that query by adding Country to the query, as shown in Listing 5.18.

Listing 5.18 Incorrect SQL statement to determine the originating country for beer with the highest alcohol level

```
SELECT Category, Country, MAX(MaxABV) AS MaxAlcohol
FROM BeerStyles
GROUP BY Category, Country;
```

The query in Listing 5.18 will return the data shown in Table 5.9, which is not what you want.

A different approach is clearly needed.

The crux of the matter is to find, for each category, the row in the table that has the largest value for MaxABV. If you were to join the table

Table 5.9 Incorrect results to determine the originating country for beer with the highest alcohol level

Category	Country	MaxAlcohol
American Beers	United States	12
British or Irish Ales	England	12
British or Irish Ales	Ireland	6
British or Irish Ales	Scotland	10
European Ales	Belgium	6.5
European Ales	France	8.5
European Ales	Germany	6
European Lagers	Austria	5.9
European Lagers	Germany	7.5

to itself so that you could look at each row and compare the value of MaxABV for that row to the value of MaxABV for all other rows for that category, you would be able to find the row of interest. The query in Listing 5.19 does just that.

Listing 5.19 Joining the BeerStyles table to itself to compare MaxABV in each row

```
SELECT l.Category, l.MaxABV AS LeftMaxABV,
   r.MaxABV AS RightMaxABV
FROM BeerStyles AS l
  LEFT JOIN BeerStyles AS r
    ON l.Category = r.Category
      AND l.MaxABV < r.MaxABV;
```

The query compares each row in the table to every other row in the table for the same Category and returns only those rows that have a larger value for MaxABV. Because it is a left join, it returns at least one row for every row in the left-hand table, even if there is no row in the right-hand table that has a larger value for MaxABV. Table 5.10 on the next page shows part of the results of the query in Listing 5.19.

Note the two rows in Table 5.10 with the null values in the RightMaxABV column. The values in the LeftMaxABV column are the maximum alcohol level for the category. Look at Table 5.8 to confirm that the highest alcohol level for British or Irish Ales is 12%, and for European Lagers is 7.5%.

Table 5.10 Partial results of comparing MaxABV in each row to all other rows

Category	LeftMaxABV	RightMaxABV
. . .	. . .	. . .
European Lagers	3.9	7.2
European Lagers	3.9	7.5
British or Irish Ales	12	NULL
British or Irish Ales	7.5	10
British or Irish Ales	7.5	12
European Ales	6.5	8.5
European Lagers	7.5	NULL
American Beers	5	11.5
American Beers	5	12
American Beers	5	9
. . .	. . .	. . .

Now that we have a way to identify each row of interest, the query in Listing 5.20 can retrieve the other columns of interest.

Listing 5.20 Returning details of the row with the largest value of MaxABV for each category

```
SELECT l.Category, l.Country, l.Style, l.MaxABV AS MaxAlcohol
FROM BeerStyles AS l
  LEFT JOIN BeerStyles AS r
    ON l.Category = r.Category
      AND l.MaxABV < r.MaxABV
WHERE r.MaxABV IS NULL
ORDER BY l.Category;
```

Table 5.11 shows the results of running the query in Listing 5.20.

Note that the query in Listing 5.20 has no aggregate function, so no GROUP BY clause is needed. Because there is no GROUP BY clause, the query can be easily joined to other tables.

We can consider the first expression in the ON clause, l.Category = r.Category, in Listing 5.20 to be functionally equivalent to the GROUP BY Category in Listing 5.18, and it is how we define the "grouping" in

Table 5.11 Details of the highest alcohol level per category

Category	Country	Style	MaxAlcohol
American Beers	United States	American Barley Wine	12
British or Irish Ales	England	English Barley Wine	12
European Ales	France	Bière de Garde	8.5
European Lagers	Germany	Maibock	7.5

our new query. We can consider the second expression, `l.MaxABV < r.MaxABV`, to be functionally equivalent to `MAX(MaxABV)`, because the `WHERE r.MaxABV IS NULL` clause allows us to select only the maximum (or minimum, if the inequality is reversed).

The entire point is to avoid both the aggregate and the `GROUP BY` that can be resource intensive. You could also solve this using `MaxAlcohol = (SELECT MAX(MaxAlcohol) FROM BeerStyles AS b2 WHERE b2.Category = BeerStyles.Category)`, but that involves not only an aggregate function but also a correlated subquery. As you will learn in Item 41, "Know the difference between correlated and non-correlated subqueries," using a correlated subquery can be very expensive because your database engine must execute the subquery for every row.

Note

These results may not hold if you are working with large tables because you will end up scanning the table twice. See Item 44, "Learn to use your system's query analyzer," to learn how to analyze your situation to see whether the approach outlined in this item is appropriate for your situation.

Things to Remember

✦ The "main" table needs to be joined to itself using `LEFT JOIN`.

✦ Every column that would have been included in the `GROUP BY` clause becomes part of the `ON` clause, using an equals (=) comparison.

✦ The column that would have been included in the `MAX()` (or `MIN()`) clause becomes part of the `ON` clause, using less than (<) or greater than (>).

✦ The columns included in the `ON` clause should be indexed for better performance, especially when you start to deal with larger data sets.

Item 34: Avoid Getting an Erroneous COUNT() When Using OUTER JOIN

Sometimes the simplest of mistakes in your SQL code can lead to an incorrect answer. Because it is a simple problem to count rows in a set, let's use a simple database. Figure 5.4 shows the design of a database to keep track of recipes that you might use at home or a chef might use in a restaurant.

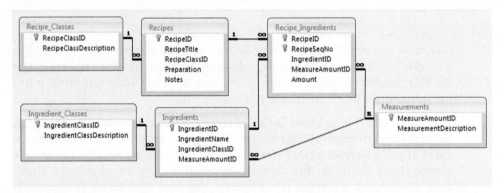

Figure 5.4 The design of a simple Recipes database

A simple problem would be to list all classes of recipes and get a count of the number of recipes in each class. We want all classes of recipes, so it would be wise to do an outer join to make sure we get them all. Listing 5.21 shows a first attempt to solve the problem.

Listing 5.21 Counting recipes in all recipe classes

```
SELECT Recipe_Classes.RecipeClassDescription,
  COUNT(*) AS RecipeCount
FROM Recipe_Classes
  LEFT OUTER JOIN Recipes
    ON Recipe_Classes.RecipeClassID = Recipes.RecipeClassID
GROUP BY Recipe_Classes.RecipeClassDescription;
```

The result might look something like Table 5.12.

It looks like we have at least one recipe per recipe class. But looks can be deceiving because the answer is actually wrong. When you use COUNT(*), you are counting the rows returned in each group. Because we did a left outer join, we will get at least one row for each recipe class, even though null values will be returned in the column(s) from the Recipes table when no recipes exist for a recipe class. (See also Item 36, "Use DISTINCT to get distinct counts.")

Table 5.12 Counting recipes in each recipe class

RecipeClassDescription	RecipeCount
Dessert	2
Hors d'oeuvres	2
Main course	7
Salad	1
Soup	1
Starch	1
Vegetable	2

One solution is to count one of the columns returned from the Recipes table. When you use a column name instead of *, the database engine ignores rows containing a null value in that column. Listing 5.22 shows the correct way to solve the problem.

Listing 5.22 Counting recipes in all recipe classes correctly

```
SELECT Recipe_Classes.RecipeClassDescription,
  COUNT(Recipes.RecipeClassID) AS RecipeCount
FROM Recipe_Classes
  LEFT OUTER JOIN Recipes
    ON Recipe_Classes.RecipeClassID = Recipes.RecipeClassID
GROUP BY Recipe_Classes.RecipeClassDescription;
```

Now we get the correct answer—there are no Soup recipes—as shown in Table 5.13.

Table 5.13 Correct count of recipes in each recipe class

RecipeClassDescription	RecipeCount
Dessert	2
Hors d'oeuvres	2
Main course	7
Salad	1
Soup	0
Starch	1
Vegetable	2

Is using LEFT OUTER JOIN and GROUP BY the most efficient way to solve this problem? Maybe not! Because there are likely to be hundreds if not thousands of rows for each recipe class, but there are only a few different classes of recipes, using a subquery to get the count could be more efficient.

Rather than fetch all the rows in the Recipes table, group them, and then count them, a simple probe using a subquery could be faster. Especially if you do a count on an indexed field, the database engine is likely to count index entries, not the actual rows. Listing 5.23 shows the alternative solution. The result is exactly the same as we saw in Table 5.13.

Listing 5.23 Using a subquery to count recipes in each recipe class

```
SELECT Recipe_Classes.RecipeClassDescription, (
    SELECT COUNT(Recipes.RecipeClassID)
    FROM Recipes
    WHERE Recipes.RecipeClassID = Recipe_Classes.RecipeClassID
    ) AS RecipeCount
FROM Recipe_Classes;
```

To verify our supposition that the subquery might be faster (even though it is a correlated subquery), we can put both queries into a query window in SQL Server and ask it to display the estimated execution plan. (For more details about using a query analyzer, see Item 44, "Learn to use your system's query analyzer." To learn more about correlated versus non-correlated subqueries, see Item 41, "Know the difference between correlated and non-correlated subqueries.") Figure 5.5 shows the result.

Even with a relatively small amount of data, we can see that using GROUP BY is more than twice as expensive (71% for GROUP BY versus 29% for the subquery) as using the subquery. However, we have demonstrated this only for the SQL Server database engine; other engines could yield the opposite results. Never be afraid to explore alternatives if you want to find a more efficient way to solve a problem in SQL. To learn more about testing the efficiency of your SQL, read Chapter 7, "Getting and Analyzing Metadata."

Things to Remember

✦ Use COUNT(*) to count all rows, including ones with null values.

✦ Use COUNT(*<column name>*) to count only the rows where the column value is not NULL.

✦ Sometimes a subquery, even a correlated subquery, can be more efficient than using a GROUP BY.

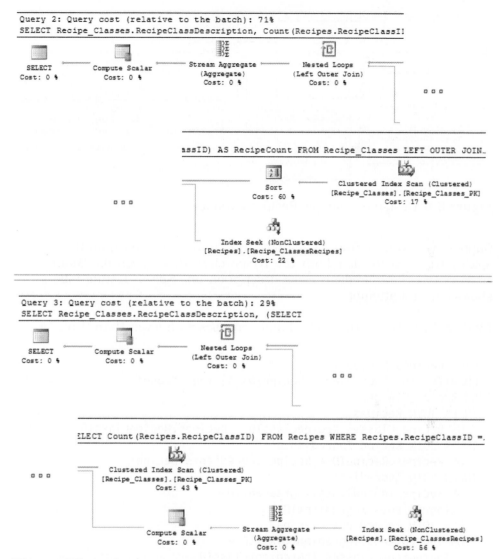

Figure 5.5 Analyzing the two queries in SQL Server

Item 35: Include Zero-Value Rows When Testing for HAVING COUNT(x) < Some Number

In this item, we show you how to include rows with zero value when applying a HAVING predicate that specifies a count less than some number.

Let's use the same little Recipes database from Item 34, "Avoid getting an erroneous COUNT() when using OUTER JOIN." Figure 5.6 on the next page shows the design.

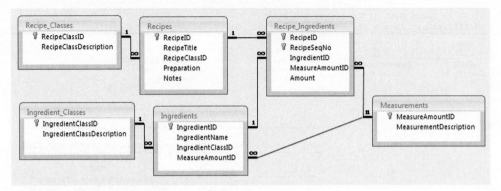

Figure 5.6 Design of a simple Recipes database

Suppose you want to find the main courses that have fewer than three spices. We need to filter both the recipe class description on "Main course" and the ingredient class description on "Spice." Listing 5.24 shows our first attempt.

Listing 5.24 Attempting to find main courses with fewer than three spices

```
SELECT Recipes.RecipeTitle,
  COUNT(Recipe_Ingredients.RecipeID) AS IngredCount
FROM Recipe_Classes
  INNER JOIN Recipes
    ON Recipe_Classes.RecipeClassID = Recipes.RecipeClassID
  INNER JOIN Recipe_Ingredients
    ON Recipes.RecipeID = Recipe_Ingredients.RecipeID
  INNER JOIN Ingredients
    ON Recipe_Ingredients.IngredientID =
      Ingredients.IngredientID
  INNER JOIN Ingredient_Classes
    ON Ingredients.IngredientClassID =
      Ingredient_Classes.IngredientClassID
WHERE Recipe_Classes.RecipeClassDescription = 'Main course'
  AND Ingredient_Classes.IngredientClassDescription = 'Spice'
GROUP BY Recipes.RecipeTitle
HAVING COUNT(Recipe_Ingredients.RecipeID) < 3;
```

The result looks like Table 5.14.

That is not the correct answer because we failed to do a left join to the Recipe_Ingredients table, so we will not get any zero counts. Listing 5.25 shows the same query, but this time using LEFT JOIN.

Table 5.14 Main courses with three or fewer spices

RecipeTitle	IngredCount
Fettuccine Alfredo	2
Salmon Filets in Parchment Paper	2

Listing 5.25 Second attempt to find main courses with fewer than three spices

```
SELECT Recipes.RecipeTitle,
  COUNT(ri.RecipeID) AS IngredCount
FROM Recipe_Classes
  INNER JOIN Recipes
    ON Recipe_Classes.RecipeClassID = Recipes.RecipeClassID
  LEFT OUTER JOIN (
    SELECT Recipe_Ingredients.RecipeID,
      Ingredient_Classes.IngredientClassDescription
    FROM Recipe_Ingredients
      INNER JOIN Ingredients
        ON Recipe_Ingredients.IngredientID =
          Ingredients.IngredientID
      INNER JOIN Ingredient_Classes
        ON Ingredients.IngredientClassID =
          Ingredient_Classes.IngredientClassID
  ) AS ri
    ON Recipes.RecipeID = ri.RecipeID
WHERE Recipe_Classes.RecipeClassDescription = 'Main course'
  AND ri.IngredientClassDescription = 'Spice'
GROUP BY Recipes.RecipeTitle
HAVING COUNT(ri.RecipeID) < 3;
```

Note

We used a subquery on the right side of the outer join to make the syntax compatible with most database implementations. For example, if we simply replace INNER with LEFT OUTER in Microsoft Access, the query would generate an "ambiguous outer join" error.

That does not work either, because filtering one of the tables on the "right" side of a "left" join negates the effect of the outer join. The second query returns the exact same results as the first. (See also Item 29, "Correctly filter the 'right' side of a 'left' join.") Listing 5.26 on the next page gets it right by moving the filter into a subquery before doing the join.

Listing 5.26 Correctly finding main courses that have fewer than three spices

```
SELECT Recipes.RecipeTitle,
  COUNT(ri.RecipeID) AS IngredCount
FROM Recipe_Classes
  INNER JOIN Recipes
    ON Recipe_Classes.RecipeClassID = Recipes.RecipeClassID
  LEFT OUTER JOIN (
    SELECT Recipe_Ingredients.RecipeID,
      Ingredient_Classes.IngredientClassDescription
    FROM Recipe_Ingredients
      INNER JOIN Ingredients
        ON Recipe_Ingredients.IngredientID =
          Ingredients.IngredientID
      INNER JOIN Ingredient_Classes
        ON Ingredients.IngredientClassID =
          Ingredient_Classes.IngredientClassID
    WHERE
      Ingredient_Classes.IngredientClassDescription = 'Spice'
    ) AS ri
    ON Recipes.RecipeID = ri.RecipeID
WHERE Recipe_Classes.RecipeClassDescription = 'Main course'
GROUP BY Recipes.RecipeTitle
HAVING COUNT(ri.RecipeID) < 3;
```

That finally gets us the correct answer, shown in Table 5.15.

Table 5.15 Main courses with three or fewer spices

RecipeTitle	IngredCount
Fettuccine Alfredo	2
Irish Stew	0
Salmon Filets in Parchment Paper	2

Frankly, we cannot imagine an Irish Stew being made with no salt and pepper, but then we would not have an interesting example. In this case, we discovered that we left out those critical ingredients, so we can fix the ingredient list.

Note that if we had made the mistake illustrated in Item 34 by using COUNT(*) instead of COUNT(RI.RecipeID), we would have seen Irish Stew, but with an incorrect count of 1. As you learned in Item 34 and this item, you have to be careful when dealing with zero values when you try to use COUNT() or HAVING less than some number.

Finally, there is also the alternative of moving the clause AND ri.IngredientClassDescription = 'Spice' from Listing 5.25 out of the WHERE clause and into the ON predicate of the JOIN clause. This will also yield the same results we got from Listing 5.26 because conditions defined in the ON predicate are filtered before joining to the outer table reference. The WHERE clause applies its predicates after the joins, which is why it is "too late" and thus we get incorrect results.

Things to Remember

+ Looking for a count of zero will not work if you use INNER JOIN.

+ If you filter the "right" side of a "left" join, you get the equivalent of an inner join. Push the filter into a subquery or use the ON predicate to filter the "right" side.

+ Looking for a count of zero when you expect a count of 1 or more can help you identify problems in your data.

Item 36: Use DISTINCT to Get Distinct Counts

The purpose of the COUNT() aggregate function should be obvious from its name. In this item, we take a closer look at some nuances the function provides.

There are three different ways in which the COUNT() aggregate function can be used to return the number of items in a group:

- COUNT(*) returns the number of items in a group, including null values and duplicates.

- COUNT(ALL <*expression*>) (which can be shortened to COUNT(<*expression*>) because ALL is the default) evaluates an expression for each row in a group and returns the number of non-null values.

- COUNT(DISTINCT <*expression*>) evaluates an expression for each row in a group and returns the number of unique, non-null values.

Usually <*expression*> is a field name, but it can be any combination of symbols and operators that evaluates to obtain a single data value.

Consider the data shown in Table 5.16 on the next page.

You can use COUNT(*) to determine that there are 25 rows in the table shown in Table 5.16.

Because all of the rows in that table have values for CustomerID, using COUNT(CustomerID) would yield the same result of 25. However, using COUNT(EmployeeID) would yield 20, because there are five rows with a null value for EmployeeID.

Table 5.16 Sample data

Order Number	OrderDate	ShipDate	Customer ID	Employee ID	Order Total
16	2012-09-02	2012-09-06	1001	707	2007.54
7	2012-09-01	2012-09-04	1001	NULL	467.85
2	2012-09-01	2012-09-03	1001	703	816.00
3	2012-09-01	2012-09-04	1002	707	11912.45
8	2012-09-01	2012-09-01	1003	703	1492.60
15	2012-09-02	2012-09-06	1004	701	2974.25
9	2012-09-01	2012-09-04	1007	NULL	69.00
4	2012-09-01	2012-09-03	1009	703	6601.73
24	2012-09-03	2012-09-05	1010	705	864.85
20	2012-09-02	2012-09-02	1011	706	4699.98
10	2012-09-01	2012-09-04	1012	701	2607.00
14	2012-09-02	2012-09-03	1013	704	6819.90
17	2012-09-02	2012-09-03	1014	702	4834.98
21	2012-09-03	2012-09-03	1014	702	709.97
6	2012-09-01	2012-09-05	1014	702	9820.29
18	2012-09-02	2012-09-03	1016	NULL	807.80
23	2012-09-03	2012-09-04	1017	705	16331.91
25	2012-09-03	2012-09-04	1017	NULL	10142.15
1	2012-09-01	2012-09-04	1018	707	12751.85
11	2012-09-02	2012-09-04	1020	706	11070.65
5	2012-09-01	2012-09-01	1024	NULL	5544.75
13	2012-09-02	2012-09-02	1024	704	7545.00
12	2012-09-02	2012-09-05	1024	706	72.00
22	2012-09-03	2012-09-07	1026	702	6456.16
19	2012-09-02	2012-09-06	1027	707	15278.98

You can use COUNT(DISTINCT CustomerID) to determine that there are 18 different values for CustomerID in those 25 rows of data.

As mentioned previously, you are not limited to simply a column name as a parameter for the COUNT() function. Let's say you want to know how many of the orders exceeded $1,000.00. You could run the query in Listing 5.27 to get the result of 18, or you could use COUNT(CASE WHEN OrderTotal > 1000 THEN CustomerID END), because the CASE function returns the CustomerID field for only those rows where OrderTotal is greater than $1,000.00 and returns a null value in the other cases.

Listing 5.27 Possible query for determining how many orders exceed $1,000.00

```
SELECT COUNT(*) AS TotalOrders
FROM Orders
WHERE OrderTotal > 1000;
```

It is even possible to use DISTINCT in conjunction with the CASE statement. You could use COUNT(DISTINCT CASE WHEN OrderTotal > 1000 THEN CustomerID END) to determine that there are 15 different customers in that group of 18 orders exceeding $1,000.00 (1001, 1002, 1003, 1004, 1009, 1011, 1012, 1013, 1014, 1017, 1018, 1020, 1024, 1026, and 1027).

If you run a single query with multiple counts, as shown in Listing 5.28, only one pass needs to be made through the table.

Listing 5.28 Multiple counts in a single query

```
SELECT COUNT(*) AS TotalRows,
  COUNT(CustomerID) AS TotalOrdersWithCustomers,
  COUNT(EmployeeID) AS TotalOrdersWithEmployees,
  COUNT(DISTINCT CustomerID) AS TotalUniqueCustomers,
  COUNT(CASE WHEN OrderTotal > 1000
    THEN CustomerID END) AS TotalLargeOrders,
  COUNT(DISTINCT CASE WHEN OrderTotal > 1000
    THEN CustomerID END) AS TotalUniqueCust_LargeOrders
FROM OrdersTable;
```

Running the query shown in Listing 5.28 yields the results shown in Table 5.17.

Table 5.17 Results of running multiple counts

Total Rows	TotalOrders WithCustomers	TotalOrders WithEmployees	TotalUnique Customers	TotalLarge Orders	TotalUniqueCust_ LargeOrders
25	25	20	18	18	15

Note

The COUNT() function returns an int value, meaning it is limited to values of up to 2,147,483,647. Both DB2 and SQL Server have a COUNT_BIG() function that returns a bigint value, which allows values of up to 9,223,372,036,854,775,807.

Access does not support using DISTINCT in conjunction with COUNT().

Things to Remember

◆ Use the appropriate form of the COUNT() function to simplify calculations.

◆ Consider using functions as the argument for the COUNT() function in order to be able to combine calculations without needing a WHERE clause.

Item 37: Know How to Use Window Functions

One area that used to be a major weakness in SQL standards prior to the SQL:2003 Standard was the ability to work with data where the results depended on adjacent rows. In the prior standards, SQL had no conception of "adjacent rows." In theory, the order of the rows should not matter as long they match the given filters. The ORDER BY clause has long been considered to be more for presentation than as truly a part of relational operations. As a consequence, certain classes of operations were very difficult to perform in SQL alone. A prime example is generating a running sum, illustrated in Table 5.18.

Table 5.18 Example of running sums

OrderNumber	CustomerID	OrderTotal	TotalByCustomer	TotalOverall
1	1	213.99	213.99	213.99
2	1	482.95	696.94	696.44
3	1	321.50	1018.44	1018.44
4	2	192.20	192.20	1210.64
5	2	451.00	643.20	1661.64
6	3	893.40	893.40	2555.04
7	3	500.01	1393.41	3055.05
8	4	720.99	720.99	3776.04

Prior to the SQL:2003 Standard, such queries would be very difficult to write and, even if they could be performed at all, likely very inefficient and slow. The SQL:2003 Standard introduced the concept of a window function where "window" refers to a set of rows that surround a considered row, either preceding or following that row. Many of the aggregate functions with which you are familiar, such as SUM(), COUNT(), AVG(), and others, can be used as window functions. Additionally, the SQL:2003 Standard introduced new functions such as ROW_NUMBER() and RANK(), which must be windowed. Several DBMS products have already implemented at least some of those in their current versions; consult the documentation to determine what window functions, if any, are available to you.

The query shown in Listing 5.29 can be used to write a running sum as demonstrated in Table 5.18.

Listing 5.29 Query to perform a running sum

```
SELECT
    o.OrderNumber, o.CustomerID, o.OrderTotal,
    SUM(o.OrderTotal) OVER (
        PARTITION BY o.CustomerID
        ORDER BY o.OrderNumber, o.CustomerID
    ) AS TotalByCustomer,
    SUM(o.OrderTotal) OVER (
        ORDER BY o.OrderNumber
    ) AS TotalOverall
FROM Orders AS o
ORDER BY o.OrderNumber, o.CustomerID;
```

There are several things to note in Listing 5.29, starting with the OVER clause. This indicates that we want to use a window over the SUM() expression. We used two predicates within the OVER clause: PARTITION BY and ORDER BY. The PARTITION BY predicate specifies how the window should be divided. If you omit it, your database system applies the function over the entire result set. For the TotalByCustomer, we specified o.CustomerID, meaning that the SUM() should be applied over the range of rows where the o.CustomerID values are the same. This is conceptually similar to the GROUP BY clause. However, a major difference is that a PARTITION predicate applies grouping only to the window created for SUM() and is independent, whereas a GROUP BY would apply grouping over the entire query and place additional constraints upon the query as discussed in Item 30, "Understand how GROUP BY works," such as disallowing a column reference that is neither grouped nor aggregated.

Note that TotalOverall does not have a PARTITION BY predicate. This is functionally equivalent to grouping over the entire set of rows returned by the query, just like when you omit the GROUP BY clause from the statement.

The next part is the ORDER BY predicate. As discussed at the start of this item, the results are sensitive to the order in which the rows are returned. In the example of a running sum, this describes the sequence of the rows that should be read into the window.

Be aware that in all cases, the predicates defined for each OVER clause can be different, and each would apply only to the aggregate function independently of one another. So it is valid to write a statement like the one in Listing 5.30.

Listing 5.30 Query with different predicates for each OVER clause

```
SELECT
  t.AccountID, t.Amount,
  SUM(t.Amount) OVER (
    PARTITION BY t.AccountID
    ORDER BY t.TransactionID DESC
  ) - t.Amount AS TotalUnspent,
  SUM(t.Amount) OVER (
    ORDER BY t.TransactionID
  ) AS TotalOverall
FROM Transactions AS t
ORDER BY t.TransactionID;
```

The query could be used for an expense report to report both overall spending and how much of the actual expenses were used up after each expenditure. In order to represent the unspent expenses, we have to use the reverse order on t.TransactionID for TotalUnspent. Table 5.19 illustrates how the data would be formed by the query in Listing 5.30.

Without the window functions, the query needed to produce the same result as Table 5.19 would likely have required several nested SELECT statements in order to represent each window independently. Because the window function allows you to specify the PARTITION BY and ORDER BY for each OVER clause, you now can write a single statement that provides aggregations over a different range of data without having to adhere to the statement-level GROUP BY clause.

In Item 38, "Create row numbers and rank a row over other rows," you will see how to deal with new aggregate functions that must be windowed, and in Item 39, "Create a moving aggregate," you will get into more advanced options for describing the size of the window.

Table 5.19 Data returned by the query in Listing 5.30

AccountID	Amount	TotalUnspent	TotalOverall
1	1237.10	606.98	1237.10
1	298.19	308.79	1535.29
1	54.39	254.40	1589.68
1	123.77	130.63	1713.45
1	49.25	81.38	1762.70
1	81.38	0.00	1844.08
2	394.29	1676.49	2238.37
2	683.39	993.10	2921.76
2	993.10	0.00	3914.86

Things to Remember

✦ Window functions are "aware" of the surrounding rows, which makes it easier to create running or moving aggregations than with the traditional aggregation functions and statement-level grouping.

✦ Window functions are great alternatives for aggregations that need to be applied over data differently and/or independently.

✦ Window functions can be used with existing aggregate functions such as SUM(), COUNT(), and AVG() and are enabled by including an OVER clause.

✦ The PARTITION BY predicate can be used to specify that grouping must be applied to the aggregation expression.

✦ The ORDER BY predicate is often important as it influences how subsequent rows will have their aggregate expression calculated.

Item 38: Create Row Numbers and Rank a Row over Other Rows

In Item 37, "Know how to use window functions," we considered how window functions help us with familiar aggregate functions such as SUM(). However, there are also new aggregate functions such as ROW_NUMBER() and RANK() that must have an OVER clause applied. This is logical, because you really cannot rank anything without defining what should rank higher than what. Let's look at how we can use both functions in Listing 5.31 on the next page.

Listing 5.31 Query with ROW_NUMBER() and RANK() functions

```
SELECT
  ROW_NUMBER() OVER (
    ORDER BY o.OrderDate, o.OrderNumber
    ) AS OrderSequence,
  ROW_NUMBER() OVER (
    PARTITION BY o.CustomerID
    ORDER BY o.OrderDate, o.OrderNumber
    ) AS CustomerOrderSequence,
  o.OrderNumber, o.CustomerID, o.OrderDate, o.OrderAmount,
  RANK() OVER (
    ORDER BY o.OrderTotal DESC
    ) AS OrderRanking,
  RANK() OVER (
    PARTITION BY o.CustomerID
    ORDER BY o.OrderTotal DESC
    ) AS CustomerOrderRanking
FROM Orders AS o
ORDER BY o.OrderDate;
```

Table 5.20 illustrates the results that the query in Listing 5.31 returns.

> **Note**
>
> Microsoft SQL Server may return ranks differently from IBM DB2, Oracle Database, and PostgreSQL. The data returned by GitHub scripts for those DBMSs will be different from what is shown in Table 5.20.

As discussed in Item 37, the PARTITION BY predicate influences the effective grouping of the ranking functions. With OrderSequence, the window was applied to the entire set, whereas CustomerSequence was grouped by CustomerID, which allows us to "restart" the ROW_NUMBER()'s sequencing and thus identify which order was the customer's first order, second, and so on in the customer rank.

With the RANK() function, we did not use the same ORDER BY predicate; we wanted to rank orders based on the amount (e.g., the largest order in terms of amount paid), and that is how we influence which row gets ranked first, second, and so forth. As with the ROW_NUMBER(), we can partition the ranking by groups, allowing us to see which order for that particular customer was its largest order placed. With CustomerOrderRanking, we had partitioning so we could see what order was the customer's largest order and so on.

It is also important to note how the RANK() function behaves when there are ties. For OrderRanking, OrderNumber 2 and 10 are tied, as

Table 5.20 Hypothetical data returned by the query in Listing 5.31

Order Sequence	Customer OrderSequence	Order Number	CustomerID	...
1	1	2	4	...
2	1	9	3	...
3	2	4	3	...
4	1	3	1	...
5	1	1	2	...
6	2	5	2	...
7	3	6	3	...
8	2	7	4	...
9	3	8	4	...
10	4	10	4	...

...	Order Date	Amount	Order Ranking	Customer OrderRanking
...	2/15	291.01	6	3
...	2/16	102.23	8	3
...	2/16	431.62	3	2
...	2/16	512.76	2	1
...	2/17	102.23	8	1
...	2/18	49.12	10	2
...	2/18	921.87	1	1
...	2/19	391.39	5	2
...	2/20	428.48	4	1
...	2/20	291.01	6	3

are 9 and 3. Consequently, we have gaps in the RANK()'s numbering. We are missing rank numbers 7 and 9 because each pair of orders shares ranks 6 and 8, respectively. If you would rather not have gaps in your ranking, you would use DENSE_RANK() instead. Alternatively, you could write your query's OVER clause so that ties are not possible.

The other thing to note about those functions is that the ORDER BY predicate is required, which is logical because the functions could give different answers if they were given different columns to sort upon.

Things to Remember

✦ ROW_NUMBER(), RANK(), and other ranking functions must always be windowed and therefore cannot appear without a corresponding OVER clause.

✦ Give consideration to how ties should be handled with ranking functions. If you need contiguous ranking, you should use DENSE_RANK() instead.

✦ The ORDER BY predicate is mandatory for this class of functions because it influences how the results will be sequenced or ranked.

Item 39: Create a Moving Aggregate

The samples in Items 37, "Know how to use window functions," and 38, "Create row numbers and rank a row over other rows," used the default bounding behavior for the window functions. However, to create a moving aggregate expression, the default bounding behavior will not work. Often, companies need to see performance compared within a smaller range than the entire set. For instance, a sales report is usually more useful when we have an average of sales for only a three-month period as opposed to the entire company's history. Or a company with seasonal cycles might want to compare sales in one month to those in the same month of the previous year instead of the previous month. In both cases, we have to specify how to set the bounds of the window frame for the functions to be applied upon. In Items 37 and 38, because we did not specify any bounding, the defaults were applied depending on whether an ORDER BY predicate was specified or not. The code in Listing 5.32 shows the equivalent code from Listing 5.29 with the default spelled out.

Listing 5.32 Window function to perform a running sum, with defaults shown

```
SELECT o.OrderNumber, o.CustomerID, o.OrderTotal
  SUM(o.OrderTotal) OVER (
    PARTITION BY o.CustomerID
    ORDER BY o.OrderNumber, o.CustomerID
    RANGE BETWEEN UNBOUNDED PRECEDING AND CURRENT ROW
  ) AS TotalByCustomer,
```

```
SUM(o.OrderTotal) OVER (
    PARTITION BY o.CustomerID
    --RANGE BETWEEN UNBOUNDED PRECEDING AND UNBOUNDED FOLLOWING
) AS TotalOverall
FROM Orders AS o
ORDER BY o.OrderID, o.CustomerID;
```

Note that for TotalOverall, the window frame definition is commented out. This is because it is not valid to define a window frame without an ORDER BY predicate. Nonetheless, this illustrates the defaults that are assumed whenever you create a window function expression. With RANGE, you have three valid bounding options:

- BETWEEN UNBOUNDED PRECEDING AND CURRENT ROW

- BETWEEN CURRENT ROW AND UNBOUNDED FOLLOWING

- BETWEEN UNBOUNDED PRECEDING AND UNBOUNDED FOLLOWING

Instead of using the BETWEEN ... AND ... syntax, you can opt to use shorthand alternatives, which are equivalent to the first and second options, respectively:

- UNBOUNDED PRECEDING

- UNBOUNDED FOLLOWING

When you use RANGE, the current row is compared to other rows and grouped based on the ORDER BY predicate. This is not always desirable; you might actually want a physical offset irrespective of whether two rows have the same results for an ORDER BY predicate. In this scenario, you would specify ROWS instead of RANGE. This gives you three options in addition to the three options enumerated previously:

- BETWEEN N PRECEDING AND CURRENT ROW

- BETWEEN CURRENT ROW AND N FOLLOWING

- BETWEEN N PRECEDING AND N FOLLOWING

. . . where N is a positive integer. You can also substitute the CURRENT ROW with either UNBOUNDED PRECEDING or UNBOUNDED FOLLOWING where it is appropriate. As you see, you must use ROWS if you want to size the window frame arbitrarily, and it can be sized only by the physical offset from the current row. You cannot use an expression to size the window frame, but you can work around this limitation by preprocessing the data before applying the window frame. For instance, you could create a common table expression that performs some grouping and then apply a window function(s) on that CTE.

With the syntax in mind, let's look at how we can create a moving average of three months. To help demonstrate that the averages are correct, we include LAG and LEAD window functions in Listing 5.33. Note that the listing does not include the CTE PurchaseStatistics, which is defined in the GitHub sample.

Listing 5.33 Demonstration of moving average window functions

```
SELECT
    s.CustomerID, s.PurchaseYear, s.PurchaseMonth,
    LAG(s.PurchaseTotal, 1) OVER (
        PARTITION BY s.CustomerID, s.PurchaseMonth
        ORDER BY s.PurchaseYear
    ) AS PreviousMonthTotal,
    s.PurchaseTotal AS CurrentMonthTotal,
    LEAD(s.PurchaseTotal, 1) OVER (
        PARTITION BY s.CustomerID, s.PurchaseMonth
        ORDER BY s.PurchaseYear
    ) AS NextMonthTotal,
    AVG(s.PurchaseTotal) OVER (
        PARTITION BY s.CustomerID, s.PurchaseMonth
        ORDER BY s.PurchaseYear
        ROWS BETWEEN 1 PRECEDING AND 1 FOLLOWING
    ) AS MonthOfYearAverage
FROM PurchaseStatistics AS s
ORDER BY s.CustomerID, s.PurchaseYear, s.PurchaseMonth;
```

Note that we define the partitioning (or grouping) to be by CustomerID and PurchaseMonth. This allows us to group all months of the year in the same group so that we are comparing one year's month to another year's, not the month before or after the current month. For that reason, we can then specify a physical offset of 1 both preceding and following as the boundary for the window frame. The selected output of data returned by the query is shown in Table 5.21.

Looking at the average sales, we can see that they were pretty good in the years 2012 and 2013. For June 2012, the 2011 total of $1,402.53 and the 2013 total of $8,400.52 were averaged with the 2012 total of $6,254.64 to give us the overall average of $5,352.56.

It is important to note that the query depends on physical offsets being consistent. The query assumes that there will be always 12 rows for each year. Otherwise the PARTITION BY and ORDER BY clauses cannot work correctly. If it were possible for there to be no sales in certain months (e.g., the company closes for a month so there are no sales made), it would be necessary to ensure that the missing months are supplied somehow. You can look at Item 56, "Create an appointment

Table 5.21 Selected rows from the query in Listing 5.33

Customer ID	Purchase Year	Purchase Month	Previous MonthTotal	Current MonthTotal	Next MonthTotal	MonthOf YearAverage
1	2011	5	NULL	1641.16	9631.94	5636.55
1	2011	6	NULL	1402.53	6254.64	3828.59
1	2011	7	NULL	2517.81	10202.26	6360.04
...	...	...	...	...	...	...
1	2012	5	1641.16	9631.94	10744.23	7339.11
1	2012	6	1402.53	6254.64	8400.52	5352.56
1	2012	7	2517.81	10202.26	12517.99	8412.69
...	...	...	...	...	...	...
1	2013	5	9631.94	10744.23	4156.48	8177.55
1	2013	6	6254.64	8400.52	6384.93	7013.36
1	2013	7	10202.26	12517.99	10871.25	11197.17
...	...	...	...	...	...	...
1	2014	5	10744.23	4156.48	11007.72	8636.14
1	2014	6	8400.52	6384.93	6569.74	7118.40
1	2014	7	12517.99	10871.25	12786.33	12058.52

calendar table with all dates enumerated in a range," for an example of creating a calendar that can then be left joined to the Purchases table to ensure that those missing months will have 0 for their totals and thus partition correctly.

When to Use RANGE or ROWS

It can be hard to see the difference between RANGE and ROWS. As mentioned, RANGE works with logical groupings so the difference is manifested only when the ORDER BY predicate returns duplicate values. The query in Listing 5.34 on the next page illustrates how we can use both with an equivalent bounding frame. For brevity, the CTE PurchaseStatistics is not shown but is defined in the GitHub scripts.

---

continues

Listing 5.34 Demonstration of a query with both RANGE and ROWS

```
SELECT
  s.CustomerID, s.PurchaseYear, s.PurchaseMonth,
  SUM(s.PurchaseCount) OVER (
    PARTITION BY s.PurchaseYear
    ORDER BY s.CustomerID
    RANGE BETWEEN UNBOUNDED PRECEDING AND CURRENT ROW
  ) AS CountByRange,
  SUM(s.PurchaseCount) OVER (
    PARTITION BY s.PurchaseYear
    ORDER BY s.CustomerID
    ROWS BETWEEN UNBOUNDED PRECEDING AND CURRENT ROW
  ) AS CountByRows
FROM PurchaseStatistics AS s
ORDER BY s.CustomerID, s.PurchaseYear, s.PurchaseMonth;
```

Note that the ORDER BY predicate is defined on s.CustomerID, which is duplicated for 12 months and thus is not unique. Table 5.22 shows a possible output.

Table 5.22 Demonstrating the difference between RANGE and ROWS

Customer ID	Purchase Year	Purchase Month	CountBy Range	CountBy Rows
1	2011	1	181	66
1	2011	2	181	78
1	2011	3	181	181
1	2011	4	181	39
1	2011	5	181	97
1	2011	6	181	153
1	2011	7	181	54
1	2011	8	181	107
1	2011	9	181	171
1	2011	10	181	11
1	2011	11	181	128
1	2011	12	181	142

Because the ORDER BY predicate does not include PurchaseMonth, there are 12 rows that have same value for CustomerID per PurchaseYear. RANGE considers those to be logically the same "group" and thus gives the same totals for all 12 rows, whereas ROWS accumulates the count as the rows come in. The counts are not in order because the engine considered those in the order it received the rows, not by the PurchaseMonth, which was not specified in the ORDER BY predicate. For that reason, March happened to be the last row received and thus was given 181, instead of December. As you learned in Item 37, ORDER BY is important and can change results drastically, so extra diligence is needed when forming both the PARTITION BY and ORDER BY predicates for window function expressions.

Things to Remember

+ Whenever you need to change the window frame's bounding to a nondefault setting, you must specify an ORDER BY predicate even when it is optional.

+ If you need to define an arbitrary size for a window frame, you must use ROWS, which allows you to input how many rows preceding or following are to be included in the window frame.

+ RANGE can accept only UNBOUNDED PRECEDING, CURRENT ROW, or UNBOUNDED FOLLOWING as valid options.

+ You can choose between RANGE for logical grouping of rows and ROWS for physical offset of the rows. If the ORDER BY predicate does not return duplicate values, the results are equivalent.

6

Subqueries

A subquery is a table expression created by embedding a complete SELECT statement inside parentheses and giving it a name. In general, you can use a subquery anywhere you can use a table name. As you will learn in this chapter, you can also use a subquery that returns a single column wherever you can use a list of values—for example, in an IN clause. A subquery that returns one column and zero or only one value can be used anywhere you can use a column name or a single literal. The subquery is a powerful construct that gives you lots of additional flexibility in SQL. The first item in this chapter explores in depth where you can use the different kinds of subqueries.

Item 40: Know Where You Can Use Subqueries

We use the term *subquery* to mean any complete SELECT statement that is enclosed in parentheses and is usually given an alias name with an AS clause outside the parentheses. You can use a subquery in several places in another SELECT, UPDATE, INSERT, or DELETE statement. In some cases, a subquery can return an entire set of data, including multiple columns and rows (also called a table subquery). In other places, a subquery must return only a single column with multiple rows (a table subquery with only one column). And finally, a subquery returning only one value (also called a scalar subquery) is useful in yet other ways. The uses of subqueries are as follows:

- A table subquery can be used anywhere you can also use the name of a table or a view, or a stored procedure or function that returns a table.

- A table subquery with one column can be used anywhere you can use a table subquery or as the list of values to be compared in an IN predicate.

- A scalar subquery can be used anywhere you could otherwise use a column name or expression on column names.

The following subsections discuss each type of subquery and show examples.

Table Subquery

Table subqueries are particularly useful in a FROM clause that joins multiple sets of data where you need to filter one or more of the sets before performing the join. Consider the problem of finding all recipes that use both beef and garlic in a typical Recipes database. One way to solve the problem is to build two separate table subqueries, one that finds recipes using beef, and a second that finds recipes using garlic, and then join the two subqueries to find recipes that contain both. The solution might look something like Listing 6.1.

Listing 6.1 Finding recipes using both beef and garlic with table subqueries

```
SELECT BeefRecipes.RecipeTitle
FROM (
  SELECT Recipes.RecipeID, Recipes.RecipeTitle
  FROM Recipes
    INNER JOIN Recipe_Ingredients
      ON Recipes.RecipeID = Recipe_Ingredients.RecipeID
    INNER JOIN Ingredients
      ON Ingredients.IngredientID =
        Recipe_Ingredients.IngredientID
  WHERE Ingredients.IngredientName = 'Beef'
  ) AS BeefRecipes
  INNER JOIN (
    SELECT Recipe_Ingredients.RecipeID
    FROM Recipe_Ingredients
    INNER JOIN Ingredients
      ON Ingredients.IngredientID =
        Recipe_Ingredients.IngredientID
  WHERE Ingredients.IngredientName = 'Garlic'
  ) AS GarlicRecipes
  ON BeefRecipes.RecipeID = GarlicRecipes.RecipeID;
```

Note that we included the RecipeTitle column in only one of the two subqueries, so we did not need to include the Recipes table in the second subquery because we need only the RecipeID value to perform the join.

Another less common use of a table subquery is in an EXISTS predicate that will accept a table subquery. Similar to the recipes problem, assume you want to find all customers who purchased both a skateboard and a helmet in the same order. You could solve the problem

using EXISTS and two correlated table subqueries that filter for the
current OrderNumber value in the outer query and either "Skateboard"
or "Helmet" in the related Products table. Listing 6.2 shows the possible solution.

Note

See Item 41, "Know the difference between correlated and non-correlated
subqueries," for more information on correlated subqueries.

Listing 6.2 Using table subqueries with the EXISTS predicate

```
SELECT Customers.CustomerID, Customers.CustFirstName,
  Customers.CustLastName, Orders.OrderNumber, Orders.OrderDate
FROM Customers
  INNER JOIN Orders
    ON Customers.CustomerID = Orders.CustomerID
WHERE EXISTS (
  SELECT NULL
  FROM Orders AS o2
    INNER JOIN Order_Details
      ON o2.OrderNumber = Order_Details.OrderNumber
    INNER JOIN Products
      ON Products.ProductNumber = Order_Details.ProductNumber
  WHERE Products.ProductName = 'Skateboard'
    AND o2.OrderNumber = Orders.OrderNumber
) AND EXISTS (
  SELECT NULL
  FROM Orders AS o3
    INNER JOIN Order_Details
      ON o3.OrderNumber = Order_Details.OrderNumber
    INNER JOIN Products
      ON Products.ProductNumber = Order_Details.ProductNumber
  WHERE Products.ProductName = 'Helmet'
    AND o3.OrderNumber = Orders.OrderNumber
);
```

Note

The actual product names in the Sales Orders sample database are not
simply Skateboard and Helmet, so the example query in Listing 6.2
returns no rows. To solve this using the sample database, you would
need to use LIKE '%Skateboard%' and LIKE '%Helmet%' to see results.
We used the simple values in the example query to make it easier to
understand.

Note that when the EXISTS predicate is used, the SELECT list is usually irrelevant, and to emphasize that point we use NULL as the lone column selection. For most database engines, * or 1 will work equally well, but for making the code self-documenting, we think NULL is the best choice.

This might not be the best way to solve the problem. The database engine must logically run both queries for every order found in the database because they depend on being filtered by the OrderNumber value in each row in the outer query. Just because you can solve a problem this way does not mean you should. We discuss some of the pros and cons further in Item 41 later in this chapter.

Table Subquery with One Column

A table subquery with one column returned can be used anywhere you can use a full table subquery. Because the subquery returns only one column, that column acts as a list of values that can certainly be used to supply the list for the IN or NOT IN predicate.

Suppose you wanted to display a list of all products that were not ordered at all in the month of December 2015. Listing 6.3 uses a single-column table subquery in the possible solution.

Listing 6.3 Finding products not ordered in December 2015 using a single-column table subquery

```
SELECT Products.ProductName
FROM Products
WHERE Products.ProductNumber NOT IN (
  SELECT Order_Details.ProductNumber
  FROM Orders
    INNER JOIN Order_Details
      ON Orders.OrderNumber = Order_Details.OrderNumber
  WHERE Orders.OrderDate
    BETWEEN '2015-12-01' AND '2015-12-31'
);
```

Of course, you can use a single-column table subquery anywhere you can use an IN clause, even within a CASE statement in the list of columns specified in the SELECT clause. Suppose you have sales reps living in several states, and you want them to focus on existing customers who live in the same state. You might want to produce a list of all employees and customers in the same state and let the employee know which customers have or have not placed an order. Listing 6.4 shows a potential solution.

Listing 6.4 Using a single-column table subquery in a CASE statement

```
SELECT Employees.EmpFirstName, Employees.EmpLastName,
  Customers.CustFirstName, Customers.CustLastName,
  Customers.CustAreaCode, Customers.CustPhoneNumber,
  CASE WHEN Customers.CustomerID IN (
    SELECT CustomerID
    FROM Orders
    WHERE Orders.EmployeeID = Employees.EmployeeID
    ) THEN 'Ordered from you.'
    ELSE ' '
  END AS CustStatus
FROM Employees
  INNER JOIN Customers
    ON Employees.EmpState = Customers.CustState;
```

Scalar Subquery

A scalar subquery returns zero or only one value in one column in a single row. You can certainly use a scalar subquery anywhere you can use a table subquery or a table subquery that returns one column. However, scalar subqueries are also usable anywhere you would otherwise use a column name or an expression. They can also be used in expressions with other columns and operators.

Let's take a look at a couple of examples using a scalar subquery. In the first example, we list all products and the latest order date for each product using the MAX() aggregate function. We know that MAX() returns a single value, so we definitely have a scalar subquery. Listing 6.5 shows the solution.

Listing 6.5 Using a scalar subquery as a column in a SELECT clause

```
SELECT Products.ProductNumber, Products.ProductName, (
    SELECT MAX(Orders.OrderDate)
    FROM Orders
      INNER JOIN Order_Details
        ON Orders.OrderNumber = Order_Details.OrderNumber
    WHERE Order_Details.ProductNumber = Products.ProductNumber
    ) AS LastOrder
FROM Products;
```

You can also use a scalar subquery to return a single value to be used in any comparison predicate. If we want to list all vendors whose average number of days to deliver all their products is greater than the average for all vendors, we might code the solution as shown in Listing 6.6 on the next page.

Listing 6.6 Using a scalar subquery in a comparison predicate

```
SELECT Vendors.VendName,
  AVG(Product_Vendors.DaysToDeliver) AS AvgDelivery
FROM Vendors
  INNER JOIN Product_Vendors
    ON Vendors.VendorID = Product_Vendors.VendorID
GROUP BY Vendors.VendName
HAVING AVG(Product_Vendors.DaysToDeliver) > (
  SELECT AVG(DaysToDeliver)
  FROM Product_Vendors
  );
```

You can see that we used a scalar subquery to generate a comparison value in the HAVING clause.

Things to Remember

✦ You can use table subqueries anywhere you could otherwise use a table or view name or name of a function or procedure that returns a table.

✦ You can use a table subquery that returns a single column anywhere you can use a table subquery and where you need to generate a list for an IN or NOT IN predicate.

✦ Scalar subqueries can be used anywhere you can use a column name—in a SELECT list, in an expression in a SELECT list, or as part of a comparison predicate.

Item 41: Know the Difference between Correlated and Non-correlated Subqueries

As you learned in Item 40, "Know where you can use subqueries," a SELECT statement embedded in parentheses within another query can be a powerful tool. A subquery is "correlated" when some condition within the subquery (in a WHERE or HAVING clause) depends on a value in the current row being processed in the outer query. A non-correlated subquery is not dependent on an external value—it could be run as a separate query when not embedded in another query. We will take a look at some examples of each type of subquery in the following sections.

Before we get started, it would help to give you the design of the database we use in this item. The database to keep track of your favorite recipes looks like Figure 6.1.

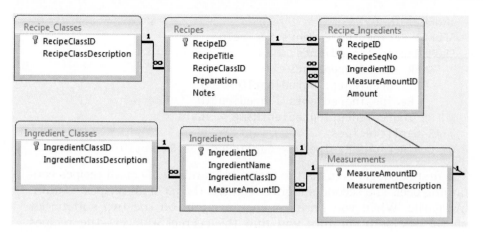

Figure 6.1 Sample design for a Recipes database

Now let's look at the two types of subqueries.

Non-correlated Subqueries

You typically use a non-correlated subquery in two cases:

- As a filtered set of data in a FROM clause

- As a single-column set of data for an IN predicate in a WHERE clause or a single value (scalar subquery) for a comparison predicate in a WHERE or HAVING clause

First, let's look at using a non-correlated subquery in a FROM clause. Listing 6.7 (which you already saw as Listing 6.1 in Item 40) shows one way to find all recipes that have both beef and garlic as an ingredient.

Listing 6.7 Finding recipes with both beef and garlic using non-correlated subqueries

```
SELECT BeefRecipes.RecipeTitle
FROM (
  SELECT Recipes.RecipeID, Recipes.RecipeTitle
  FROM Recipes
    INNER JOIN Recipe_Ingredients
      ON Recipes.RecipeID = Recipe_Ingredients.RecipeID
    INNER JOIN Ingredients
      ON Ingredients.IngredientID =
        Recipe_Ingredients.IngredientID
  WHERE Ingredients.IngredientName = 'Beef'
) AS BeefRecipes
```

```
INNER JOIN (
SELECT Recipe_Ingredients.RecipeID
FROM Recipe_Ingredients
  INNER JOIN Ingredients
    ON Ingredients.IngredientID =
      Recipe_Ingredients.IngredientID
WHERE Ingredients.IngredientName = 'Garlic'
) AS GarlicRecipes
ON BeefRecipes.RecipeID = GarlicRecipes.RecipeID;
```

The first subquery returns the recipe title and the ID of all recipes containing beef. The second subquery returns the ID of all recipes containing garlic. When you perform an inner join on the two subqueries on the RecipeID column, you find the correct answer—the recipes that contain both ingredients. Note that both queries are filtered, but the filter in the WHERE clause does not depend on any value returned outside the subquery. You could take either subquery and run it independently.

Now let's look at using a non-correlated subquery to use as a filter for an IN predicate in a WHERE clause. Listing 6.8 shows an example.

Listing 6.8 Listing recipes that are a salad, a soup, or a main course

```
SELECT Recipes.RecipeTitle
FROM Recipes
WHERE Recipes.RecipeClassID IN (
  SELECT rc.RecipeClassID
  FROM Recipe_Classes AS rc
  WHERE rc.RecipeClassDescription IN
    ('Salad', 'Soup', 'Main course')
  );
```

Again, you could run the subquery that provides values to the IN predicate separately because it does not depend on any value returned outside the subquery. You could also solve this problem by doing an inner join between the Recipes table and the Recipe_Classes table in the main FROM clause and using a simple IN clause. However, using the subquery turns out to be slightly more efficient (at least in SQL Server) than using JOIN.

Finally, let's look at using a scalar subquery in a WHERE clause. The SQL in Listing 6.9 shows a method for finding the recipe that uses the most garlic (just for you garlic lovers). Note that the standard measure amount (in this case, cloves of garlic) is specified in the Ingredients table, so we can assume that all quantities in the RecipeIngredients table use the same measure.

Listing 6.9 Finding the recipe that uses the most garlic

```
SELECT DISTINCT Recipes.RecipeTitle
FROM Recipes
  INNER JOIN Recipe_Ingredients
    ON Recipes.RecipeID = Recipe_Ingredients.RecipeID
  INNER JOIN Ingredients
    ON Recipe_Ingredients.IngredientID
      = Ingredients.IngredientID
WHERE Ingredients.IngredientName = 'Garlic'
  AND Recipe_Ingredients.Amount = (
      SELECT MAX(Amount)
      FROM Recipe_Ingredients
        INNER JOIN Ingredients
          ON Recipe_Ingredients.IngredientID =
            Ingredients.IngredientID
      WHERE IngredientName = 'Garlic'
      );
```

As with any non-correlated subquery, you could run the SELECT MAX subquery by itself with no problems. Because the MAX aggregate function returns a single value, we can use the subquery to return a comparison value for an equals predicate in the WHERE clause.

Correlated Subqueries

A correlated subquery uses one or more filters in either a WHERE or a HAVING clause that depend on a value provided by the outer query. Because of this dependence, the subquery is "co-related" to the outer query, and your database engine must run the subquery once for every row returned by the outer query. This can, potentially, make using a subquery like this run more slowly than other techniques, but that is not always the case because some database systems smartly optimize queries that contain a correlated subquery.

You are not likely to use a correlated subquery as one of the sets in a FROM clause because it is simpler and more straightforward to use JOIN instead. (In fact, many database systems use JOIN in the execution plan to optimize correlated subqueries.) You can use a correlated scalar subquery to return a value in a SELECT clause, to provide a single value to test in a comparison predicate in a WHERE or HAVING clause, to provide a single-column list for the IN predicate in a WHERE or HAVING clause, or to provide a set for testing in an EXISTS predicate in a WHERE or HAVING clause.

Let's first look at using a scalar correlated subquery to return a value in a SELECT clause. Listing 6.10 on the next page shows one way to list all recipe classes along with a count of the recipes in each class.

Listing 6.10 Getting a count of rows using a correlated subquery

```
SELECT Recipe_Classes.RecipeClassDescription, (
    SELECT COUNT(*)
    FROM Recipes
    WHERE Recipes.RecipeClassID =
      Recipe_Classes.RecipeClassID
    ) AS RecipeCount
FROM Recipe_Classes;
```

The subquery is correlated because it must be filtered on a value from the Recipe_Classes table in the outer query—that is, your database system must run the subquery once for every row in the Recipe_Classes table. You might be wondering why we did not just use JOIN and GROUP BY to get the answer. We did it this way for two reasons: (1) the query with the correlated subquery actually runs faster on most database systems, and (2) you will get the wrong answer if you use the GROUP BY technique. For more details about why the second reason is true, consult Item 34, "Avoid getting an erroneous COUNT() when using OUTER JOIN."

Now let's look at using a correlated subquery to return a set for testing in an EXISTS predicate. Earlier in Listing 6.7, we showed you how to find all recipes that have both beef and garlic. You get the same answer using correlated subqueries and an existence test. Listing 6.11 shows how.

Listing 6.11 Finding recipes with both beef and garlic using correlated subqueries

```
SELECT Recipes.RecipeTitle
FROM Recipes
WHERE EXISTS (
  SELECT NULL
  FROM Ingredients
    INNER JOIN Recipe_Ingredients
      ON Ingredients.IngredientID =
        Recipe_Ingredients.IngredientID
  WHERE Ingredients.IngredientName = 'Beef'
    AND Recipe_Ingredients.RecipeID = Recipes.RecipeID
  ) AND EXISTS (
  SELECT NULL
  FROM Ingredients
    INNER JOIN Recipe_Ingredients
      ON Ingredients.IngredientID =
        Recipe_Ingredients.IngredientID
  WHERE Ingredients.IngredientName = 'Garlic'
    AND Recipe_Ingredients.RecipeID = Recipes.RecipeID
  );
```

Because each subquery references the Recipes table in the outer query, your database system must run both subqueries for every row in the Recipes table. You might expect that this second version of the query would run much more slowly (or less efficiently) than the first version. It does take a few more resources (55% versus 45% in SQL Server), but it is not horrendously awful because most database systems optimize the second query discussed in next paragraph. Note, however, that there is no index defined on the IngredientName column. If we add an index to that column, the EXISTS version wins handily. This simply points out how important an index can be when you use a sargable predicate. See Item 28, "Write sargable queries to ensure that the engine will use indexes," for more details.

As you might expect, you could also solve the query using IN. Instead of EXISTS (SELECT Recipe_Ingredients.RecipeID ...), you could use Recipes.RecipeID IN (SELECT Recipe_Ingredients.RecipeID ...). It turns out that the IN version uses about the same amount of resources as the EXISTS version, but only because there is no index on the IngredientName column. If we add an index to that column, the EXISTS version runs faster. Without an index, EXISTS may still run faster because most optimizers stop running the subquery as soon as the engine finds the first row, but IN usually retrieves all rows. A regular JOIN clause can create duplicate rows when joining a pair of tables that participate in a one-to-many relationship. With an EXISTS predicate, the optimizer optimizes it as a "semi-join," in which case the outermost table's rows do not get duplicated and the optimizer does not need to actually process the entire contents of the inner table as it would with an IN predicate.

Things to Remember

- ✦ A correlated subquery uses a reference in a WHERE or HAVING clause that depends on a value from the query in which the subquery is embedded.

- ✦ A non-correlated subquery has no dependence on the outer query and could be run by itself.

- ✦ You typically use a non-correlated subquery as either a filtered set of data in a FROM clause, as a single-column set of data for an IN predicate, or to return a scalar value for a comparison predicate in a WHERE or HAVING clause.

- ✦ You use a correlated subquery to return a scalar value in a SELECT clause, to provide a single value to test in a comparison predicate in a WHERE or HAVING clause, or to provide a set for existence testing in an EXISTS clause.

- ✦ A correlated subquery is not necessarily slower than some other method, and it may be the only way to return the correct answer.

Item 42: If Possible, Use Common Table Expressions Instead of Subqueries

In Item 25, "Know techniques to solve multiple-criteria problems," we showed you how to solve a complex problem to find customers who purchased all of four different products. We also showed you how to find customers who purchased a potentially dangerous product (a skateboard) but who did not buy all the necessary protective gear (helmet, gloves, and knee pads). In that item, we suggested that you could create a function that evaluates a complex join and filters it based on a parameter to make your final SQL simpler.

Note

Neither Microsoft Access nor MySQL supports common table expressions.

Figure 6.2 shows the design of the Sales Orders database that we use in this item.

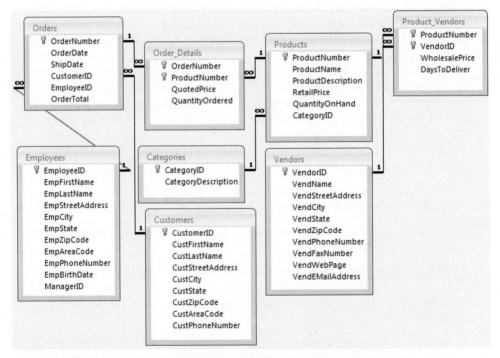

Figure 6.2 Design of a typical Sales Orders database

One of the disadvantages of a function is that you cannot see what the function is doing in your final SQL. Also, you or someone else could inadvertently change the separate function and break the query that depends on it. There is a better way to do this: a common table expression (CTE), provided your database system supports that feature. (IBM DB2, Microsoft SQL Server, Oracle, and PostgreSQL all support CTEs; Microsoft Access as of 2016 and MySQL as of 5.7 do not.)

Using a CTE to Simplify a Query

First, let's review the original query used to find the customers who purchased skateboards, helmets, knee pads, and gloves—all four products. Listing 6.12 shows the original solution.

> ### Note
>
> The actual product names in the Sales Orders sample database are not simply Skateboard and Helmet, so the example queries in this item return no rows. To solve these using the sample database, you would need to use LIKE '%Skateboard%' and LIKE '%Helmet%' to see results. We used the simple values in the example queries to make them easier to understand.

Listing 6.12 Finding customers who purchased all four products

```
SELECT c.CustomerID, c.CustFirstName, c.CustLastName
FROM Customers AS c
  INNER JOIN (
  SELECT DISTINCT Orders.CustomerID
  FROM Orders
    INNER JOIN Order_Details
      ON Orders.OrderNumber = Order_Details.OrderNumber
    INNER JOIN Products
      ON Products.ProductNumber = Order_Details.ProductNumber
  WHERE Products.ProductName = 'Skateboard'
  ) AS OSk
    ON c.CustomerID = OSk.CustomerID
  INNER JOIN (
  SELECT DISTINCT Orders.CustomerID
  FROM Orders
    INNER JOIN Order_Details
      ON Orders.OrderNumber = Order_Details.OrderNumber
    INNER JOIN Products
      ON Products.ProductNumber = Order_Details.ProductNumber
  WHERE Products.ProductName = 'Helmet'
  ) AS OHel
    ON c.CustomerID = OHel.CustomerID
```

```
INNER JOIN (
SELECT DISTINCT Orders.CustomerID
FROM Orders
  INNER JOIN Order_Details
    ON Orders.OrderNumber = Order_Details.OrderNumber
  INNER JOIN Products
    ON Products.ProductNumber = Order_Details.ProductNumber
WHERE Products.ProductName = 'Knee Pads'
) AS OKn
ON c.CustomerID = OKn.CustomerID
INNER JOIN (
SELECT DISTINCT Orders.CustomerID
FROM Orders
  INNER JOIN Order_Details
    ON Orders.OrderNumber = Order_Details.OrderNumber
  INNER JOIN Products
    ON Products.ProductNumber = Order_Details.ProductNumber
WHERE Products.ProductName = 'Gloves'
) AS OGl
ON c.CustomerID = OGl.CustomerID;
```

The four table subqueries make the query difficult to read and understand. The only difference among the four is the value of the ProductName selected. If you include the ProductName column in a CTE within the query, you can reference the name of the CTE as though it were a table and apply the necessary filter. Listing 6.13 shows how to simplify this query using a CTE. You define a CTE using a WITH clause.

Listing 6.13 Finding customers who purchased all four products using a CTE

```
WITH CustProd AS (
  SELECT Orders.CustomerID, Products.ProductName
  FROM Orders
    INNER JOIN Order_Details
      ON Orders.OrderNumber = Order_Details.OrderNumber
    INNER JOIN Products
      ON Products.ProductNumber = Order_Details.ProductNumber
  ),
SkateboardOrders AS (
  SELECT DISTINCT CustomerID
  FROM CustProd
  WHERE ProductName = 'Skateboard'
  ),
HelmetOrders AS (
  SELECT DISTINCT CustomerID
```

```
    FROM CustProd
    WHERE ProductName = 'Helmet'
    ),
KneepadsOrders AS (
    SELECT DISTINCT CustomerID
    FROM CustProd
    WHERE ProductName = 'Knee Pads'
    ),
GlovesOrders AS (
    SELECT DISTINCT CustomerID
    FROM CustProd
    WHERE ProductName = 'Gloves'
)
SELECT c.CustomerID, c.CustFirstName, c.CustLastName
FROM Customers AS c
    INNER JOIN SkateboardOrders AS OSk
        ON c.CustomerID = OSk.CustomerID
    INNER JOIN HelmetOrders AS OHel
        ON c.CustomerID = OHel.CustomerID
    INNER JOIN KneepadsOrders AS OKn
        ON c.CustomerID = OKn.CustomerID
    INNER JOIN GlovesOrders AS OGl
        ON c.CustomerID = OGl.CustomerID;
```

As you can see, using a CTE in the query greatly shortens and simplifies it. You can readily see what CustProd returns without having to look up a separate function. Note that we had to include the ProductName column in the output of the CTE so that we could apply the appropriate filter.

You can also see that you can create multiple CTEs and have those CTEs refer back to other CTEs if you want. The biggest advantage of using a CTE is that it enables you to build a complex query by reading the subqueries from top to bottom instead of from inside out as it has been traditionally done. This is particularly useful when you need to build a query for reporting, and you must perform aggregations with a different grouping. The other big advantage is that you can reuse CTEs in multiple places within a query statement.

Some might have approached the problem by creating multiple views, then joining them together. However, this is much harder to maintain because one must examine each view's definition to piece together the final query and deal with proliferation of several views that are not directly usable. CTEs enable you to create a "private" view that is contained within the view's definition and thus maintain definitions in one place. You could certainly turn the preceding SQL into a view by placing a CREATE VIEW statement at the beginning.

Using a Recursive CTE

One of the interesting things you can do with a CTE is make it recursive—that is, have the CTE call itself to generate additional rows. When you make a CTE recursive, most databases restrict what you can do. For example, Microsoft SQL Server disallows DISTINCT, GROUP BY, HAVING, scalar aggregation, subqueries, and LEFT or RIGHT JOIN (INNER JOIN is allowed).

The ISO SQL Standard dictates that you must use the RECURSIVE keyword after the WITH keyword if you intend to make the CTE recursive. However, only PostgreSQL requires that keyword. In all other database systems that support CTEs, you either do not need the keyword or the keyword is not recognized.

Let's look at a simple example that generates a list of numbers from 1 to 100. Listing 6.14 shows how. (Note that we did not include the RECURSIVE keyword.)

Listing 6.14 Generating a list of numbers from 1 to 100

```
WITH SeqNumTbl AS (
   SELECT 1 AS SeqNum
   UNION ALL
   SELECT SeqNum + 1
   FROM SeqNumTbl
   WHERE SeqNum < 100
)
SELECT SeqNum
FROM SeqNumTbl;
```

The second SELECT in the UNION query calls the CTE again and adds 1 to the last number generated but stops when the number reaches 100. When you get to Chapter 9, "Tally Tables," you will find that we often use a list of numbers similar to this in a saved table to do some creative things with SQL. Although you could use the CTE shown here instead of a saved tally table, using the saved table may be faster because you can index the values in a saved table, but the columns generated by a CTE can never be indexed.

Another interesting thing to do with a recursive CTE is to traverse a hierarchy in a self-referencing table. Let's use the ManagerID column in the Employees table in the sample Sales Orders database matched with EmployeeID to list all employees and their managers. The sample data looks like Table 6.1.

You can create a list of managers and employees by using a recursive CTE similar to that found in Listing 6.15.

Table 6.1 Relevant columns from the Employees table

EmployeeID	EmpFirstName	EmpLastName	ManagerID
701	Ann	Patterson	NULL
702	Mary	Thompson	701
703	Jim	Smith	701
704	Carol	Viescas	NULL
705	Michael	Johnson	704
706	David	Viescas	704
707	Kathryn	Patterson	704
708	Susan	Smith	706

Listing 6.15 Displaying managers and all employees

```
WITH MgrEmps (
    ManagerID, ManagerName, EmployeeID, EmployeeName,
    EmployeeLevel
) AS (
  SELECT ManagerID, CAST(' ' AS varchar(50)), EmployeeID,
    CAST(CONCAT(EmpFirstName, ' ', EmpLastName)
      AS varchar(50)), 0 AS EmployeeLevel
  FROM Employees
  WHERE ManagerID IS NULL
  UNION ALL
  SELECT e.ManagerID, d.EmployeeName, e.EmployeeID,
    CAST(CONCAT(e.EmpFirstName, ' ', e.EmpLastName)
      AS varchar(50)), EmployeeLevel + 1
  FROM Employees AS e
    INNER JOIN MgrEmps AS d
      ON e.ManagerID = d.EmployeeID
)
SELECT ManagerID, ManagerName, EmployeeID, EmployeeName,
  EmployeeLevel
FROM MgrEmps
ORDER BY ManagerID;
```

The first query in the CTE finds the employees who do not have a
ManagerID specified to get the starting root rows. We use CAST to ensure
that the data types of all the name columns are compatible so that
the UNION will work. The second query joins the CTE (recursively) with

the original Employees table to match managers with their employees. The query returns the results shown in Table 6.2.

Table 6.2 Listing managers and their employees using a recursive CTE

Manager ID	ManagerName	Employee ID	EmployeeName	Employee Level
NULL	NULL	701	Ann Patterson	0
NULL	NULL	704	Carol Viescas	0
701	Ann Patterson	702	Mary Thompson	1
701	Ann Patterson	703	Jim Smith	1
704	Carol Viescas	705	Michael Johnson	1
704	Carol Viescas	706	David Viescas	1
704	Carol Viescas	707	Kathryn Patterson	1
706	David Viescas	708	Susan Smith	2

The first two rows list the managers who do not report to anyone else in the table. The remaining rows show the employees of those managers, and you can see that Susan Smith reports to David Viescas who then reports to Carol Viescas.

You will most likely use CTEs to simplify complex queries that use the same subquery more than once. You can also see that recursive CTEs let you do creative things in SQL that you might not have imagined.

Things to Remember

✦ Common table expressions (CTEs) let you simplify complex queries that use the same subquery more than once.

✦ CTEs free you from using a function that might be inadvertently changed, thus making your query that uses that function not work correctly.

✦ CTEs let you define the subquery that you are embedding in another query directly in the same SQL, so the query is easier to understand.

✦ Although you can use a recursive CTE to generate values you might otherwise find in a tally table (see also Chapter 9), the stored tally table is more efficient because you can index it.

✦ Recursive CTEs let you navigate a hierarchical relationship and display the information in a meaningful way.

Item 43: Create More Efficient Queries Using Joins Rather than Subqueries

There are often many different ways to achieve the same results when querying a database, but some ways are better than others. In this item, we look at using joins rather than subqueries.

Consider the data model shown in Figure 6.3.

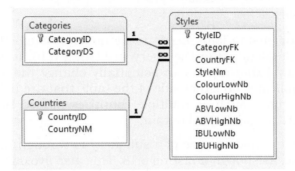

Figure 6.3 Beer Styles data model

If we wanted a list of all of the beer styles that are associated with Belgium, we could use the query shown in Listing 6.16.

Listing 6.16 Selecting beer styles from Belgium using a subquery

```
SELECT StyleNm
FROM Styles
WHERE CountryFK IN (
  SELECT CountryID
  FROM Countries
  WHERE CountryNM = 'Belgium'
  );
```

This would appear to be a reasonable way to solve the problem. "Get the facts from table A, conditional on the facts from table B" makes logical sense. Because Styles contains CountryFK, not CountryNM, you first run a subquery against Countries to determine the value of the ID, then, by using the IN clause, you determine the styles that have that value.

However, note that the entire subquery must be processed before the overall query can evaluate the IN clause to match the values in the Styles table to the values returned by the subquery. Unless the table in the subquery is very small (which fortunately it is in this case!), it is generally more efficient to use a join, as shown in Listing 6.17, because the database engine is usually able to optimize it better.

Listing 6.17 Selecting beer styles from Belgium using JOIN

```sql
SELECT s.StyleNm
FROM Styles AS s
  INNER JOIN Countries AS c
    ON s.CountryFK = c.CountryID
WHERE c.CountryNM = 'Belgium';
```

A caveat about using joins needs to be noted. Though the query in Listing 6.17 is identical to the query in Listing 6.16, it is important to keep in mind that a join can potentially change the output. So if there are duplicates on either side of the table that are not part of the intended outcome, such as multiple countries named Belgium, this might not return the desired output.

Another way to avoid the use of a subquery is through the use of an EXISTS clause, as shown in Listing 6.18. This also avoids the potential problem of generating duplicate output with joins.

Listing 6.18 Selecting beer styles from Belgium using an EXISTS clause

```sql
SELECT s.StyleNm
FROM Styles AS s
WHERE EXISTS (
  SELECT NULL
  FROM Countries
  WHERE CountryNM = 'Belgium'
    AND Countries.CountryID = s.CountryFK
);
```

Although this is not as intuitive as the join or using the subquery, the database simply needs to check the relationship specified to return true or false as opposed to having to evaluate the entire subquery. Also, in spite of the fact that an EXISTS operator expects a subquery, the optimizer may transform it into a semi-join (discussed in Item 41, "Know the difference between correlated and non-correlated subqueries").

Note

Realistically, this is optimizer specific, DBMS version specific, and query specific. Some optimizers prefer a join to a subquery, and some may go the other way. You should always check the specifics of your DBMS, using the information found in Chapter 7, "Getting and Analyzing Metadata."

There are other reasons to prefer using a join. Although Countries has only two columns in this example, should you need to include columns from the second table, using a join makes that possible. In addition, if there is a possibility that the foreign key might not have a value, it is easy to use a left join to retrieve those rows that match the criterion or do not have a value, as shown in Listing 6.19.

Listing 6.19 Selecting beer styles from Belgium or unknown using LEFT JOIN

```
SELECT s.StyleNm
FROM Styles AS s
  LEFT JOIN Countries AS c
    ON s.CountryFK = c.CountryID
WHERE c.CountryNM = 'Belgium'
   OR c.CountryNM IS NULL;
```

Note

See Item 29, "Correctly filter the 'right' side of a 'left' join," for a discussion of the query shown in Listing 6.19.

Things to Remember

✦ Do not always assume that breaking the problem down sequentially is the preferred way. SQL works best with a set, not row by row.

✦ Test the specifics of how the optimizer for your DBMS handles the various approaches to decide on the preferred solution.

✦ Make sure to have the appropriate indexes for any joins.

Getting and Analyzing Metadata

Sometimes just data is not enough. You need data about data. You might even need data about how you are getting the data. In some cases it might even be convenient to get the metadata using SQL, and indeed, you can for several vendors. You can then incorporate the results into your other scripts such as conditionally creating a table only if it is not already created and so forth.

Another type of metadata is how well a query performs. Though in principle SQL is supposed to abstract us away from the mechanics of locating and retrieving data, it is an abstraction nonetheless. And as Joel Spolsky[1] has written, all abstractions are leaky. So it is possible to write a query that forces a suboptimal execution plan, and thus you must dig into the physical aspects of the DBMS product to understand how to improve the performance. This chapter will get you started on the basics, though because it is product specific, it is at most a starting point that you can then supplement with other resources.

Item 44: Learn to Use Your System's Query Analyzer

You have read in many of the items in this book that certain features vary from DBMS to DBMS, and that an approach that might work well on, say, Microsoft SQL Server will not work as well on, say, Oracle. You may be wondering how you can determine which approach to use for your DBMS. In this item we try to give you some tools to help you make your decision.

Before any DBMS can execute an SQL statement, its optimizer has to determine how best to run it. It does this by creating an execution plan, which it then follows step by step. You can think of the optimizer

---

1. Joel Spolsky is a software engineer and writer, author of *Joel on Software* and a blog of the same name.

as being similar to a compiler. Compilers convert source code into executable programs; optimizers convert SQL statements into execution plans. Looking at the execution plan for a particular SQL statement you intend to run can help you to identify performance issues.

Note

Because the specifics of each optimizer vary from DBMS to DBMS and even from one version of a specific DBMS to another, we cannot go in depth for any specific database. Consult your documentation for more details.

IBM DB2

Before you can get an execution plan from DB2, you need to ensure that certain system tables exist. If they do not, you need to create them. You can run the code in Listing 7.1 to create these tables using the SYSINSTALLOBJECTS procedure.

Listing 7.1 Creating DB2 explain tables

```
CALL SYSPROC.SYSINSTALLOBJECTS('EXPLAIN', 'C',
    CAST(NULL AS varchar(128)), CAST(NULL AS varchar(128)))
```

Note

The SYSPROC.SYSINSTALLOBJECTS procedure does not exist in DB2 for z/OS.

After you have installed the necessary tables in the SYSTOOLS schema, you can determine the execution plan for any SQL statement by prefixing the statement with the words EXPLAIN PLAN FOR, as shown in Listing 7.2.

Listing 7.2 Creating an execution plan in DB2

```
EXPLAIN PLAN FOR SELECT CustomerID, SUM(OrderTotal)
FROM Orders
GROUP BY CustomerID;
```

Note that using EXPLAIN PLAN FOR does not actually show the execution plan. What it does is store the plan in the tables created by Listing 7.1.

IBM provides some tools to help analyze the explain information, such as the db2exfmt tool to display explain information in formatted output and the db2expln tool to see the access plan information that is available for one or more packages of static SQL, or you can write your own queries against the explain tables. Writing your own queries allows you to customize the output and lets you do comparisons among different queries, or executions of the same query over time, but it does require knowledge of how the data is stored in the explain tables. IBM also provides the capability to generate a diagram of the current access plan through its freely downloadable Data Studio tool (version 3.1 and later). You can download the Data Studio tool at www-03.ibm.com/software/products/en/data-studio. Figure 7.1 illustrates how Data Studio displays the execution plan (using the term "Access Plan Diagram").

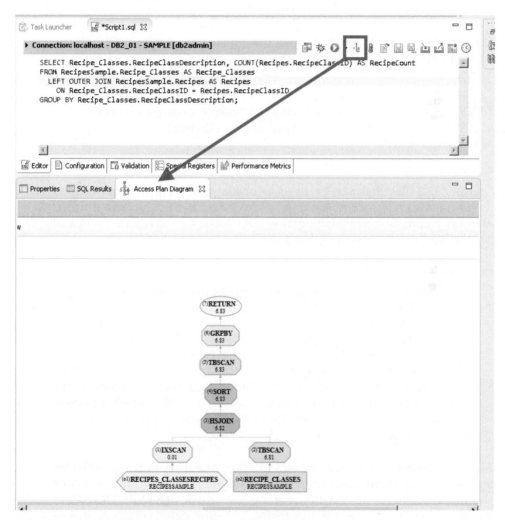

Figure 7.1 IBM Data Studio Access Plan Diagram

Microsoft Access

Obtaining an execution plan in Access can be a bit of an adventure. In essence, you turn on a flag telling the database engine to create a text file, SHOWPLAN.OUT, every time it compiles a query, but how you turn that flag on (and where SHOWPLAN.OUT appears) depends on the version of Access you are using.

Turning the flag on involves updating your system registry. For the x86 version of Access 2013 on an x64 operating system, you would use the registry key shown in Listing 7.3.

Listing 7.3 Registry key to turn Show Plan on for Access 2013 x86 on Windows x64

```
Windows Registry Editor Version 5.00

[HKEY_LOCAL_MACHINE\SOFTWARE\WOW6432Node\Microsoft\Office↲
\15.0\Access Connectivity Engine\Engines\Debug]
"JETSHOWPLAN"="ON"
```

> **Note**
>
> The .REG files that can be used to update your registry are included in the Microsoft Access/Chapter 07 folder on the GitHub site (https://github.com/TexanInParis/Effective-SQL). Make sure to read the name of the file carefully to ensure that you use the correct one for your setup.

> **Note**
>
> As mentioned, the exact registry key varies depending on the version of Access being run, and whether you are running a 32-bit or 64-bit version of Access. For example, for Access 2013 on an x86 operating system, the key would be [HKEY_LOCAL_MACHINE\SOFTWARE\Microsoft\Office\15.0\Access Connectivity Engine\Engines\Debug]. For Access 2010 on an x64 operating system, it would be [HKEY_LOCAL_MACHINE\SOFTWARE\WOW6432Node\Microsoft\Office\14.0\Access Connectivity Engine\Engines\Debug]. For Access 2010 on an x86 operating system, it would be [HKEY_LOCAL_MACHINE\SOFTWARE\Microsoft\Office\14.0\Access Connectivity Engine\Engines\Debug].

After you have created that registry entry, you simply run your queries as usual. Every time you run a query, the Access query engine writes the query's plan to a text file. For Access 2013, SHOWPLAN.OUT is written to your My Documents folder. In some older versions, it was written to the current default folder.

Once you have analyzed all the queries you wish, remember to turn off the flag in your system registry. Again, for the x86 version of

Access 2013 on an x64 operating system, you would use the registry key shown in Listing 7.4, but the exact key depends on whichever one you used to turn it on. Unfortunately, there is no built-in tool for graphical viewing of the plan.

Listing 7.4 Registry key to turn Show Plan off for Access 2013 x86 on Windows x64

```
Windows Registry Editor Version 5.00

[HKEY_LOCAL_MACHINE\SOFTWARE\WOW6432Node\Microsoft\Office↲
\15.0\Access Connectivity Engine\Engines\Debug]
"JETSHOWPLAN"="OFF"
```

Note

Former Access MVP Sascha Trowitzsch has written a free Showplan Capturer tool for Access 2010 and earlier, which can be downloaded at www.mosstools.de/index.php?option=com_content&view=article&id=54. This tool allows you to see execution plans without having to update your registry and locate the SHOWPLAN.OUT file.

Microsoft SQL Server

SQL Server provides several ways to fetch an execution plan. A graphical representation is easily accessible in the Management Studio, but because some of the information is visible only when you move the mouse over a particular operation, it is harder to share details with others. Figure 7.2 shows the two different icons on the toolbar, which can be used to produce a graphical execution plan.

Figure 7.2 How to produce a graphical execution plan in SQL Server

Regardless of which button is used to produce the plan, you will end up with a diagram similar to Figure 7.3 on the next page.

You can compare two queries by placing the SQL for both queries in a new query window, highlighting the SQL for both, and then clicking the Display Estimated Execution Plan button. Management Studio shows you the two estimated plans in the results window. You can obtain an XML version of the execution plan by profiling the execution of an SQL statement. You run the code in Listing 7.5 on the next page to enable it.

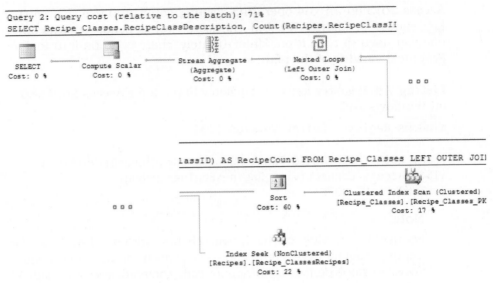

```
Query 2: Query cost (relative to the batch): 71%
SELECT Recipe_Classes.RecipeClassDescription, Count(Recipes.RecipeClassII
```

Figure 7.3 Sample SQL Server graphical execution plan

Listing 7.5 Enabling execution profiling in SQL Server

```
SET STATISTICS XML ON;
```

After you have enabled profiling, every time you execute a statement, you will get an extra result set. For example, if you run a SELECT statement, you will get two result sets: the result of the SELECT statement first, followed by the execution plan in a well-formed XML document.

Note

It is possible to get the output in tabular form, rather than in an XML document, by using SET STATISTICS PROFILE ON (and SET STATISTICS PROFILE OFF). Unfortunately, the tabular execution plan can be hard to read, especially in SQL Server Management Studio, because the information contained in StmtText is too wide to fit on a screen. However, you can copy the information and reformat it to make it more useful. Unlike the graphical plan, you can see all the information at once. We recommend the use of XML instead, especially because Microsoft has indicated that SET STATISTICS PROFILE will be deprecated.

After you have captured all the information you want, you can disable profiling by running the code in Listing 7.6.

Listing 7.6 Disabling execution profiling in SQL Server

```
SET STATISTICS XML OFF;
```

MySQL

Similar to the case for DB2, you can determine the execution plan for any SQL statement in MySQL by prefixing the statement with the word EXPLAIN, as shown in Listing 7.7. (Unlike in DB2, you do not have to do anything first to enable the action.)

Listing 7.7 Creating an execution plan in MySQL

```
EXPLAIN SELECT CustomerID, SUM(OrderTotal)
FROM Orders
GROUP BY CustomerID;
```

MySQL shows you the plan in tabular form. It is also possible to use the "Visual Explain" feature of the MySQL Workbench 6.2 to provide a visualization of the execution plan, as demonstrated in Figure 7.4.

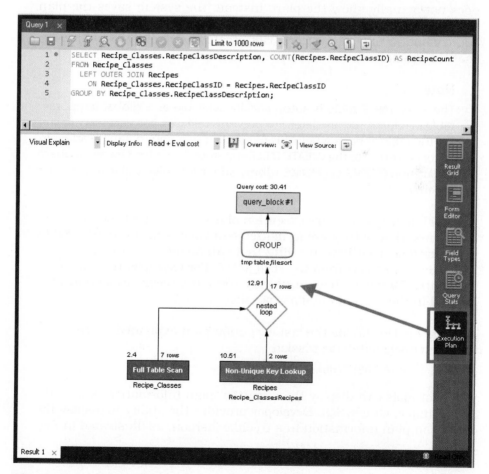

Figure 7.4 MySQL Workbench execution plan pane

Oracle

To view an execution plan in Oracle, perform these two steps:

1. Save the execution plan in the PLAN_TABLE.

2. Format and display the execution plan.

To create the execution plan, you prefix the SQL statement with the keywords EXPLAIN PLAN FOR, as shown in Listing 7.8.

Listing 7.8 Creating an execution plan in Oracle

```
EXPLAIN PLAN FOR SELECT CustomerID, SUM(OrderTotal)
FROM Orders
GROUP BY CustomerID;
```

As was the case for DB2, executing the EXPLAIN PLAN FOR command does not actually show the plan. Instead, the system saves the plan into a table named PLAN_TABLE. You should note that the EXPLAIN PLAN FOR command may not necessarily create the same execution plan that the system will use when executing the statement.

> **Note**
>
> The PLAN_TABLE table is automatically available as a global temporary table in release 10g and later. For previous releases, it is necessary to create the table in each schema as needed. You or your database administrator can execute the CREATE TABLE statement from the Oracle database installation ($ORACLE_HOME/rdbms/admin/utlxplan.sql) in any desired schema.

Although it is easy to show execution plans in the Oracle development environment, how they are formatted can vary. A package DBMS_XPLAN was introduced with release 9iR2 that can be used to format and display execution plans from the PLAN_TABLE. For example, the statement in Listing 7.9 shows how to display the most recent execution plan created in the current database session.

Listing 7.9 Displaying the last execution plan explained in the current Oracle database session

```
SELECT * FROM TABLE(dbms_xplan.display)
```

Different tools can display the execution plan information differently. For example, Oracle SQL Developer provides the ability to display the execution plan information in a treelike fashion, as illustrated in Figure 7.5.

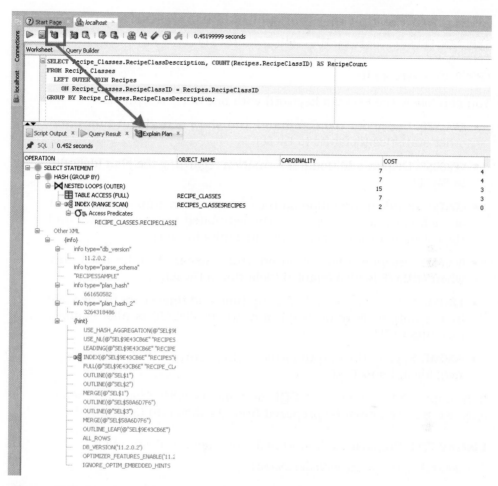

Figure 7.5 Oracle SQL Developer's Explain Plan tab

Note that some tools are known not to display all of the information, even though it may exist in the PLAN_TABLE.

Note

There are cases when the plan generated by EXPLAIN PLAN FOR and the actual runtime plan do not match, for example, when there are BIND variables with data skew. We advise you to read the Oracle documentation.

PostgreSQL

You can display execution plans in PostgreSQL by prefixing the SQL statement with the keyword EXPLAIN, as shown in Listing 7.10 on the next page.

Listing 7.10 Creating an execution plan in PostgreSQL

```
EXPLAIN SELECT CustomerID, SUM(OrderTotal)
FROM Orders
GROUP BY CustomerID;
```

You can follow the EXPLAIN keyword with one of these options:

- **ANALYZE**: Carry out the command and show actual run times and other statistics (defaults to FALSE).

- **VERBOSE**: Display additional information regarding the plan (defaults to FALSE).

- **COSTS**: Include information on the estimated start-up and total cost of each plan node, as well as the estimated number of rows and the estimated width of each row (defaults to TRUE).

- **BUFFERS**: Include information on buffer usage. May be used only when ANALYZE is also enabled (defaults to FALSE).

- **TIMING**: Include the actual start-up time and time spent in the node in the output. May be used only when ANALYZE is also enabled (defaults to TRUE).

- **FORMAT**: Specify the output format, which can be TEXT, XML, JSON, or YAML (defaults to TEXT).

It is important to note that SQL statements with BIND parameters (e.g., $1, $2, etc.) must be prepared first, as shown in Listing 7.11.

Listing 7.11 Preparing a bound SQL statement in PostgreSQL

```
SET search_path = SalesOrdersSample;

PREPARE stmt (int) AS
SELECT * FROM Customers AS c
WHERE c.CustomerID = $1;
```

After the statement has been prepared, its execution can be explained using the statement shown in Listing 7.12.

Listing 7.12 Explaining a prepared SQL statement in PostgreSQL

```
EXPLAIN EXECUTE stmt(1001);
```

> **Note**
>
> In PostgreSQL 9.1 version and older, the execution plan was created with the PREPARE call, so it could not consider the actual values provided with the EXECUTE call. Since PostgreSQL 9.2, the execution plan is not created until execution, so it can consider the actual values for the BIND parameters.

PostgreSQL also provides the pgAdmin tool that can be used to provide a graphical representation of the execution plan via the Explain tab, as Figure 7.6 shows.

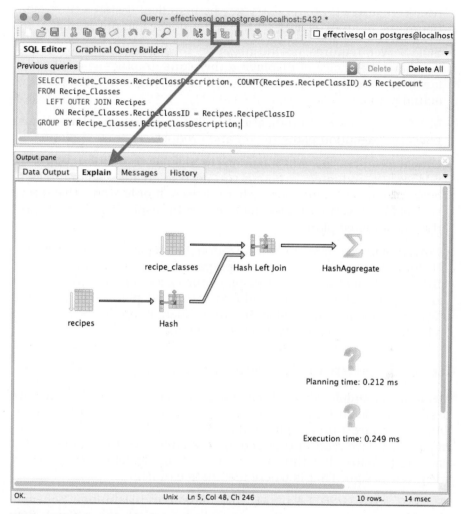

Figure 7.6 PostgreSQL pgAdmin Explain tab

Things to Remember

✦ Learn how to obtain execution plans for your DBMS.

✦ Consult the documentation for your DBMS to learn how to interpret the execution plans it produces.

✦ Remember that the information shown in execution plans can change over time.

+ DB2 requires that system tables be created first. It stores the execution plans in those system tables, as opposed to displaying them. It produces estimated plans.

+ Access requires that a registry key be installed. It stores the execution plans in an external text file and produces actual plans.

+ SQL Server requires no initialization to display execution plans. You have the choice of displaying the plans graphically or in tabular form. You also have the choice of producing estimated plans or actual plans.

+ MySQL requires no initialization to display execution plans. It displays the execution plans to you and produces estimated plans.

+ Oracle requires no initialization to display execution plans in release 10g and later, although you need to create system tables in each schema of interest for earlier releases. It only stores the execution plans in system tables, as opposed to displaying them. It produces estimated plans.

+ PostgreSQL requires no initialization to display execution plans. It does, however, require you to prepare SQL statements that have BIND parameters in them. It displays the execution plan for you. For basic SQL statements, it produces estimated plans. For prepared SQL statements, in version 9.1 and older, it produces estimated plans, but since 9.2 it produces actual plans.

Item 45: Learn to Get Metadata about Your Database

Metadata is simply "data about data." Although you may well have designed an ideal logical database model and worked hard with the DBAs to ensure a proper physical database model (ideally using techniques you have read in this book!), it is often nice to be able to step back and ensure that things were, in fact, implemented consistently with your design. That is where metadata can help.

ISO/IEC 9075-11:2011 Part 11: Information and Definition Schemas (SQL/Schemata) is an often-overlooked part of the official SQL Standards. This standard defines the INFORMATION_SCHEMA, which is intended to make SQL databases and objects self-describing.

When a physical data model is implemented in a compliant DBMS, not only are each of the objects such as tables, columns, and views created in the database, but also your system stores information about each of those objects in system tables. A set of read-only views exists on those system tables, and those views can provide information about all the tables, views, columns, procedures, constraints, and everything else necessary to re-create the structure of a database.

Note

Although INFORMATION_SCHEMA is an official standard of the SQL language, the standard is not always followed. While IBM DB2, Microsoft SQL Server, MySQL, and PostgreSQL all provide INFORMATION_SCHEMA views, Microsoft Access and Oracle do not at present (although Oracle does provide internal metadata that can serve the same needs).

There are a variety of third-party products that can provide you with information about your database. Most of them do so by retrieving information from the INFORMATION_SCHEMA views. You do not need a third-party tool, though, to be able to get useful information from those views.

Let's assume you have been given access to a new database, and you want to find out details about it.

You can query the INFORMATION_SCHEMA.TABLES view to get a list of the tables and views that exist in the database, as shown in Listing 7.13, the results of which are shown in Table 7.1.

Listing 7.13 Get a list of tables and views

```
SELECT t.TABLE_NAME, t.TABLE_TYPE
FROM INFORMATION_SCHEMA.TABLES AS t
WHERE t.TABLE_TYPE IN ('BASE TABLE', 'VIEW');
```

Table 7.1 List of tables and views from Listing 7.13

TABLE_NAME	TABLE_TYPE
Categories	BASE TABLE
Countries	BASE TABLE
Styles	BASE TABLE
BeerStyles	VIEW

You can query the INFORMATION_SCHEMA TABLE_CONSTRAINTS view to get a list of what constraints have been created on those tables, as shown in Listing 7.14, with results shown in Table 7.2 on the next page.

Listing 7.14 Get a list of constraints

```
SELECT tc.CONSTRAINT_NAME, tc.TABLE_NAME, tc.CONSTRAINT_TYPE
FROM INFORMATION_SCHEMA.TABLE_CONSTRAINTS AS tc;
```

Table 7.2 List of constraints from Listing 7.14

CONSTRAINT_NAME	TABLE_NAME	CONSTRAINT_TYPE
Categories_PK	Categories	PRIMARY KEY
Styles_PK	Styles	PRIMARY KEY
Styles_FK00	Styles	FOREIGN KEY

Yes, there are definitely other ways to obtain that same information. However, the fact that the information is available in views allows you to determine more information. For example, since you know all of the tables in your database and you know all of the table constraints that have been defined, you can easily determine which tables in your database do not have a primary key, as shown in Listing 7.15, with results shown in Table 7.3.

Listing 7.15 Get a list of tables without a primary key

```
SELECT t.TABLE_NAME
FROM (
  SELECT TABLE_NAME
  FROM INFORMATION_SCHEMA.TABLES
  WHERE TABLE_TYPE = 'BASE TABLE'
  ) AS t
  LEFT JOIN (
    SELECT TABLE_NAME, CONSTRAINT_NAME, CONSTRAINT_TYPE
    FROM INFORMATION_SCHEMA.TABLE_CONSTRAINTS
    WHERE CONSTRAINT_TYPE = 'PRIMARY KEY'
    ) AS tc
      ON t.TABLE_NAME = tc.TABLE_NAME
WHERE tc.TABLE_NAME IS NULL;
```

Table 7.3 List of tables without a
primary key from Listing 7.15

TABLE_NAME
Countries

Should you be considering making a change to a particular column, you can use the INFORMATION_SCHEMA.VIEW_COLUMN_USAGE view to see which table columns are being used in any view, as shown in Listing 7.16.

Listing 7.16 Get a list of all tables and columns used in any view

```
SELECT vcu.VIEW_NAME, vcu.TABLE_NAME, vcu.COLUMN_NAME
FROM INFORMATION_SCHEMA.VIEW_COLUMN_USAGE AS vcu;
```

As shown in Table 7.4, it does not matter whether or not you have used an alias for any of the column names, or even if the column appears only in the WHERE or ON clause of the view. This information allows you to see quickly whether your possible change might have any impacts.

Table 7.4 List of all tables and columns used in any view from Listing 7.16

VIEW_NAME	TABLE_NAME	COLUMN_NAME
BeerStyles	Categories	CategoryID
BeerStyles	Categories	CategoryDS
BeerStyles	Countries	CountryID
BeerStyles	Countries	CountryNM
BeerStyles	Styles	CategoryFK
BeerStyles	Styles	CountryFK
BeerStyles	Styles	StyleNM
BeerStyles	Styles	ABVHighNb

Listing 7.17 shows the SQL used to create the BeerStyles view. You can see that INFORMATION_SCHEMA.VIEW_COLUMN_USAGE reports on all columns used, whether they are in the SELECT clause, the ON clause, or anywhere else in the CREATE VIEW statement.

Listing 7.17 CREATE VIEW statement for the view documented in Table 7.4

```
CREATE VIEW BeerStyles AS
SELECT Cat.CategoryDS AS Category, Cou.CountryNM AS Country,
  Sty.StyleNM AS Style, Sty.ABVHighNb AS MaxABV
FROM Styles AS Sty
  INNER JOIN Categories AS Cat
    ON Sty.CategoryFK = Cat.CategoryID
  INNER JOIN Countries AS Cou
    ON Sty.CountryFK = Cou.CountryID;
```

A major advantage of using INFORMATION_SCHEMA rather than DBMS-specific metadata tables is that because INFORMATION_SCHEMA is an SQL standard, any queries you write should be portable from DBMS to DBMS, as well as from release to release of any specific DBMS.

That being said, you should probably be aware that there can be issues with using INFORMATION_SCHEMA. For one thing, despite being a standard, INFORMATION_SCHEMA is not actually implemented consistently from DBMS to DBMS. The INFORMATION_SCHEMA.VIEW_COLUMN_USAGE view that we showed in Listing 7.16 does not exist in MySQL, but it does in SQL Server and PostgreSQL.

Additionally, because INFORMATION_SCHEMA is a standard, it is designed to document only features that exist in the standards. And even when the feature is permitted, it is still possible that INFORMATION_SCHEMA may not be capable of documenting it. An example of this is creating FOREIGN KEY constraints that reference unique indexes (as opposed to primary key indexes). Usually you would document FOREIGN KEY constraints by joining the REFERENTIAL_CONSTRAINTS, TABLE_CONSTRAINTS, and CONSTRAINT_COLUMN_USAGE views in INFORMATION_SCHEMA, but because a unique index is not a constraint, there is no data in TABLE_CONSTRAINTS (or in any other constraint-related view), and you cannot determine which columns are used in the "constraint."

Fortunately, all DBMSs have other metadata sources available, and you can use them to determine information as well. The downside, of course, is that what you have learned that works in one DBMS may not work in another DBMS.

For instance, you could retrieve the same information retrieved in Listing 7.13 in SQL Server using the SQL statement in Listing 7.18.

Listing 7.18 Get a list of tables and views using SQL Server system tables

```
SELECT name, type_desc
FROM sys.objects
WHERE type_desc IN ('USER_TABLE', 'VIEW');
```

Alternatively you can use the SQL statement in Listing 7.19 to get the same information in SQL Server as provided by Listing 7.18.

Listing 7.19 Get a list of tables and views using different SQL Server system tables

```
SELECT name, type_desc
FROM sys.tables
UNION
SELECT name, type_desc
FROM sys.views;
```

It is perhaps telling that even Microsoft seems not to trust INFORMATION_SCHEMA: there are many places on MSDN, such as https://msdn.microsoft.com/en-us/library/ms186224.aspx, where they state:

Important Do not use INFORMATION_SCHEMA views to determine the schema of an object. The only reliable way to find the schema of an object is to query the sys.objects catalog view. INFORMATION_SCHEMA views could be incomplete because they are not updated for all new features.

Note

Many DBMSs offer alternative means of getting to their metadata. For example, DB2 has a db2look command, MySQL has a SHOW command, Oracle has a DESCRIBE command, and PostgreSQL's command-line interface psql has a \d command, all of which can be used to query data. Consult your documentation to determine what options you have. However, those commands do not permit you to query the metadata using SQL as shown in the previous listings, so also check the documentation for system tables or schema if you need to collect information from several objects at once or within the context of an SQL query.

Things to Remember

+ Use the SQL standard INFORMATION_SCHEMA views whenever possible.

+ Remember that INFORMATION_SCHEMA is not the same across DBMSs.

+ Learn any nonstandard command your DBMS may have to display metadata.

+ Accept that INFORMATION_SCHEMA does not contain 100% of the necessary metadata, and learn the system tables associated with your DBMS.

Item 46: Understand How the Execution Plan Works

Because this is a book about SQL, and not about any particular vendor's product, it is difficult to be very specific, because the execution plan is dependent on the physical implementation. Each vendor has a different implementation and uses different terminology for the same concepts. However, it is an essential skill for anyone working with an SQL database to understand how to read and understand what an execution plan means in order to be able to optimize SQL queries or make any needed schema changes, especially on indices or model design. Thus we will focus on some general principles that you might find useful when reading an execution plan for your SQL database, regardless of which vendor's product you use. This item is intended to be supplemented with additional readings in the vendor's documentation on reading and interpreting the execution plan.

We also want to remind readers that the goal of SQL is to free developers from the menial task of describing the physical steps to retrieve the data, especially in an efficient manner. It is meant to be declarative, describing what data we want to get back and leaving it up to the optimizer to figure out the best way to get it. When we discuss execution plans, and therefore the physical implementation, we are breaking the abstraction that SQL offers.

A common mistake that even computer-literate people make is to assume that because a task is done by a computer, it is magically different from the way it would be done by a person. It just ain't so. Yes, a computer might execute and complete a task much faster and more accurately, but the physical steps it must take are no different from those of an actual person doing the same task. Consequently, when you read an execution plan, you get an outline of physical steps the database engine performs to satisfy a query. You can then ask yourself, if you were doing it yourself, whether you would get the best result.

Consider a card catalog in a library. If you wanted to locate a book named *Effective SQL*, you would go to the catalog and locate the drawer that contains cards for books starting with the letter *E* (maybe it will actually be labeled *D–G*). You would then open the drawer and flip through the index cards until you find the card you are looking for. The card says the book is located at 601.389, so you must then locate the section somewhere within the library that houses the 600 class. Arriving there, you have to find the bookshelves holding 600–610. After you have located the correct bookshelves, you have to scan the sections until you get to 601, and then scan the shelves until you find the 601.3XX books before pinpointing the book with 601.389.

In an electronic database system, it is no different. The database engine needs to first access its index on data, locate the index page(s) that contains the letter *E*, then look within the page to get the pointer back to the data page that contains the sought data. It will jump to the address of the data page and read the data within that page(s). Ergo, an index in a database is just like the catalog in a library. Data pages are just like bookshelves, and the rows are like the books themselves. The drawers in the catalog and the bookshelves represent the B-tree structure for both index and data pages.

We made you walk through this to emphasize the point that when you read the execution plan, you can easily apply the physical action, as though you were doing the same thing with papers, folders, books and index cards, labels, and the classification system. Let's do one more thought experiment. Now that you have found the *Effective SQL* book that John Viescas coauthored, you want to find out what other books he has written. You cannot go back to the catalog because that catalog sorts the index cards by book title, not by author. Without a catalog available, the only way to answer the question is to painstakingly go through every bookshelf, each of the shelves, and each book to see what other books John has authored. If you found that such questions were commonly asked, it would be more expedient to build a new catalog, sorted by author, and put it beside the original catalog. Now it is easy to find all books that John has authored or coauthored just by looking in the new catalog—no more trips to the bookshelves. But what if the question changes and is now "How many pages are there in each book that John wrote?" Well, that extra piece of information is not in the index cards. So it is back to the bookshelves to find out the page counts in each book.

This illustrates the next key point: the index system you set up depends heavily on what kind of queries you will typically use against your database. You needed two catalogs to support different types of queries. Even so, there were still some gaps. Is the correct answer to add page counts to the index cards in one of the catalogs? Maybe, maybe not. It depends more on whether it is essential that you get the information quickly.

It is also possible to have queries where you never need to actually go to the bookshelves. For example, if you wanted a list of all authors with whom John has written books, you could look up all books that John has co-written, but the catalog does not list the other authors for those books. But you can then look in the book titles catalog, look up the title that you got from the author catalog, and thus get the list of coauthors. You were able to do all this standing at the catalogs without going to the bookshelves at all. Thus, this is the fastest way to retrieve data.

The preceding thought experiments should make it clear that when you read the execution plan, you can act out the physical actions in your mind. So, if you saw an execution plan that scans a table, and you know you have an index that exists but apparently is not used in the plan (as though you had walked past the catalog and gone directly to the bookshelves), you can tell something is amiss and start your analysis.

Note

The examples provided in the rest of the items are heavily dependent on the data stored in the database, the existing index structure, and other things. Therefore, it might not always be possible to reproduce the exact same execution plan. The examples also use the Microsoft SQL Server execution plan, as it provides a graphical view. Other vendors might yield similar plans but use different terms.

With the mental scaffolding set up, let's look at some examples, starting with Listing 7.20.

Listing 7.20 Query to find customers' cities based on an area code

```
SELECT CustCity
FROM Customers
WHERE CustAreaCode = 530;
```

In a large enough table, we might get the plan illustrated in Figure 7.7.

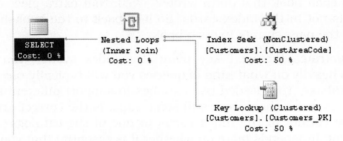

Figure 7.7 Initial execution plan with a key lookup

To translate this into physical actions, think of it as going to a catalog containing the CustAreaCode and location code on the index cards. For each index card found, we then go to the bookshelves, locate the record to read the CustCity value, then return to the catalog to read the next index. That is what is meant when you see a "Key Lookup" operation. An "Index Seek" operation represents looking through the catalog, whereas "Key Lookup" means you are going to the bookshelves to get the additional information that is not contained on the index card.

For a table with few records, it is not that bad. But if it turns out that we found many index cards and shuttled between the bookshelves and the catalog, that is a lot of wasted time. Let's say there are several possible matches. If the query is commonly asked, it makes sense to update the index to include the CustCity. One way to do this is with the SQL statement in Listing 7.21.

Listing 7.21 Improved index definition

```
CREATE INDEX IX_Customers_CustArea
ON Customers (CustAreaCode, CustCity);
```

This changes the execution plan to what is shown in Figure 7.8 for the same query.

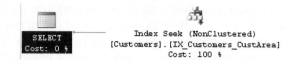

Figure 7.8 Example of splitting data into tables by subject

So we are back to standing at the new catalog and reading through the index cards without going to the bookshelves at all. That is much more efficient even though we now have one more catalog in the library.

It is also important to note that sometimes the physical steps described by a generated execution plan can be quite different from the logical steps described by the SQL query itself. Consider the query that does an EXISTS correlated subquery in Listing 7.22.

Listing 7.22 Query to find customers who have not placed any orders

```
SELECT p.*
FROM Products AS p
WHERE NOT EXISTS (
    SELECT NULL
    FROM Order_Details AS d
    WHERE p.ProductNumber = d.ProductNumber
);
```

At a glance, it looks as if the engine must query the subquery for each row in the Products table because we are using a correlated subquery. Let's consider the execution plan in Figure 7.9.

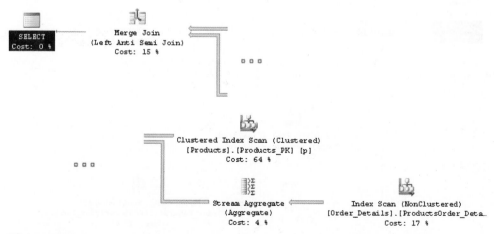

Figure 7.9 Execution plan for a query with a correlated NOT EXISTS subquery

To translate the execution plan into physical actions: with "Clustered Index Scan" on Products, we first grab a stack of index cards from one catalog that detail the products we have on hand. With "Index Scan" on Order_Details, we grab another stack of index cards from the catalog containing orders. For "Stream Aggregate," we group all index cards containing the same ProductNumber. Then for "Merge Join," we sort through both stacks, taking out a product index card only if we do not have a matching card from the Order_Details stack. That gives us the answer. Take note that the merge join is a "left anti-semi-join"; this is a relational operation that has no direct representation in the SQL language. Conceptually, a semi-join is like a join except that you select a row that matches only once rather than for all matching rows. Therefore, an anti-semi-join selects distinct rows that do not match the other side.

So in this specific example, the engine was smart enough to see a better way of doing things and rearranged the execution plan accordingly. However, it bears emphasizing that the engine itself is constrained by the user asking the queries. If we send it poorly written queries, it has no choice but to generate poor execution plans.

When you read your execution plans, you check whether the engine is making sane choices as to how it should collect the data and doing it in the most efficient manner. Because the execution plan is a sequence of physical actions, it can vary drastically even for the same query if the data volume and distribution change. For example, using the same query from Listing 7.22 on a smaller set of data, we might get the plan shown in Figure 7.10.

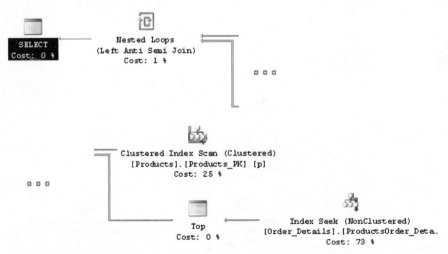

Figure 7.10 Another possible execution plan for a query with a correlated NOT EXISTS subquery

What is not apparent is that the "Index Seek" on the Order_Details table has a predicate to take a value from the "Clustered Index Scan" on the Products table. The "Top" operation then restricts the output to only one row and matches to the records from the Products table. This is similar to the key lookup we saw earlier. Because the data set was small enough, the database engine decided it was good enough to do a key lookup instead of taking a stack, because that is less setup to do.

That then brings us to the problem of "elephant and mouse." By now you should realize that there are many possible sequences of physical actions to get the same results. However, which sequence is more effective depends on the data distribution. So it is possible to have a parameterized query that performs great for a particular value but is awful with a different value. This is a particular problem for any engines that cache an execution plan for a parameterized query (which might be a stored procedure, for instance). Consider the simple parameterized query in Listing 7.23.

Listing 7.23 Query to find order details for a particular product

```
SELECT o.OrderNumber, o.CustomerID
FROM Orders AS o
WHERE EmployeeID = ?;
```

Suppose we pass in EmployeeID = 751. That employee made 99 orders out of 160,944 rows in the Orders table. Because there are comparatively few records, the engine might create a plan like the one in Figure 7.11.

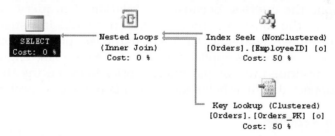

Figure 7.11 Execution plan for few records in an index

Contrast that with the plan where we pass in EmployeeID = 708 who has worked on 5,414 orders in Figure 7.12.

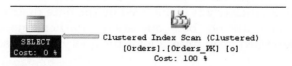

Figure 7.12 Execution plan for a large number of records in an index

Because the engine saw that there were so many records scattered, it decided it was just as fast to wade through all the data. This is obviously suboptimal, and we can improve it by adding an index specifically for this query as shown in Listing 7.24.

Listing 7.24 Index to cover the query in Listing 7.23

```
CREATE INDEX IX_Orders_EmployeeID_Included
ON Orders (EmployeeID)
INCLUDE (OrderNumber, CustomerID);
```

Because the index covers both queries, this improves the plan for both "mouse" and "elephant" significantly, as shown in Figure 7.13.

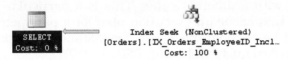

Figure 7.13 Improved execution plan for the query in Listing 7.23

However, this might not be possible in all cases. In a complicated query, it might not make sense to create an index that would be usable in only one query. You want to have an index that is useful in several queries. For that reason, you might elect to modify the columns indexed or included in an index and even exclude some.

In those situations, the "mouse and elephant" problem can still appear for parameterized queries. In those situations, it is likely best to recompile the queries, because compilation of a query is usually a fraction of the total execution time. You should investigate what options you have available for your database product for forcing recompilation where it is applicable. With some database engines such as Oracle, peeking into the parameters prior to executing the cached plan is supported, which helps alleviate this particular problem.

Things to Remember

+ Whenever you read an execution plan, translate it into physical actions, analyze whether you have indices that are not being used, and determine why they are not being used.

+ Analyze the individual steps and consider whether they are effective. Note that efficiency is influenced by the data distribution. Consequently, there are no "bad" operations. Rather, analyze whether the operation used is appropriate for the query being used.

◆ Do not fixate on one query and add indices to get a good execution plan. You must consider the overall usage of the database to ensure that indices serve as many queries as possible.

◆ Watch out for a "mouse and elephant" situation, where the data distribution is unequal and thus requires different optimizations for an identical query. That is especially problematic when execution plans are cached and reused (typically the case with stored procedures or client-side prepared statements).

Cartesian Products

In Item 22, "Understand relational algebra and how it is implemented in SQL," you read about Cartesian Products, which are the results of combining all rows in one table or row set with all rows in a second table or row set. Although perhaps not as common as other join types, the CROSS JOIN (which is how you create a Cartesian Product in SQL) is often a necessary input when creating SQL statements.

In this chapter we show you several real-world situations where it would not be possible to answer the underlying question without the use of a Cartesian Product. Note that we are not talking about unintentional Cartesian Products that you might produce by forgetting to include one or more columns required for a multiple-column join. All the problems we discuss use intentional Cartesian Products and no join criteria.

We think that once you see the usefulness of this capability, you will see many other opportunities to use it to solve your problems.

Item 47: Produce Combinations of Rows between Two Tables and Flag Rows in the Second That Indirectly Relate to the First

Sometimes you need to generate a list of every possible combination in order to be able to determine which records have been processed and which have not.

Assume you wish to see, for each customer, which products that customer has purchased and which he or she has not purchased. A straightforward approach would be:

1. Produce a list of all possible combinations of customers and products.

2. Produce a list of all purchases each customer made.

3. Use a left join between the list of all possible combinations and the list of actual purchases to allow you to mark the actual purchases.

Simply having a list of what each customer has purchased is not sufficient to be able to determine what the customer has not purchased. You must also have a list of all possible purchases (i.e., the Cartesian Product). When you use a left join between those two result sets (with the Cartesian Product as the "left" table and the actual purchases as the "right" table), you can identify what was not purchased by finding the null values on the "right" side.

You can use a Cartesian Product to produce a list showing every combination of Customers and Products using the SQL shown in Listing 8.1.

Listing 8.1 Using a Cartesian Product to obtain a list of every customer and every product

```
SELECT c.CustomerID, c.CustFirstName, c.CustLastName,
  p.ProductNumber, p.ProductName, p.ProductDescription
FROM Customers AS c, Products AS p;
```

> **Note**
> Although all DBMSs support listing the tables in a FROM clause with no JOIN clause, some will change the FROM clause to FROM Customer AS c CROSS JOIN Products AS p.

You can produce a list of what products each customer has purchased by joining the Orders and Order_Details tables, as shown in Listing 8.2.

Listing 8.2 Determining all products sold

```
SELECT o.OrderNumber, o.CustomerID, od.ProductNumber
FROM Orders AS o
  INNER JOIN Order_Details AS od
    ON o.OrderNumber = od.OrderNumber;
```

Armed with those two queries, you can use a left join to determine which rows in the Cartesian Product have been purchased and which have not, as shown in Listing 8.3.

Listing 8.3 Listing all customers and all products, flagging products already purchased by each customer

```
SELECT CustProd.CustomerID, CustProd.CustFirstName,
  CustProd.CustLastName, CustProd.ProductNumber,
```

```
  CustProd.ProductName,
  (CASE WHEN OrdDet.OrderCount > 0
    THEN 'You purchased this!'
    ELSE ' '
  END) AS ProductOrdered
FROM
(SELECT c.CustomerID, c.CustFirstName, c.CustLastName,
   p.ProductNumber, p.ProductName, p.ProductDescription
 FROM Customers AS c, Products AS p) AS CustProd
   LEFT JOIN
     (SELECT o.CustomerID, od.ProductNumber,
        COUNT(*) AS OrderCount
      FROM Orders AS o
        INNER JOIN Order_Details AS od
          ON o.OrderNumber = od.OrderNumber
       GROUP BY o.CustomerID, od.ProductNumber) AS OrdDet
    ON CustProd.CustomerID = OrdDet.CustomerID
      AND CustProd.ProductNumber = OrdDet.ProductNumber
ORDER BY CustProd.CustomerID, CustProd.ProductName;
```

Rather than using LEFT JOIN, another approach is to use IN to determine whether the given customer purchased the given product, as shown in Listing 8.4. Unfortunately, we cannot tell you whether one approach is better than the other, because performance depends on the amount of data, the indexes, and which DBMS you use.

Listing 8.4 Alternative approach for listing all customers and all products, flagging products already purchased by each customer

```
SELECT c.CustomerID, c.CustFirstName, c.CustLastName,
  p.ProductNumber, p.ProductName,
  (CASE WHEN c.CustomerID IN
    (SELECT Orders.CustomerID
     FROM Orders
       INNER JOIN Order_Details
         ON Orders.OrderNumber = Order_Details.OrderNumber
      WHERE Order_Details.ProductNumber = p.ProductNumber)
    THEN 'You purchased this!'
    ELSE ' '
  END) AS ProductOrdered
FROM Customers AS c, Products AS p
ORDER BY c.CustomerID, p.ProductNumber;
```

The results from either query might look something like Table 8.1 on the next page.

Table 8.1 Partial results from a list of all customers and products, with those purchased noted

Customer ID	CustFirst Name	CustLast Name	Product Number	Product Name	Product Ordered
1004	Doug	Steele	28	Turbo Twin Tires	You purchased this!
1004	Doug	Steele	40	Ultimate Export 2G Car Rack	You purchased this!
1004	Doug	Steele	29	Ultra-2K Competition Tire	You purchased this!
1004	Doug	Steele	30	Ultra-Pro Knee Pads	You purchased this!
1004	Doug	Steele	23	Ultra-Pro Skateboard	
1004	Doug	Steele	4	Victoria Pro All Weather Tires	
1004	Doug	Steele	7	Viscount C-500 Wireless Bike Computer	You purchased this!
1004	Doug	Steele	18	Viscount CardioSport Sport Watch	You purchased this!

Things to Remember

+ Use a Cartesian Product to produce every possible combination of records between two tables.

+ Use INNER JOIN to determine those combinations that actually did occur.

+ Consider using LEFT JOIN to compare the result of the Cartesian Product to the list of combinations that actually occurred.

+ You can also use an IN subquery in a CASE statement in the SELECT clause to produce the same result as using a Cartesian Product and LEFT JOIN, but the relative performance depends on the amount of data, indexes, and the particular DBMS used.

Item 48: Understand How to Rank Rows by Equal Quantiles

When analyzing and comparing results—whether it be product sales or student grades—it is often useful to know not just which is the best or worst but also where a particular value lies in comparison to others. To do this, you need to break the ranked rows into even quantiles—for example, quartiles (four even groups), quintiles (five even groups), or deciles (ten groups). This gives you, for example, not just the best students or the best-selling products, but also those who rank in the top 10 or 20 or 25%. In this item we explore how to do this sort of ranking and rate the results in 20% (or quintile) bands.

For this example, we use the Sales Orders sample database. Figure 8.1 shows the design.

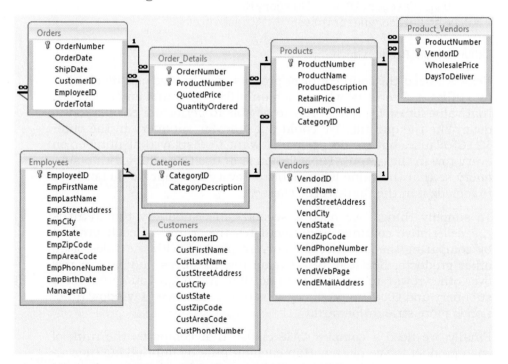

Figure 8.1 Design of a sample Sales Orders database

It would be interesting to find out how the sales of products in a particular category rank with respect to one another. In the sample database, the Accessories category has the most products, so that should produce more interesting results.

We need the sales by product several times in this query, so it makes sense to use a common table expression (CTE) that returns the total sales for each product number in the Accessories category. You can see the SQL for the CTE in Listing 8.5.

Listing 8.5 Calculating total sales by product for each product in Accessories

```
SELECT od.ProductNumber,
  SUM(od.QuantityOrdered * od.QuotedPrice) AS ProductSales
FROM Order_Details AS od
WHERE od.ProductNumber IN (
  SELECT p.ProductNumber
  FROM Products AS p
    INNER JOIN Categories AS c
      ON p.CategoryID = c.CategoryID
  WHERE c.CategoryDescription = 'Accessories'
  )
GROUP BY od.ProductNumber;
```

Next, we need the total count of products so that we can divide that into fifths to determine where each quintile begins and ends. We need that value for each product row to be able to perform a calculation to determine the quintile. We could put a scalar subquery in the outer SELECT clause, but we do not really want to display that number on every row in the output. The solution is to use CROSS JOIN with a subquery so that the value is available on every row, but we do not have to include it in the final SELECT clause.

To simplify things, we need a second table subquery that returns the descriptive columns and calculates the "rank" of each product by comparing the sales for the current product with the sales of all other products. See Item 38, "Create row numbers and rank a row over other rows," to recall how to do that. Although you could use a subquery and COUNT to produce the ranking, the RANK() window function is more straightforward.

Finally, we need a complex CASE clause that compares the rank of each product to the place within each quintile by multiplying the values 0.2, 0.4, 0.6, and 0.8 (the boundaries of each quintile) by the total number of products. The final solution is in Listing 8.6.

Listing 8.6 Ranking Accessories by total sales and calculating the quintile

```
WITH ProdSale AS (
  SELECT od.ProductNumber,
    SUM(od.QuantityOrdered * od.QuotedPrice) AS ProductSales
```

```
    FROM Order_Details AS od
    WHERE od.ProductNumber IN (
      SELECT p.ProductNumber
      FROM Products AS p
        INNER JOIN Categories AS c
          ON p.CategoryID = c.CategoryID
      WHERE c.CategoryDescription = 'Accessories'
      )
    GROUP BY od.ProductNumber
),
RankedCategories AS (
  SELECT Categories.CategoryDescription, Products.ProductName,
    ProdSale.ProductSales,
    RANK() OVER (
      ORDER BY ProdSale.ProductSales DESC
    ) AS RankInCategory
  FROM Categories
    INNER JOIN Products
      ON Categories.CategoryID = Products.CategoryID
    INNER JOIN ProdSale
      ON ProdSale.ProductNumber = Products.ProductNumber
),
ProdCount AS (
  SELECT COUNT(ProductNumber) AS NumProducts
  FROM ProdSale
)
SELECT p1.CategoryDescription, p1.ProductName,
  p1.ProductSales, p1.RankInCategory,
  CASE
    WHEN RankInCategory <= ROUND(0.2 * NumProducts, 0)
      THEN 'First'
    WHEN RankInCategory <= ROUND(0.4 * NumProducts, 0)
      THEN 'Second'
    WHEN RankInCategory <= ROUND(0.6 * NumProducts, 0)
      THEN 'Third'
    WHEN RankInCategory <= ROUND(0.8 * NumProducts, 0)
      THEN 'Fourth'
    ELSE 'Fifth'
  END AS Quintile
FROM RankedCategories AS p1
  CROSS JOIN ProdCount
ORDER BY p1.ProductSales DESC;
```

Note that the ROUND() function is not defined in the ISO SQL Standard, but all major implementations support it. You can see the final result in Table 8.2 on the next page.

Table 8.2 Accessories ranked by sales with a calculated quintile

Category Description	ProductName	Product Sales	RankIn Category	Quintile
Accessories	Cycle-Doc Pro Repair Stand	62157.04	1	First
Accessories	King Cobra Helmet	57572.41	2	First
Accessories	Glide-O-Matic Cycling Helmet	56286.25	3	First
Accessories	Dog Ear Aero-Flow Floor Pump	36029.40	4	First
Accessories	Viscount CardioSport Sport Watch	27954.43	5	Second
Accessories	Pro-Sport 'Dillo Shades	20336.82	6	Second
Accessories	Viscount C-500 Wireless Bike Computer	18046.70	7	Second
Accessories	Viscount Tru-Beat Heart Transmitter	17720.41	8	Second
Accessories	HP Deluxe Panniers	15984.54	9	Third
Accessories	ProFormance Knee Pads	14792.96	10	Third
Accessories	Ultra-Pro Knee Pads	14581.35	11	Third
Accessories	Nikoma Lok-Tight U-Lock	12488.85	12	Fourth
Accessories	TransPort Bicycle Rack	9442.44	13	Fourth
Accessories	True Grip Competition Gloves	7465.70	14	Fourth
Accessories	Kryptonite Advanced 2000 U-Lock	5999.50	15	Fourth
Accessories	Viscount Microshell Helmet	4219.20	16	Fifth
Accessories	Dog Ear Monster Grip Gloves	2779.50	17	Fifth
Accessories	Dog Ear Cyclecomputer	2238.75	18	Fifth
Accessories	Dog Ear Helmet Mount Mirrors	767.73	19	Fifth

If you do not use ROUND(), the first quintile will have three members, and all the rest will have four. Using ROUND() when the total count is not evenly divisible by five pushes the "odd" quintile down to the middle.

Note

If your database system does not support RANK(), you can generate a rank within each category by using a SELECT COUNT subquery. We used this technique in the Microsoft Access version of the Sales Orders database in the query named Listing 8-006-RankedCategories, available on the GitHub site at https://github.com/TexanInParis/Effective-SQL.

You can use the same technique to divide any set of ranked data into equal percentages. To calculate the multiplier numbers, divide 1 by the number of equal groups you want, and then use a multiple of that result to split up the groups. For example, if you want to divide into deciles, 1/10 = 0.10, so you would use 0.10, 0.20, . . . , 0.80, and 0.90.

Things to Remember

+ Breaking a set of quantified data into ranking partitions can be an interesting and useful way to evaluate information.

+ Use the RANK() window function to easily create a ranking value.

+ Divide 1 by the number of groups you want to create the count multiplier for each group.

Item 49: Know How to Pair Rows in a Table with All Other Rows

Finding all possible combinations of a set of data can often be useful. The simplest example is to create a list of all combinations of all teams taken two at a time—perhaps to create a competition schedule for a softball or bowling league. Let's suppose we have a Teams table created with the SQL in Listing 8.7.

Listing 8.7 Table structure for a Teams table

```
CREATE TABLE Teams (
  TeamID int NOT NULL PRIMARY KEY,
  TeamName varchar(50) NOT NULL,
  CaptainID int NULL
);
```

To create a schedule that shows each team playing every other team, you need to get all the combinations (not the permutations) of teams taken two at a time.[1] When you have at least one column that is unique, it is a simple matter to pair each team with any other team that has a lower or higher unique ID. You can create a Cartesian Product of two copies of the table and apply a filter on TeamID, as shown in Listing 8.8.

Listing 8.8 Fetching all combinations of teams taken two at a time using a Cartesian Product

```
SELECT Teams1.TeamID AS Team1ID,
  Teams1.TeamName AS Team1Name,
  Teams2.TeamID AS Team2ID,
  Teams2.TeamName AS Team2Name
FROM Teams AS Teams1
  CROSS JOIN Teams AS Teams2
WHERE Teams2.TeamID > Teams1.TeamID
ORDER BY Teams1.TeamID, Teams2.TeamID;
```

Or you can solve it with a non-equijoin as shown in Listing 8.9. In SQL Server, both queries use the same resources, but you might find one to be faster than the other on another system.

Listing 8.9 Fetching all combinations of teams taken two at a time using a non-equijoin

```
SELECT Teams1.TeamID AS Team1ID,
  Teams1.TeamName AS Team1Name,
  Teams2.TeamID AS Team2ID,
  Teams2.TeamName AS Team2Name
FROM Teams AS Teams1
  INNER JOIN Teams AS Teams2
    ON Teams2.TeamID > Teams1.TeamID
ORDER BY Teams1.TeamID, Teams2.TeamID;
```

Note

In some DBMSs, the optimizer might yield the same plan for both Listing 8.8 and Listing 8.9, and the optimizer might also be able to transform a cross join into an inner join. Refer to Chapter 7, "Getting and Analyzing Metadata," for details on reading execution plans.

---

1. Combinations are the sets of unique numbers, regardless of position. For example, given the set 1, 2, 3, 4, 5, the combinations of two at a time are 1-2, 1-3, 1-4, 1-5, 2-3, 2-4, 2-5, 3-4, 3-5, and 4-5. Permutations are the sets of combinations and positions. The permutations of the set 1, 2, 3, 4, 5 taken two at a time include the ten combinations and another ten sets with the numbers reversed. So, both 1-2 and 2-1 participate in the permutation, but only 1-2 or 2-1 participates in the combination.

If you understand a bit of mathematics, the formula for calculating the number of combinations you should get for a set of N items taken K at a time is as follows:

$$\frac{N!}{K!(N-K)!}$$

If we are pairing ten teams, we would expect to get

$$\frac{10!}{2!(10-2)!} = \frac{10 * 9 * 8 * 7 * 6 * 5 * 4 * 3 * 2 * 1}{2 * 1(8 * 7 * 6 * 5 * 4 * 3 * 2 * 1)}$$

When you cancel 8 factorial (8 * 7 * 6 * 5 * 4 * 3 * 2 * 1) from above and below the dividing line, you end up with 10 * 9 divided by 2, or 45 rows. Table 8.3 is the result, and it has exactly 45 rows.

Table 8.3 All teams paired with each other

Team1ID	Team1Name	Team2ID	Team2Name
1	Marlins	2	Sharks
1	Marlins	3	Terrapins
1	Marlins	4	Barracudas
1	Marlins	5	Dolphins
1	Marlins	6	Orcas
1	Marlins	7	Manatees
1	Marlins	8	Swordfish
1	Marlins	9	Huckleberrys
1	Marlins	10	MintJuleps
2	Sharks	3	Terrapins
2	Sharks	4	Barracudas
2	Sharks	5	Dolphins
2	Sharks	6	Orcas
2	Sharks	7	Manatees
2	Sharks	8	Swordfish

continues

Table 8.3 All teams paired with each other (*continued*)

Team1ID	Team1Name	Team2ID	Team2Name
2	Sharks	9	Huckleberrys
2	Sharks	10	MintJuleps
… 22 additional rows …			
7	Manatees	8	Swordfish
7	Manatees	9	Huckleberrys
7	Manatees	10	MintJuleps
8	Swordfish	9	Huckleberrys
8	Swordfish	10	MintJuleps
9	Huckleberrys	10	MintJuleps

Assuming these are left and right lane or home and away team assignments, you can UNION the SQL with another copy that uses Teams2.TeamID < Teams1.TeamID to extend the assignments to a second round where the team assignments are reversed. If you want to create one round where home and away assignments are alternated so that each team has roughly the same number of home and away games, you can use the SQL that uses window functions shown in Listing 8.10. (See Item 37, "Know how to use window functions," for more details.)

Listing 8.10 Using window functions to allocate home and away games

```
WITH TeamPairs AS (
  SELECT
    ROW_NUMBER() OVER (
      ORDER BY Teams1.TeamID, Teams2.TeamID
      ) AS GameSeq,
    Teams1.TeamID AS Team1ID, Teams1.TeamName AS Team1Name,
    Teams2.TeamID AS Team2ID, Teams2.TeamName AS Team2Name
  FROM Teams AS Teams1
    CROSS JOIN Teams AS Teams2
  WHERE Teams2.TeamID > Teams1.TeamID
)
SELECT TeamPairs.GameSeq,
  CASE ROW_NUMBER() OVER (
    PARTITION BY TeamPairs.Team1ID
    ORDER BY GameSeq
    ) MOD 2
```

```
   WHEN 0 THEN
     CASE RANK() OVER (ORDER BY TeamPairs.Team1ID) MOD 3
       WHEN 0 THEN 'Home' ELSE 'Away' END
   ELSE
     CASE RANK() OVER (ORDER BY TeamPairs.Team1ID) MOD 3
       WHEN 0 THEN 'Away' ELSE 'Home' END
   END AS Team1PlayingAt,
 TeamPairs.Team1ID, TeamPairs.Team1Name,
 TeamPairs.Team2ID, TeamPairs.Team2Name
FROM TeamPairs
ORDER BY TeamPairs.GameSeq;
```

Note

The modulus operator in SQL Server and PostgreSQL is %, not MOD. In DB2 and Oracle, use the MOD function. PostgreSQL also supports the MOD function.

The TeamPairs CTE is our original query with a row number added to each pair. In the main query, we examine every other row (MOD 2) to decide whether to assign "home" or "away" to the first team. Because there is a bias toward assigning "home" to the first game of every team, we then look at every third row to make the assignments in reverse order. If we do not do that, we end up with 25 home games and 20 away games. See also Item 42, "If possible, use common table expressions instead of subqueries," for more information about CTEs.

Creating combinations of things can be useful in many other ways. Suppose you are the manager of a grocery store, and you are interested in which combinations of items sell best together. For example, do a lot of shoppers frequently buy pretzels and potato chips with beer? When you find popular combinations of three items, one marketing theory might suggest that you place those three items together in the store to make it easier for shoppers to find them. Yet another theory might be to separate those three products as far as possible from each other so that a shopper has to pass many other tempting items to pick up the three popular ones.

Let's assume you have a Products table that has a ProductNumber primary key column and a ProductName column. You can find all combinations of products taken three at a time using the SQL in Listing 8.11.

Listing 8.11 Finding all combinations of products taken three at a time

```
SELECT Prod1.ProductNumber AS P1Num,
  Prod1.ProductName AS P1Name, Prod2.ProductNumber AS P2Num,
  Prod2.ProductName AS P2Name, Prod3.ProductNumber AS P3Num,
  Prod3.ProductName AS P3Name
```

```
FROM Products AS Prod1 CROSS JOIN Products AS Prod2
  CROSS JOIN Products AS Prod3
WHERE Prod1.ProductNumber < Prod2.ProductNumber
  AND Prod2.ProductNumber < Prod3.ProductNumber;
```

Note that the choice of > or < as a comparison operator does not matter as long as you use the same one in all your comparisons. You might think that <> would also work, but that gets all the permutations when all you want are the combinations.

Of course, the typical grocery store has tens of thousands of products, so finding the combination of all products taken three at a time could produce more than 200 billion rows! A wise store manager would perhaps choose a few related product categories or products from one vendor.

You can use the result to drive finding orders that contain a particular combination of three products, then count the orders for each combination to determine which occur most often. We showed you ways to solve problems with multiple criteria like this ("Find the orders that contain all three products") in Item 25, "Know techniques to solve multiple-criteria problems."

Things to Remember

+ Finding all combinations of *N* things taken *K* at a time can be useful.

+ The technique to find combinations when you have a unique column is quite straightforward.

+ To increase the number of items chosen per combination, simply add another copy of the target table to your query.

+ Be careful when working with large sets of data because you could end up with billions of rows.

Item 50: Understand How to List Categories and the Count of First, Second, or Third Preferences

When you want to compare qualifications to a list of attributes, you might not get a perfect match. When you do not get a perfect match, you are probably interested in finding the closest matches, and that is more easily done if you can rank the importance of qualifications with respect to attributes.

One of our sample databases handles scheduling of entertainers with customers. In that database, we list all the styles of music that each entertainer plays. We also have a table that contains the musical preferences of each customer. You can see the design of the database in Figure 8.2.

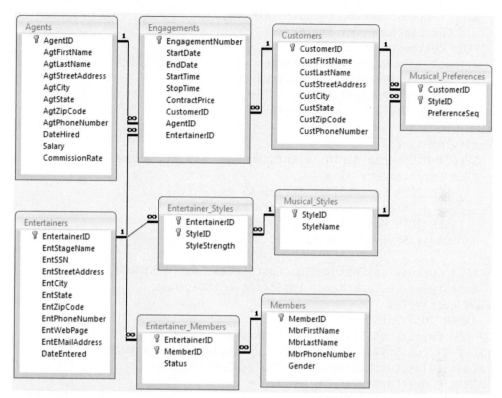

Figure 8.2 Design of a database to track entertainment bookings

You can see that the Musical_Preferences table contains a column to rank the customer preferences using a sequence number. In this database, a 1 indicates the customer's first preference, a 2 the second preference, and so on. There is also a column in the Entertainer_ Styles table that lists for each style that an entertainer can play the relative strength of that style. For example, customer Zachary Johnson has specified a preference for Rhythm and Blues, Jazz, and Salsa in that order. Entertainer Jazz Persuasion says they focus on Rhythm and Blues, Salsa, and Jazz in that order.

First, let's see if any of the sets of styles for any entertainer fully matches the preferences listed for each customer. We can do that using one of the techniques that we showed you in Item 26, "Divide your data if you need a perfect match." Listing 8.12 on the next page shows how.

Listing 8.12 Finding out if any entertainers match all customer preferences

```
WITH CustStyles AS (
  SELECT c.CustomerID, c.CustFirstName,
    c.CustLastName, ms.StyleName
  FROM Customers AS c
    INNER JOIN Musical_Preferences AS mp
      ON c.CustomerID = mp.CustomerID
    INNER JOIN Musical_Styles AS ms
      ON mp.StyleID = ms.StyleID
),
EntStyles AS (
  SELECT e.EntertainerID, e.EntStageName, ms.StyleName
  FROM Entertainers AS e
    INNER JOIN Entertainer_Styles AS es
      ON e.EntertainerID = es.EntertainerID
    INNER JOIN Musical_Styles AS ms
      ON es.StyleID = ms.StyleID
)
SELECT CustStyles.CustomerID, CustStyles.CustFirstName,
  CustStyles.CustLastName, EntStyles.EntStageName
FROM CustStyles
  INNER JOIN EntStyles
    ON CustStyles.StyleName = EntStyles.StyleName
GROUP BY CustStyles.CustomerID, CustStyles.CustFirstName,
  CustStyles.CustLastName, EntStyles.EntStageName
HAVING COUNT(EntStyles.StyleName) = (
  SELECT COUNT(StyleName)
  FROM CustStyles AS cs1
  WHERE cs1.CustomerID = CustStyles.CustomerID
  )
ORDER BY CustStyles.CustomerID;
```

Because there are multiple sets of requirements (customer preferences) that potentially match multiple sets of attributes (entertainer styles), the query in Listing 8.12 is a variation on the second technique we showed you in Item 26. We added a WHERE clause in the subquery that counts style names so that we only count the styles for each customer. As it turns out, there are perfect matches for seven of the 15 customers in the database, as shown in Table 8.4. (Note that one customer has two perfect matches.)

It is actually a good result to find that many entertainers who match all of a customer's preferences! But we would like to find the best

Table 8.4 List of customers for whom entertainers exist that match all their preferences

CustomerID	CustFirstName	CustLastName	EntStageName
10002	Deb	Smith	JV & the Deep Six
10003	Ben	Clothier	Topazz
10005	Elizabeth	Hallmark	Julia Schnebly
10005	Elizabeth	Hallmark	Katherine Ehrlich
10008	Darren	Davidson	Carol Peacock Trio
10010	Zachary	Johnson	Jazz Persuasion
10012	Kerry	Patterson	Carol Peacock Trio
10013	Louise	Johnson	Jazz Persuasion

entertainers for each customer. Let's assume that the best entertainer for a given customer is one whose top two styles match the top two preferences in any order.

To do that, we need to "pivot" the top three preferences into first, second, and third place and do the same for entertainer strengths. Then, if the top two match in any order, we have found our best matches. Listing 8.13 shows how.

Listing 8.13 Selecting the best matches by comparing the top two preferences

```
WITH CustPreferences AS (
  SELECT c.CustomerID, c.CustFirstName, c.CustLastName,
    MAX((CASE WHEN mp.PreferenceSeq = 1
            THEN mp.StyleID
            ELSE Null END)) AS FirstPreference,
    MAX((CASE WHEN mp.PreferenceSeq = 2
            THEN mp.StyleID
            ELSE Null END)) AS SecondPreference,
    MAX((CASE WHEN mp.PreferenceSeq = 3
            THEN mp.StyleID
            ELSE Null END)) AS ThirdPreference
  FROM Musical_Preferences AS mp
    INNER JOIN Customers AS c
      ON mp.CustomerID = c.CustomerID
  GROUP BY c.CustomerID, c.CustFirstName, c.CustLastName
),
```

```
EntStrengths AS (
  SELECT e.EntertainerID, e.EntStageName,
    MAX((CASE WHEN es.StyleStrength = 1
              THEN es.StyleID
              ELSE Null END)) AS FirstStrength,
    MAX((CASE WHEN es.StyleStrength = 2
              THEN es.StyleID
              ELSE Null END)) AS SecondStrength,
    MAX((CASE WHEN es.StyleStrength = 3
              THEN es.StyleID
              ELSE Null END)) AS ThirdStrength
  FROM Entertainer_Styles AS es
    INNER JOIN Entertainers AS e
      ON es.EntertainerID = e.EntertainerID
  GROUP BY e.EntertainerID, e.EntStageName
)
SELECT CustomerID, CustFirstName, CustLastName,
  EntertainerID, EntStageName
FROM CustPreferences
  CROSS JOIN EntStrengths
WHERE (
  FirstPreference = FirstStrength
    AND SecondPreference = SecondStrength
  ) OR (
  SecondPreference = FirstStrength
    AND FirstPreference = SecondStrength
  )
ORDER BY CustomerID;
```

As you can imagine, you can use any combination of tests in the WHERE clause to expand what is acceptable. For example, you could accept any match where the customer's first and second preferences match any of the entertainer's three strengths. Table 8.5 shows the result.

As you can see, we have many of the same matches that the first query picked out, but we have added a recommendation for customer 10009 because at least two of the preferences and strengths match. However, dropped from this list are customers 10008 (Darren Davidson) and 10010 (Zachary Johnson) because even though all three preferences match, they do not match in first and second place in either order.

Certainly, a Divide operation will find all complete matches, but when you want to find the best partial matches, you have to get a bit more creative. Finding matches on two out of three helps you decide what recommendations to make to your marketing staff.

Table 8.5 Finding entertainers whose first and second strengths match the first and second preferences of any customer

Customer ID	CustFirst Name	CustLast Name	Entertainer ID	EntStageName
10002	Deb	Smith	1003	JV & the Deep Six
10003	Ben	Clothier	1002	Topazz
10005	Elizabeth	Hallmark	1009	Katherine Ehrlich
10005	Elizabeth	Hallmark	1011	Julia Schnebly
10009	Sarah	Thompson	1007	Coldwater Cattle Company
10012	Kerry	Patterson	1001	Carol Peacock Trio

Things to Remember

- A Divide operation finds all perfect matches.

- If you are willing to accept partial matches, you need to apply other techniques.

- Having ranking data in your tables can help you decide on the best alternative matches.

Tally Tables

In Chapter 8, "Cartesian Products," you read about Cartesian Products and how they can provide necessary data for SQL statements.

Another useful tool is the *tally table*, usually a table with a single column of sequential numbers, with values starting from 1 (or 0) to a maximum number appropriate for the situation. It can also be a single column of sequential dates that cover a range of interest, or something more complex to aid in "pivoting" a set of summaries. These allow us to solve problems that cannot be solved with Cartesian Products because Cartesian Products are dependent on actual values in the underlying tables, whereas tally tables cover all possibilities. In this chapter we show you examples of such problems and how tally tables can help.

As with Cartesian Products, we think you will see many other examples of where you can use tally tables to solve your problems.

Item 51: Use a Tally Table to Generate Null Rows Based on a Parameter

Sometimes it is useful to be able to generate null or blank rows in your data, particularly with data that is being fetched for a report. One example is a report that has a header and several detail rows per page, and the bottom line of a box drawn around the detail rows always gets placed after the last row in each group. When there are not enough detail lines in a group (or at the end of a group) to completely fill a page, you need blank rows of data sent to the report engine to push the bottom border down to the correct location.

Another, perhaps simpler, example is data being formatted to print mailing labels. The last time you ran the report, you used up a few of the labels at the top of the last page. Rather than throw away the partially used page, it would be nice to be able to generate *n* blank rows at the beginning of the mailing list data to skip over the labels already used on the first page.

What you need in order to do either task is a set of integer numbers from 1 to the maximum number of lines in a report group or the maximum number of labels on a page. With that, you can use a parameter or calculated value to generate the necessary blank rows. In Item 42, "If possible, use common table expressions instead of subqueries," we showed you that it is possible to generate a list of numbers using a recursive CTE. Let's solve the "skip used mailing labels" problem using a CTE, as shown in Listing 9.1. We assume for this example that we need to skip three used labels; we will add the parameter later.

Listing 9.1 Using a generated list to skip blank labels

```
WITH SeqNumTbl AS (
  SELECT 1 AS SeqNum
  UNION ALL
  SELECT SeqNum + 1
  FROM SeqNumTbl
  WHERE SeqNum < 100
  ),
SeqList AS (
  SELECT SeqNum
  FROM SeqNumTbl
  )
SELECT ' ' AS CustName, ' ' AS CustStreetAddress,
     ' ' AS CustCityState, ' ' AS CustZipCode
FROM SeqList
WHERE SeqNum <= 3
UNION ALL
SELECT CONCAT(c.CustFirstName, ' ', c.CustLastName)
      AS CustName,
    c.CustStreetAddress,
    CONCAT(c.CustCity, ', ', c.CustState, ' ', c.CustZipCode)
      AS CustCityState, c.CustZipCode
FROM Customers AS c
ORDER BY CustZipCode;
```

Note

IBM DB2, Microsoft SQL Server, MySQL, Oracle, and PostgreSQL all support the CONCAT() function; however, DB2 and Oracle accept only two arguments, so you must nest CONCAT() functions to concatenate multiple strings. The ISO Standard defines only the operator || to perform concatenation. DB2, Oracle, and PostgreSQL accept the || concatenation operator, and MySQL accepts it if the server sql_mode is set to PIPES_AS_CONCAT. In SQL Server, you can use + as a concatenation operator. Microsoft Access does not support the CONCAT() function, but you can concatenate strings using either & or +.

Remember that neither MySQL as of 5.7 nor Microsoft Access as of 2016 supports CTEs, including recursive CTEs.

That gives us three blank rows followed by the data we want to print. Note that we used UNION ALL not because some duplicates might be omitted (highly unlikely) but because it is more efficient. When you use UNION, your database must do extra work to check for and eliminate duplicates. The first eight rows of the output look like Table 9.1.

Table 9.1 Skipping used labels in a mailing list

CustName	CustStreetAddress	CustCityState	CustZip
Deborah Smith	2500 Rosales Lane	Dallas, TX 75260	75260
Doug Steele	672 Lamont Ave.	Houston, TX 77201	77201
Kirk Johnson	455 West Palm Ave.	San Antonio, TX 78284	78284
Angel Kennedy	667 Red River Road	Austin, TX 78710	78710
Mark Smith	323 Advocate Lane	El Paso, TX 79915	79915

Another way to do this is to use a tally table to provide the number sequence. In our sample Sales Orders database, we just happen to have a handy table called ztblSeqNumbers that contains the numbers from 1 to 60. Listing 9.2 shows how to use the tally table.

Listing 9.2 Using a tally table to skip blank labels

```
SELECT ' ' AS CustName, ' ' AS CustStreetAddress,
     ' ' AS CustCityState, ' ' AS CustZipCode
FROM ztblSeqNumbers
WHERE Sequence <= 3
UNION ALL
SELECT CONCAT(c.CustFirstName, ' ', c.CustLastName)
     AS CustName,
```

```
      c.CustStreetAddress,
      CONCAT(c.CustCity, ', ', c.CustState, ' ', c.CustZipCode)
          AS CustCityState, c.CustZipCode
FROM Customers AS c
ORDER BY CustZipCode;
```

In this simple example using SQL Server, there is a negligible difference in performance between the two techniques—perhaps because there are only 28 customers in the sample Customers table. In some systems, a tally table may be more efficient than using the CTE because the Sequence column can be indexed in the table.

Looking at the two solutions just presented, you will see that the value 3 was hard-coded into the SQL. Because the number of labels to be skipped will vary over time, it would obviously be more flexible to pass the number of labels to be skipped as a parameter. To be able to do that, we need to add the SQL to a function that names the parameter, applies the filter on the sequence number using that parameter, and returns the result as a table. Each time you run the report, you simply change the parameter value in the table name that you use in the SELECT statement that is the source of the report. Listing 9.3 shows the SQL for the function and the SELECT statement used to call the function to skip five rows.

Listing 9.3 Skipping blank labels using a function

```
CREATE FUNCTION MailingLabels (@skip AS int = 0)
RETURNS Table
AS RETURN (
  SELECT ' ' AS CustName, ' ' AS CustStreetAddress,
    ' ' AS CustCityState, ' ' AS CustZipCode
  FROM ztblSeqNumbers
  WHERE Sequence <= @skip
  UNION ALL
  SELECT
    CONCAT(c.CustFirstName, ' ', c.CustLastName) AS CustName,
    c.CustStreetAddress,
    CONCAT(c.CustCity, ', ', c.CustState, ' ', c.CustZipCode)
        AS CustCityState, c.CustZipCode
  FROM Customers AS c
);

SELECT * FROM MailingLabels(5)
ORDER BY CustZipCode;
```

Table-Valued Functions

Functions can certainly be useful to return a scalar value that you can use anywhere you would otherwise use a column name. When you have a complex calculation that you use in several views or stored procedures, you can put that calculation once in a function and then call the function whenever you need the complex calculation performed.

But functions that return an entire table are even more useful. When you want to run a query that depends on a changing variable value in a filter, a table-valued function lets you write what is perhaps complex SQL once and use the parameter value to return the filtered set of data. You can use a table-valued function anywhere you would otherwise use a table reference in a FROM clause. You can think of a table-valued function as a "parameterized" view. The parameter value can be supplied as a constant or as a value from a column reference to another table or subquery.

From a performance standpoint, a table-valued function is likely to be better than an equivalent SQL query using scalar functions. As discussed in Item 12, "Use indexes for more than just filtering," the database engine may use different algorithms for joining the data from different tables. An SQL query with a scalar function is far more likely to severely limit the engine's choices, and for practical purposes the engine must treat it as a black box that must be completely processed before it can be used further. That is usually the logical consequence of needing to execute a scalar function once (or more!) per row. A table-valued function, on the other hand, can be transparent, and the engine is able to see the "inside" of the function and use that information to form a better execution plan. This is what we usually call "inlining." So an engine might be able to inline a table-valued function, but almost never a query whose filtering or joining depends on a scalar function. If you come from a programming background where functions are second nature to you, you must shift your paradigm when writing SQL queries and think about sets, not rows. As usual, consult your database documentation to determine cases when the database can inline a table-valued function and when it cannot.

Of course, you need to execute the CREATE statement only once. Note that we perform the final sort in the query that calls the function because most implementations do not allow ORDER BY inside a function that returns a table. After your database system saves the function, it is a simple matter to change the parameter value each time you run your mailing labels report.

Things to Remember

✦ Generating blank rows can be useful, particularly for reports.

✦ You can use either a recursive CTE or a tally table to help you generate blank rows. In some cases, using the table may be faster.

✦ To make it easy to supply a parameter value for the number of blank rows, create a function that accepts the parameter so that you can call it from a SELECT statement.

Item 52: Use a Tally Table and Window Functions for Sequencing

This item deals with a case where tally tables excel with window functions, discussed in Item 37, "Know how to use window functions," to obtain results that depend on adjacent rows (e.g., numbering, ranking, etc.). This is useful for generating records or sequencing when there is no preexisting data. If your database engine supports window functions (see Item 37), this item is for you.

Suppose you are working in a database for a brokerage that sells and buys stocks. They are required by their country's laws to keep a record of all sales. But the complicating factor is that they will buy stocks at one price and then sell the same stocks at a different price, and they do not necessarily buy or sell the same quantities of a stock every time. In some situations, those variances could be sorted out by simply totaling the margins. However, this is not always possible, especially if we need to work with complex formulas or certain conditions where the output is markedly influenced by what order we use for calculating margin. How is that relevant to our hypothetical broker? Let's start with this formula:

gross margin = revenue of product – cost of product

So what is the cost of that *particular* unit of stock? And for how much was that *particular* unit of stock actually sold? Let's look at a broker's data model, noting also the tally table that is a single-column table in Figure 9.1.

The broker keeps records of all the different stocks they may buy or sell. The actual purchases and sales are kept in a common transaction table, with a transaction type to differentiate whether the transaction is a purchase or a sale of that stock.

Now, observe that we have our usual columns for quantity and price. Let's consider how our transaction table looks in Table 9.2 with the assumption that we consider only one stock.

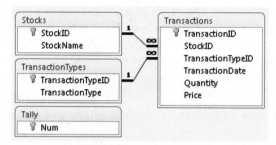

Figure 9.1 Data model of the broker's database, simplified

Table 9.2 Content of a broker's
transaction table

ID	Type	Date	Qty	Price
1	Buy	2/24	12	27.10
2	Sell	2/25	7	29.90
3	Buy	2/25	3	26.35
4	Sell	2/25	6	30.20
5	Buy	2/26	15	22.10
6	Sell	2/27	5	26.25

With that in mind, here is the pop question: What is the gross margin of the tenth unit of stock? Because the tenth unit was bought in the first buy transaction, at $27.10, that is the cost of the product. But it was not sold in the first sale; only seven units of stock were sold. It is actually in the second sale that the tenth unit was sold. So that means it earned $30.20. Therefore, the gross margin for that *particular* stock unit is $3.10. And here is the important question: How do we figure all that with SQL? We do not even have the luxury of keys on which to do joins!

We cannot very well tell brokers to start entering each *single* unit of stock bought or sold as a record. That is just tedious. And that is where tally tables and window functions (discussed in Item 37) come to our rescue. The idea here is that we need to assign a "row" for each single unit of stock and assign a cost and matching revenue to that row so that we can then calculate the margin for each option. If you are familiar with accounting, you might have heard of "First In, First Out" (FIFO) accounting, meaning that when a product is sold, its cost is assumed to be the cost at which it was first bought. So the first and second sales must use the first buy transaction's price (the cost of the product) with the exception that the sixth unit of the second sale actually comes from the second buy transaction. Therefore, we need to use the tally table twice: once to calculate the cost of the product (e.g., the price of a "buy"), and again to calculate the revenue of the same product (e.g., the price of a "sell").

To get started, let's look at the complete query in Listing 9.4.

Listing 9.4 Complete query for breaking out the individual stocks sold and bought

```
WITH Buys AS (
  SELECT
    ROW_NUMBER() OVER (
      PARTITION BY t.StockID
      ORDER BY t.TransactionDate, t.TransactionID, c.Num
      ) AS TransactionSeq,
    c.Num AS StockSeq,
    t.StockID,
    t.TransactionID,
    t.TransactionDate,
    t.Price AS CostOfProduct
  FROM Tally AS c
    INNER JOIN Transactions AS t
      ON c.Num <= t.Quantity
  WHERE t.TransactionTypeID = 1
  ),
Sells AS (
  SELECT
    ROW_NUMBER() OVER (
      PARTITION BY t.StockID
      ORDER BY t.TransactionDate, t.TransactionID, c.Num
      ) AS TransactionSeq,
    c.Num AS StockSeq,
    t.StockID,
    t.TransactionID,
    t.TransactionDate,
    t.Price AS RevenueOfProduct
  FROM Tally AS c
    INNER JOIN Transactions AS t
      ON c.Num <= t.Quantity
  WHERE t.TransactionTypeID = 2
  )
```

```
SELECT
  b.StockID,
  b.TransactionSeq,
  b.TransactionID AS BuyID,
  s.TransactionID AS SellID,
  b.TransactionDate AS BuyDate,
  s.TransactionDate AS SellDate,
  b.CostOfProduct,
  s.RevenueOfProduct,
  s.RevenueOfProduct - b.CostOfProduct AS GrossMargin
FROM Buys AS b
  INNER JOIN Sells AS s
    ON b.StockID = s.StockID
      AND b.TransactionSeq = s.TransactionSeq
ORDER BY b.TransactionSeq;
```

Table 9.3 shows a selected listing of the data returned by the query.

Table 9.3 Data returned by the query in Listing 9.4

Stock ID	Transaction Seq	Buy ID	Sell ID	Buy Date	Sell Date	Cost	Revenue	Margin
1	1	1	2	2/24	2/25	27.10	29.90	2.80
1	2	1	2	2/24	2/25	27.10	29.90	2.80
	. . .		. . .				. . .	
1	7	1	2	2/24	2/25	27.10	29.90	2.80
1	8	1	4	2/24	2/25	27.10	30.20	3.10
	. . .		. . .				. . .	
1	12	1	4	2/24	2/25	27.10	30.20	3.10
1	13	3	4	2/25	2/25	26.35	30.20	3.85
1	14	3	6	2/25	2/27	26.35	26.25	−0.10

As you can see, we need to perform three logical steps: break out the "buy" stocks, then do the same for "sells," and then finally match one unit's cost to revenue based on the specified order. Let's look more closely at the Buys CTE in Listing 9.5 on the next page.

Note

See also Item 42, "If possible, use common table expressions instead of subqueries," for more examples of using CTEs.

Listing 9.5 Buys CTE

```
SELECT
  ROW_NUMBER() OVER (
    PARTITION BY t.StockID
    ORDER BY t.TransactionDate, t.TransactionID, c.Num
    ) AS TransactionSeq,
  ...
FROM Tally AS c
  INNER JOIN Transactions AS t
    ON c.Num <= t.Quantity
WHERE t.TransactionTypeID = 1
```

We use the non-equijoin, which you can read about in Item 33, "Find maximum or minimum values without using GROUP BY," between the transaction table and the tally table to generate a single row for each unit of the quantity bought. This works brilliantly for giving us the correct sequence of individual stocks, but we also need a global sequence across all "buys" so that we can then match them to the corresponding unit among "sells." For that, we turn to the ROW_NUMBER() window function, which you can read more about in Item 38, "Create row numbers and rank a row over other rows," where we pass in the transaction date and the ID in addition to the number from the tally table to ensure unique and consistent sorting. We include the ID to act as a tiebreaker in cases where we have two "buys" (or "sells") on the same date. Though in this book we consider only one stock for brevity, note that the window function has a PARTITION clause so that it will work across all different stocks that the broker might sell, resetting the sequence for each stock being considered.

The Sells CTE is actually similar, the only differences being the filter of 2 rather than 1 to indicate that we want only transactions that are "sells," and we use RevenueOfProduct rather than CostOfProduct.

The final SELECT then joins the Buys and Sells CTEs together using the same global sequence that we created with the ROW_NUMBER(). Because that sequence is based on the same logic (sorted by transaction date, then ID), we can be assured that the answer will remain consistent every time we run the query, and the same individual unit of a stock will get the correct cost and revenue assigned to it, enabling us to calculate the gross margin for that particular unit of stock in a consistent manner.

You might wonder what happens if the broker has more "buys" than "sells" or vice versa. In the query from Listing 9.4, those excess rows would be excluded because we did an inner join. It would depend on the firm's accounting—they might simply consider excess buys to be inventory and thus of no interest for the purpose of calculating the margins, or they might mark them as losses (especially if the product in question is perishable, such as a crate of fruit rather than a unit of stock). If it is necessary, you could consider using LEFT JOIN or even FULL OUTER JOIN to ensure that the excess buys are accounted for.

Things to Remember

✦ Tally tables can be used in tandem with window functions to provide more ways to sequence or otherwise describe formulas that require a window.

✦ Non-equijoins with tally tables are useful when you need to create records out of thin air.

Item 53: Generate Multiple Rows Based on Range Values in a Tally Table

You learned in Item 51, "Use a tally table to generate null rows based on a parameter," that a tally table is handy for generating multiple artificial rows based on a comparison to a numeric value. Let's take that one step further and use one tally table to select a row count based on a range of values, and then a second tally table to generate a row count based on a value stored in the first tally table.

For this item, we will again use the sample Sales Orders database. You can see the design in Figure 9.2 on the next page; notice that it includes the two tally tables that we will use.

Let's assume you are a marketing manager for a company that had great sales volumes in the previous December. You would like to reward your best customers by mailing them one or more coupons for $10 off (on a $100 minimum purchase) based on how much they spent in December of 2015. If they spent more than $1,000, you will send them one coupon. If they spent more than $2,000, you will send them two coupons. If they spent more than $5,000, you will send them four coupons. And so on up to 50 coupons for spending more than $50,000.

You cannot easily calculate the correct number of coupons using a mathematical formula because the ranges and respective amounts do not follow a linear algorithm. But you can build a tally table to contain the ranges and respective coupon amounts. Table 9.4 on the next page shows a sample table (ztblPurchaseCoupons) with the values decided by the manager.

The second tally table, ztblSeqNumbers, is a simple table with one column that contains ascending integer values from 1 to 60.

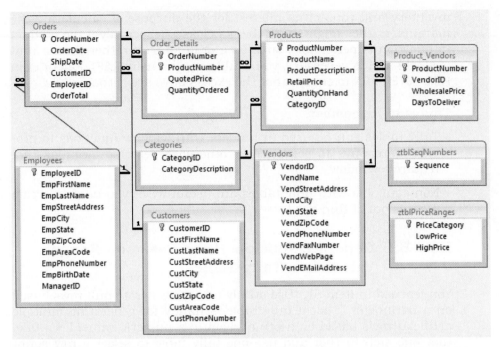

Figure 9.2 The design of the sample Sales Orders database, including tally tables

Table 9.4 A tally table to define a coupon count based on spending amount

LowSpend	HighSpend	NumCoupons
1000.00	1999.99	1
2000.00	4999.99	2
5000.00	9999.99	4
10000.00	29999.99	9
30000.00	49999.99	20
50000.00	999999.99	50

Clearly, we need to figure out the total amount each customer spent in December 2015, look up that value in the first tally table, and then use the NumCoupons column value to generate multiple rows per customer. Let's first calculate the purchase total by customer. Listing 9.6 shows the first CTE that you can use in the final query. (See Item 42,

"If possible, use common table expressions instead of subqueries," for details about using CTEs.) Notice that we left a comma at the end of the listing because we are going to add a second CTE.

Listing 9.6 Calculating the total December 2015 purchase amount per customer

```
WITH CustDecPurch AS (
  SELECT Orders.CustomerID,
    SUM((QuotedPrice)*(QuantityOrdered)) AS Purchase
  FROM Orders
    INNER JOIN Order_Details
      ON Orders.OrderNumber = Order_Details.OrderNumber
  WHERE Orders.OrderDate BETWEEN '2015-12-01'
      AND '2015-12-31'
  GROUP BY Orders.CustomerID
), ...
```

Next, let's take that total and figure out the number of coupons. Listing 9.7 shows the second CTE we will add that uses the value from the first CTE to look up the correct number from our tally table.

Listing 9.7 Using the result from the first CTE to find the number of coupons

```
... Coupons AS (
  SELECT CustDecPurch.CustomerID,
    ztblPurchaseCoupons.NumCoupons
  FROM CustDecPurch
    CROSS JOIN ztblPurchaseCoupons
  WHERE CustDecPurch.Purchase BETWEEN
    ztblPurchaseCoupons.LowSpend AND
    ztblPurchaseCoupons.HighSpend
) ...
```

Finally, we have identified the customers who have earned coupons and the number of $10 off coupons they should receive. Listing 9.8 shows the final SQL in the query to generate customer names and addresses repeated the appropriate number of times based on the coupon count.

Listing 9.8 Generating one line per customer per coupon

```
...
SELECT c.CustFirstName, c.CustLastName,
  c.CustStreetAddress, c.CustCity, c.CustState,
  c.CustZipCode, cp.NumCoupons
```

```
FROM Coupons AS cp
  INNER JOIN Customers AS c
    ON cp.CustomerID = c.CustomerID
  CROSS JOIN ztblSeqNumbers AS z
WHERE z.Sequence <= cp.NumCoupons;
```

Put all three listings together to build the final query. The end result is 321 rows—some customers will get one coupon (one row), some will get two, some will get four, some will get nine, a few will get 20, and two customers will get the maximum of 50 coupons. The query can then be sent to a printing application to print the specified number of coupons for each customer. The first several rows of the result look like Table 9.5. Note that the repeated customer rows correspond to the count reported in the NumCoupons column.

Table 9.5 Partial results from the query

CustFirst Name	CustLast Name	CustStreet Address	CustCity	Cust State	Cust ZipCode	Num Coupons
Suzanne	Viescas	15127 NE 24th, #383	Redmond	WA	98052	2
Suzanne	Viescas	15127 NE 24th, #383	Redmond	WA	98052	2
William	Thompson	122 Spring River Drive	Duvall	WA	98019	9
William	Thompson	122 Spring River Drive	Duvall	WA	98019	9
William	Thompson	122 Spring River Drive	Duvall	WA	98019	9
William	Thompson	122 Spring River Drive	Duvall	WA	98019	9
William	Thompson	122 Spring River Drive	Duvall	WA	98019	9

In the end, we used one tally table to calculate the number of coupons a particular customer should receive, and another tally table to expand that number into one row per customer per coupon. You could use a CTE and a complex CASE expression to generate the range values, which might be preferable if this needs to be done only one time. But if you need to do this again in the future using different ranges, it is much easier to simply change the values in the tally table rather than fix the code in your CTE and CASE expression.

Things to Remember

+ Use a tally table to generate values not otherwise found in your database.

+ When a tally table contains a range of values, you can compare the ranges to live data to generate a related calculated value.

+ You can use a sequential tally table to generate rows based on a value from another tally table.

Item 54: Convert a Value in One Table Based on a Range of Values in a Tally Table

You learned in Chapter 5, "Aggregation," how to aggregate data for the purpose of analysis. One potential issue with GROUP BY, as with most computer things, is that it is very literal: values must be the same before they can be aggregated together. Sometimes you may wish to treat ranges of values in the same way. We explore how to do that in this item.

Consider a Student Grades database with data as shown in Table 9.6. (The Advanced SQL teacher obviously believed in giving bonus marks!)

Table 9.6 Sample Student Grades data

Student	Subject	FinalGrade
Ben	Advanced SQL	102
Ben	Arithmetic	99
Ben	Reading	88.5
Ben	Writing	87
Doug	Advanced SQL	90
Doug	Arithmetic	72.3
Doug	Reading	60
Doug	Recess	100
Doug	Writing	59
Doug	Zymurgy	99.9
John	Advanced SQL	104
John	Arithmetic	75

continues

Table 9.6 Sample Student Grades data (*continued*)

Student	Subject	FinalGrade
John	Reading	61
John	Recess	95
John	Writing	92

Because no two grades have the same value, it is difficult to create summaries of that data. A query such as that shown in Listing 9.9 would return counts of 1 for each combination of subject and final grade, as shown in Table 9.7.

Listing 9.9 Attempt to summarize Student Grades data

```
WITH StudentGrades (Student, Subject, FinalGrade) AS (
  SELECT stu.StudentFirstNM AS Student,
    sub.SubjectNM AS Subject, ss.FinalGrade
  FROM StudentSubjects AS ss
  INNER JOIN Students AS stu
    ON ss.StudentID = stu.StudentID
  INNER JOIN Subjects AS sub
    ON ss.SubjectID = sub.SubjectID
  )
SELECT Subject, FinalGrade, COUNT(*) AS NumberOfStudents
FROM StudentGrades
GROUP BY Subject, FinalGrade
ORDER BY Subject, FinalGrade;
```

Table 9.7 Results of the summarization attempt in Listing 9.9

Subject	FinalGrade	NumberOfStudents
Advanced SQL	90	1
Advanced SQL	102	1
Advanced SQL	104	1
Arithmetic	72.3	1
Arithmetic	75	1
Arithmetic	99	1
Reading	60	1

Table 9.7 Results of the summarization attempt in Listing 9.9 (*continued*)

Subject	FinalGrade	NumberOfStudents
Reading	61	1
Reading	88.5	1
Recess	95	1
Recess	100	1
Writing	59	1
Writing	87	1
Writing	92	1
Zymurgy	99.9	1

As summaries go, that is not particularly useful. It would help if you could group the grades, such as a letter grade covering a range of numeric grades. Table 9.8 shows one possible tally table that could be used for that purpose.

Table 9.8 Tally table to convert ranges of numeric grades to letter grades

LetterGrade	LowGradePoint	HighGradePoint
A+	97	120
A	93	96.99
A–	90	92.99
B+	87	89.99
B	83	86.99
B–	80	82.99
C+	77	79.99
C	73	76.99
C–	70	72.99
D+	67	69.99

continues

Table 9.8 Tally table to convert ranges of numeric grades to letter grades (*continued*)

LetterGrade	LowGradePoint	HighGradePoint
D	63	66.99
D–	60	62.99
F	0	59.99

Listing 9.10 shows how the GradeRanges tally table can be joined to the StudentGrades table to produce the results shown in Table 9.9.

Listing 9.10 Joining the GradeRanges tally table to convert numeric grades to letter grades

```
WITH StudentGrades (Student, Subject, FinalGrade) AS (
  SELECT stu.StudentFirstNM AS Student,
    sub.SubjectNM AS Subject, ss.FinalGrade
  FROM StudentSubjects AS ss
  INNER JOIN Students AS stu
    ON ss.StudentID = stu.StudentID
  INNER JOIN Subjects AS sub
    ON ss.SubjectID = sub.SubjectID
  )
SELECT sg.Student, sg.Subject, sg.FinalGrade, gr.LetterGrade
FROM StudentGrades AS sg INNER JOIN GradeRanges AS gr
  ON sg.FinalGrade >= gr.LowGradePoint
  AND sg.FinalGrade <= gr.HighGradePoint
ORDER BY sg.Student, sg.Subject;
```

Table 9.9 Sample Student Grades data with letter grades

Student	Subject	FinalGrade	LetterGrade
Ben	Advanced SQL	102	A+
Ben	Arithmetic	99	A+
Ben	Reading	88.5	B+
Ben	Writing	87	B+
Doug	Advanced SQL	90	A–
Doug	Arithmetic	72.3	C–

Table 9.9 Sample Student Grades data with letter grades (*continued*)

Student	Subject	FinalGrade	LetterGrade
Doug	Reading	60	D–
Doug	Recess	100	A+
Doug	Writing	59	F
Doug	Zymurgy	99.9	A+
John	Advanced SQL	104	A+
John	Arithmetic	75	C
John	Reading	61	D–
John	Recess	95	A
John	Writing	92	A–

You can now summarize the marks by LetterGrade, as shown in Listing 9.11, with the results shown in Table 9.10 on the next page.

Listing 9.11 Summarizing Student Grades data by letter grade

```
WITH StudentGrades (Student, Subject, FinalGrade) AS (
  SELECT stu.StudentFirstNM AS Student,
    sub.SubjectNM AS Subject, ss.FinalGrade
  FROM StudentSubjects AS ss
  INNER JOIN Students AS stu
    ON ss.StudentID = stu.StudentID
  INNER JOIN Subjects AS sub
    ON ss.SubjectID = sub.SubjectID
  )
SELECT ag.Subject, gr.LetterGrade, COUNT(*) AS NumberOfStudents
FROM StudentGrades AS sg
  INNER JOIN GradeRanges AS gr
    ON sg.FinalGrade >= gr.LowGradePoint
    AND sg.FinalGrade <= gr.HighGradePoint
GROUP BY sg.Subject, gr.LetterGrade
ORDER BY sg.Subject, gr.LetterGrade;
```

Although the small sample size in the example means there are still many counts of 1, at least you can see that some aggregation has occurred.

Table 9.10 The results of summarizing Student Grades data by letter grade

Subject	LetterGrade	NumberOfStudents
Advanced SQL	A+	2
Advanced SQL	A–	1
Arithmetic	A+	1
Arithmetic	C	1
Arithmetic	C–	1
Reading	B+	1
Reading	D	2
Recess	A	1
Recess	A+	1
Writing	A–	1
Writing	B+	1
Writing	F	1
Zymurgy	A+	1

There are a few things to keep in mind when designing tally tables for conversions such as this. It is important to ensure that all possible ranges are covered. The last thing you want to do is lose data because some values fall outside the range of acceptable values. There are two general approaches to handling that problem: (1) you can prohibit invalid values at entry time with a CHECK constraint, or (2) you can add rows to the tally table including the invalid value ranges and return "Invalid Values."

Assuming that the intent is to group data for summary purposes, you want to ensure that your ranges are of appropriate sizes. It does not provide much benefit if each range has only a few values in it. Depending on your specific situation, there is no reason why the size of each range has to be the same.

The type of data being considered can mean that you may need to have each low range value equal to the previous high range value, as shown in Table 9.11. This is especially common when the value being compared is subject to issues with decimal precision.

Table 9.11 Tally table to convert continuous ranges of numeric grades to letter grades

LetterGrade	LowGradePoint	HighGradePoint
A+	97	120
A	93	97
A−	90	93
B+	87	90
B	83	87
B−	80	83
C+	77	80
C	73	77
C−	70	73
D+	67	70
D	63	67
D−	60	63
F	0	60

Of course, if you use ranges such as those shown in Table 9.11, you must remember to change the inequalities being used in your ON clauses from <= to < (as shown in Listing 9.12) to ensure that no value falls into two groups.

Listing 9.12 Joining the GradeRanges tally table to convert continuous numeric grades to letter grades

```
WITH StudentGrades (Student, Subject, FinalGrade) AS (
  SELECT stu.StudentFirstNM AS Student,
    sub.SubjectNM AS Subject, ss.FinalGrade
  FROM StudentSubjects AS ss
  INNER JOIN Students AS stu
    ON ss.StudentID = stu.StudentID
  INNER JOIN Subjects AS sub
    ON ss.SubjectID = sub.SubjectID
  )
SELECT sg.Student, sg.Subject, sg.FinalGrade, gr.LetterGrade,
FROM StudentGrades AS sg
  INNER JOIN GradeRanges AS gr
```

```
    ON sg.FinalGrade >= gr.LowGradePoint
    AND sg.FinalGrade < gr.HighGradePoint
ORDER BY sg.Student, sg.Subject;
```

Note

It is possible to construct conversion tally tables that define the ranges using only one number. Rather than having a low value and a high value for each range, you can simply have only one value that represents either the bottom of the range or the top of the range, with the other limit being implied by the value in either the preceding row or the following row for each row. However, we feel that specifying both the low and high values for each range leads to less confusion and easier SQL statements.

Things to Remember

✦ Ensure that your conversion tally table is designed appropriately for your data.

✦ Ensure that the inequalities used in your non-equijoins are appropriate for the tally table being used.

Item 55: Use a Date Table to Simplify Date Calculation

Dates and times rank high on the list of problematic data types. Compared to other data types, they require several functions just to do something useful, and in some cases it might even be necessary to wrap one date-based function in yet another date-based function. Some people cheat and use shortcuts, such as performing arithmetic on dates using numbers instead of interval data types, which is in fact illogical. The challenge is magnified when we consider that most DBMSs do not completely implement the SQL Standards with regard to data types, functions, and allowed operations for dates and times.

To illustrate the problem, consider a typical query that might be used for a business report on shipping performance, shown in Listing 9.13. Note that the query might return zero rows due to the fact that the query only searches for the last two months.

Listing 9.13 Possible query with several date functions

```
SELECT DATENAME(weekday, o.OrderDate) AS OrderDateWeekDay,
    o.OrderDate,
    DATENAME(weekday, o.ShipDate) AS ShipDateWeekDay,
    o.ShipDate,
    DATEDIFF(day, o.OrderDate, o.ShipDate) AS DeliveryLead
```

```
FROM Orders AS o
WHERE o.OrderDate >=
    DATEADD(month, -2,
      DATEFROMPARTS(YEAR(GETDATE()), MONTH(GETDATE()), 1))
  AND o.OrderDate <
    DATEFROMPARTS(YEAR(GETDATE()), MONTH(GETDATE()), 1);
```

Note

Listing 9.13 uses several date functions specific to SQL Server, and some are not available prior to the 2012 version. Consult the Appendix, "Date and Time Types, Operations, and Functions," for equivalent date functions for other DBMSs.

As you can see, even this small query with fairly modest requirements is already loaded with several function invocations and literals. More code means less readability. If not for aliases, it would be hard to see what the query is doing. But aliases will not help us validate whether the logic is correct. After all, calling a pig by another name does not make it less of a pig.

When a lot of business decisions or the business performance heavily depends on dates in a database, it might be beneficial to adopt a different approach: create a date table and use it as your reference table in place of using several date functions. Listing 9.14 shows a possible creation DDL for a date table.

Listing 9.14 Possible table creation DDL for a date table

```
CREATE TABLE DimDate (
  DateKey int NOT NULL,
  DateValue date NOT NULL PRIMARY KEY,
  NextDayValue date NOT NULL,
  YearValue smallint NOT NULL,
  YearQuarter int NOT NULL,
  YearMonth int NOT NULL,
  YearDayOfYear int NOT NULL,
  QuarterValue tinyint NOT NULL,
  MonthValue tinyint NOT NULL,
  DayOfYear smallint NOT NULL,
  DayOfMonth smallint NOT NULL,
  DayOfWeek tinyint NOT NULL,
  YearName varchar(4) NOT NULL,
  YearQuarterName varchar(7) NOT NULL,
  QuarterName varchar(8) NOT NULL,
  MonthName varchar(3) NOT NULL,
  MonthNameLong varchar(9) NOT NULL,
```

```
WeekdayName varchar(3) NOT NULL,
WeekDayNameLong varchar(9) NOT NULL,
StartOfYearDate date NOT NULL,
EndOfYearDate date NOT NULL,
StartOfQuarterDate date NOT NULL,
EndOfQuarterDate date NOT NULL,
StartOfMonthDate date NOT NULL,
EndOfMonthDate date NOT NULL,
StartOfWeekStartingSunDate date NOT NULL,
EndOfWeekStartingSunDate date NOT NULL,
StartOfWeekStartingMonDate date NOT NULL,
EndOfWeekStartingMonDate date NOT NULL,
StartOfWeekStartingTueDate date NOT NULL,
EndOfWeekStartingTueDate date NOT NULL,
StartOfWeekStartingWedDate date NOT NULL,
EndOfWeekStartingWedDate date NOT NULL,
StartOfWeekStartingThuDate date NOT NULL,
EndOfWeekStartingThuDate date NOT NULL,
StartOfWeekStartingFriDate date NOT NULL,
EndOfWeekStartingFriDate date NOT NULL,
StartOfWeekStartingSatDate date NOT NULL,
EndOfWeekStartingSatDate date NOT NULL,
QuarterSeqNo int NOT NULL,
MonthSeqNo int NOT NULL,
WeekStartingSunSeq int NOT NULL,
WeekStartingMonSeq int NOT NULL,
WeekStartingTueSeq int NOT NULL,
WeekStartingWedSeq int NOT NULL,
WeekStartingThuSeq int NOT NULL,
WeekStartingFriSeq int NOT NULL,
WeekStartingSatSeq int NOT NULL,
JulianDate int NOT NULL,
ModifiedJulianDate int NOT NULL,
ISODate varchar(10) NOT NULL,
ISOYearWeekNo int NOT NULL,
ISOWeekNo smallint NOT NULL,
ISODayOfWeek tinyint NOT NULL,
ISOYearWeekName varchar(8) NOT NULL,
ISOYearWeekDayOfWeekName varchar(10) NOT NULL);
```

Instead of invoking different functions with different literals, we create a single table with a large number of columns used to store precalculated values in the table. The actual script to populate the date table is too long to include in the item. However, you can get the script at the GitHub site: https://github.com/TexanInParis/Effective-SQL.

Returning to the query shown in Listing 9.13, we can then modify it as shown in Listing 9.15.

Listing 9.15 Modified query from Listing 9.13

```
SELECT od.WeekDayNameLong AS OrderDateWeekDay,
  o.OrderDate,
  sd.WeekDayNameLong AS ShipDateWeekDay,
  o.ShipDate,
  sd.DateKey - od.DateKey AS DeliveryLead
FROM Orders AS o
  INNER JOIN DimDate AS od
    ON o.OrderDate = od.DateValue
  INNER JOIN DimDate AS sd
    ON o.ShipDate = sd.DateValue
  INNER JOIN DimDate AS td
    ON td.DateValue = CAST(GETDATE() AS date)
WHERE od.MonthSeqNo = (td.MonthSeqNo - 1);
```

Instead of several functions and complex predicates, we now have simple joins and simple arithmetic. Pay attention to the fact that we join the DimDate table three times, each time to different date columns. More descriptive aliases could make it clearer what WeekdayNameLong we are going to get.

Note that because the DimDate table already precalculates the sequential numbering, it is now possible to do simple arithmetic that normally would be dangerous to do. Consider the sampling of the DimDate table in Table 9.12.

Table 9.12 Sampled data from the DimDate table

DateValue	Year Value	Month Value	Year Month	YearMonth NameLong	Month SeqNo
2015-12-30	2015	12	201512	2015 December	1392
2015-12-31	2015	12	201512	2015 December	1392
2016-01-01	2016	1	201601	2016 January	1393
2016-01-02	2016	1	201601	2016 January	1393
	. . .			. . .	
2016-01-30	2016	1	201601	2016 January	1393
2016-01-31	2016	1	201601	2016 January	1393

continues

Table 9.12 Sampled data from the `DimDate` table (*continued*)

DateValue	Year Value	Month Value	Year Month	YearMonth NameLong	Month SeqNo
2016-02-01	2016	2	201602	2016 February	1394
2016-02-02	2016	2	201602	2016 February	1394

As you can see, we have our typical 1 to 12 for the `MonthValue` field, and we also have `MonthSeqNo`, which increases continuously for each month. By using the `***SeqNo` fields, it becomes easy to perform arithmetic on different parts of the dates without having to invoke a function. More importantly, those columns can be indexed, which enables you to create sargable queries more easily.

In Listing 9.13 we had to use two predicates to correctly filter dates, as discussed in Item 27, "Know how to correctly filter a range of dates on a column containing both date and time," with several function invocations. All of that was necessary to create a sargable query that could locate an order within the last month. Things can get much worse when we start to do week calculations, especially when we incorporate business calendar items such as workdays or fiscal years.

It is important to note that the date table can be extended to support the workdays and other business-specific domains for which there are no easy algorithms to figure out what's what. You could go to the trouble of calculating all the logic for the next five or ten years or even more. The extra work up front can mean that date-heavy queries become much simpler.

However, be aware that you are also likely trading CPU usage for disk I/O. The date table is now stored on disk, whereas the date functions are calculated in memory. Even if the date table is cached in memory, you still have to consider that a table requires more processing than a simple inline function does. In fact, the query from Listing 9.15 will perform more slowly than the one from Listing 9.13 because of all the extra reads being performed on the `DimDate` table. However, the date table should win out in queries where several dates from different sources must be read, and calculations depend on those.

Another thing you should remember is that because the `DimDate` table will not change and will be added to only periodically, you can create several indices on the table, just as though you were indexing a dimension table in a data warehouse. That then gives the database engine the ability to pick an index and read from it instead of from the entire table, which should reduce the I/O. When explicitly loading a table into memory is an option, you can choose that option so that it loads and resides in memory, thus eliminating any disk access required to read from the data. Not all DBMS products give you the ability to do this, but when it is available, it can make the date table even faster because the optimizer is able to assume that the table will always be available in memory.

Optimizing Queries with Date Tables

Applying the concepts that you learned in Item 11, "Carefully consider creation of indexes to minimize index and data scanning," Item 12, "Use indexes for more than just filtering," and Item 46, "Understand how the execution plan works," you should have enough knowledge to analyze how best to use your date table. Continuing with the query from Listing 9.15, if we did not add any other indices beyond the primary key, the execution plan for the query would likely be suboptimal because there are several details that the query needs to extract in order to make the determination.

For one thing, we are looking up the WeekDayNameLong column in the DimDate table for the OrderDate and ShipDate columns from the Orders table. So we could create an index to quickly extract the weekday's name using dates with Listing 9.16.

Listing 9.16 First try to index the DimDate table

```
CREATE INDEX DimDate_WeekDayLong
ON DimDate (DateValue, WeekdayNameLong);
```

However, that is not the only thing we do with the DimDate table in that query. For one thing, we use the MonthSeqNo; we compare the td.MonthSeqNo with the od.MonthSeqNo. So let's make sure we include this as shown in Listing 9.17.

Listing 9.17 Second try to index the DimDate table

```
CREATE INDEX DimDate_WeekDayLong
ON DimDate (DateValue, WeekdayNameLong, MonthSeqNo);
```

Now this covers all columns that we used for the query in Listing 9.15. However, just having all columns covered in an index is not the end of the story. For one thing, the index is sorted on the DateValue column, and we cannot directly access the MonthSeqNo column even though it is used in the WHERE clause of the query. Let's create an index that sorts on MonthSeqNo first in Listing 9.18 on the next page.

continues

Listing 9.18 Indexing by MonthSeqNo in the DimDate table

```
CREATE INDEX DimDate_MonthSeqNo
ON DimDate (MonthSeqNo, DateValue, WeekdayNameLong);
```

If you have been checking the execution plans between tries, you should have seen the plans getting better and better, replacing hash joins with nested loops, and scans with seeks. However, DimDate is only one part of the equation. We also have the Orders table. We are looking up both the OrderDate and ShipDate columns, and we are filtering on the OrderDate indirectly via the od.MonthSeqNo in the WHERE clause. So, we should have an index that gives us both date columns, sorting by OrderDate as shown in Listing 9.19.

Listing 9.19 Indexing on the Orders table's dates

```
CREATE INDEX Orders_OrderDate_ShipDate
ON Orders (OrderDate, ShipDate);
```

At this point, the query should be quite optimized, being able to use much smaller indices throughout its execution plan to give the answer as quickly as possible for this particular query. On some DBMSs, using a filtered index might go even further. It pays to experiment.

It is unlikely that this will be the only query using the DimDate table, but because the content within DimDate will not be updated frequently, you can create as many indices as you need to provide the database engine with as many choices as possible to quickly satisfy requests by using index access, without actually touching the data pages. This means faster I/O, whether it is on a spinning platter or in RAM chips.

Things to Remember

+ For applications that are heavy on dates and date-based calculations, a date table may simplify the logic significantly.

+ The date table can be extended to include application-specific domains such as working days, holidays, or fiscal years.

+ Because the date table is basically a dimension table, it can be indexed heavily, even for an online transaction processing (OLTP) database. If possible, storing the table explicitly in memory can avoid the disk access penalty and help improve the optimizer's estimates.

Item 56: Create an Appointment Calendar Table with All Dates Enumerated in a Range

You saw the concept of a date table in Item 55, "Use a date table to simplify date calculation," and you saw how to use a left join to produce more comprehensive lists in Item 47, "Produce combinations of rows between two tables and flag rows in the second that indirectly relate to the first." You can use the same approach to produce listings of appointments (or any other events you want to display on a calendar).

Consider the Appointments table shown in Listing 9.20.

Listing 9.20 Table creation DDL for an Appointments table

```
CREATE TABLE Appointments (
  AppointmentID int IDENTITY (1, 1) PRIMARY KEY,
  ApptStartDate date NOT NULL,
  ApptStartTime time NOT NULL,
  ApptEndDate date NOT NULL,
  ApptEndTime time NOT NULL,
  ApptDescription varchar(50) NULL
);
```

Note

Not all DBMSs support the time data type. See the Appendix, "Date and Time Types, Operations, and Functions," for details.

Storing dates as integer values (in yyyymmdd format) might lead to more efficient queries. However, we chose not to add that complication to this example.

Although it is true that there are both date and time components associated with the start and end of each appointment, and thus the DateTime or Timestamp data type might seem more appropriate, we suggest storing the values in separate date and time fields to make it easier to write sargable queries. (See Item 28, "Write sargable queries to ensure that the engine will use indexes," for an explanation.)

Note

Some DBMSs now provide temporal support in accordance with the SQL:2011 Standard. Consider using temporal support where available.

For the purpose of this item, all that is required in the way of a date table is what is shown in Listing 9.21 on the next page, with one row for each day. Of course, if you have a more complete date table, having additional columns is not an issue.

Listing 9.21 Table creation DDL for a date table

```
CREATE TABLE DimDate (
  DateKey int PRIMARY KEY,
  FullDate date NOT NULL
  );
CREATE INDEX iFullDate
  ON DimDate (FullDate);
```

> **Note**
>
> See Item 55 for a discussion of how to create and populate a date table. Because date tables are often used in information warehouses, the primary key is usually not a date field.

You can now create a query, shown in Listing 9.22, that will show every day in the date table and what appointments you have. (Note that the query will result in more rows than are in the date table, unless you have the unusual situation where you never have more than one appointment on a given day!)

Listing 9.22 SQL statement to return calendar details

```
SELECT d.FullDate,
  a.ApptDescription,
  a.ApptStartDate + a.ApptStartTime AS ApptStart,
  a.ApptEndDate + a.ApptEndTime AS ApptEnd
FROM DimDate AS d
  LEFT JOIN Appointments AS a
    ON d.FullDate = a.ApptStartDate
ORDER BY d.FullDate;
```

> **Note**
>
> Not all DBMSs allow you to add dates and times as in Listing 9.22. See the Appendix, "Date and Time Types, Operations, and Functions," for alternatives for your DBMS.

Should you wish to see appointments for only a specific time period, remember that, as was mentioned in Item 35, "Include zero-value rows when testing for HAVING COUNT(x) < some number," the WHERE clause should refer to columns in DimDate, not columns in Appointments, because the dates may not exist in Appointments.

If you run the query in Listing 9.22 against the sample data shown in Table 9.13, you will get the results shown in Table 9.14.

Table 9.13 Sample data for the Appointments table

Appointment ID	ApptStart Date	ApptStart Time	ApptEnd Date	ApptEnd Time	Appt Description
1	2017-01-03	10:30	2017-01-03	11:00	Meet with John
2	2017-01-03	11:15	2017-01-03	12:00	Design cover page
3	2017-01-05	09:00	2017-01-05	15:00	Teach SQL course
4	2017-01-05	15:30	2017-01-05	16:30	Review with Ben
5	2017-01-06	10:00	2017-01-06	11:30	Plan for lunch

Table 9.14 Results of running Listing 9.22

FullDate	ApptDescription	ApptStart	ApptEnd
2017-01-01			
2017-01-02			
2017-01-03	Meet with John	2017-01-03 10:30	2017-01-03 11:00
2017-01-03	Design cover page	2017-01-03 11:15	2017-01-03 12:00
2017-01-04			
2017-01-05	Teach SQL course	2017-01-05 09:00	2017-01-05 15:00
2017-01-05	Review with Ben	2017-01-05 15:30	2017-01-05 16:30
2017-01-06	Plan for lunch	2017-01-06 10:00	2017-01-06 11:30
2017-01-07			

Things to Remember

+ Ensure that your date table has the appropriate indexing.

+ Learn the appropriate date and time handling for your DBMS and design to accommodate it.

+ Ensure that your WHERE clause tests values from the appropriate tables.

Item 57: Pivot Data Using a Tally Table

To create output information to use in a report, it is often useful to "pivot" the data to get a denormalized result that looks more like a spreadsheet. You typically want to do that with a query that outputs a SUM() or a COUNT() that is grouped on two column values—for example, count of orders by sales rep and month, or sum of contracts signed by agent and by month. By "pivot," we mean use the values in one of the columns as column headings. The result places the aggregate value at the intersection of the remaining grouped columns and the values in the grouped column that you pivoted.

For the examples in this item, let's use the sample Entertainment Agency database that you can find on GitHub at https://github.com/TexanInParis/Effective-SQL. The database design (including the tally table we will use) looks like Figure 9.3.

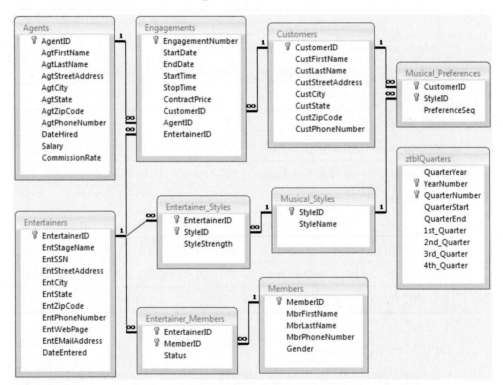

Figure 9.3 Design of the sample Entertainment Agency database

Let's assume that your marketing manager has asked for a report that shows the total value of entertainment contracts booked by each agent per month in 2015. Your first effort might look like the SQL shown in Listing 9.23.

Listing 9.23 Calculating contract totals by agent and month

```
SELECT a.AgtFirstName, a.AgtLastName,
  MONTH(e.StartDate) AS ContractMonth,
  SUM(e.ContractPrice) AS TotalContractValue
FROM Agents AS a
  INNER JOIN Engagements AS e
    ON a.AgentID = e.AgentID
WHERE YEAR(e.StartDate) = 2015
GROUP BY a.AgtFirstName, a.AgtLastName, MONTH(e.StartDate);
```

In our sample database, the SQL in this listing returns 25 rows. You can see the first several rows in Table 9.15.

Table 9.15 Generating contract value totals by month in 2015

AgtFirstName	AgtLastName	ContractMonth	TotalContractValue
Caleb	Viescas	9	2300.00
Caleb	Viescas	10	3460.00
Caleb	Viescas	12	1000.00
Carol	Viescas	9	6560.00
Carol	Viescas	10	6170.00
Carol	Viescas	11	3620.00
Carol	Viescas	12	1900.00

That gets the data requested, but the manager takes one look at the output and says, "Well, I know that's what I asked for, but I really want to see the data by fiscal quarter. And I want the quarters across the top, the agents down the side, and the contract values by agent and quarter in the intersection. That will let me see the performance of each agent from quarter to quarter and compare the performance of the various agents in a given quarter. Oh, and remember that our first quarter begins on May 1. And I also want to see all agents whether they've booked anything or not."

You knew this was coming, but at least it now appears that you have all the requirements! Wanting to see all agents regardless of activity adds an interesting twist, but you are sure you can handle it. (See also Item 29, "Correctly filter the 'right' side of a 'left' join," for more details.)

Sadly, there is nothing in the current ISO SQL Standard that will let you do this easily. Various database systems have implemented custom solutions. Some versions of IBM DB2 use DECODE, Microsoft SQL

Server uses PIVOT, Microsoft Access uses TRANSFORM, Oracle uses PIVOT and DECODE, and PostgreSQL uses CROSSTAB (which requires installing an extension "tablefunc").

If the requirement remained total by month, you could solve the problem without a tally table using standard SQL. Your solution might look something like Listing 9.24.

Listing 9.24 Calculating and pivoting contract totals by month using standard SQL

```
SELECT a.AgtFirstName, a.AgtLastName,
  YEAR(e.StartDate) AS ContractYear,
  SUM(CASE WHEN MONTH(e.StartDate) = 1
        THEN e.ContractPrice
      END) AS January,
  SUM(CASE WHEN MONTH(e.StartDate) = 2
        THEN e.ContractPrice
      END) AS February,
  SUM(CASE WHEN MONTH(e.StartDate) = 3
        THEN e.ContractPrice
      END) AS March,
  SUM(CASE WHEN MONTH(e.StartDate) = 4
        THEN e.ContractPrice
      END) AS April,
  SUM(CASE WHEN MONTH(e.StartDate) = 5
        THEN e.ContractPrice
      END) AS May,
  SUM(CASE WHEN MONTH(e.StartDate) = 6
        THEN e.ContractPrice
      END) AS June,
  SUM(CASE WHEN MONTH(e.StartDate) = 7
        THEN e.ContractPrice
      END) AS July,
  SUM(CASE WHEN MONTH(e.StartDate) = 8
        THEN e.ContractPrice
      END) AS August,
  SUM(CASE WHEN MONTH(e.StartDate) = 9
        THEN e.ContractPrice
      END) AS September,
  SUM(CASE WHEN MONTH(e.StartDate) = 10
        THEN e.ContractPrice
      END) AS October,
  SUM(CASE WHEN MONTH(e.StartDate) = 11
        THEN e.ContractPrice
      END) AS November,
```

```
      SUM(CASE WHEN MONTH(e.StartDate) = 12
            THEN e.ContractPrice
          END) AS December
FROM Agents AS a
  LEFT JOIN (
    SELECT en.AgentID, en.StartDate, en.ContractPrice
    FROM Engagements AS en
    WHERE en.StartDate >= '2015-01-01'
      AND en.StartDate < '2016-01-01'
    ) AS e
    ON a.AgentID = e.AgentID
GROUP BY AgtFirstName, AgtLastName, YEAR(e.StartDate);
```

Of course, you could make this completely flexible by defining this as a function that returns the result as a table and that accepts the year you want as a parameter. But now the requirement is to arrange the data by fiscal quarter, and the first quarter starts on an odd date, so you cannot use any built-in functions to find out the quarter number. You could add more complex WHEN clauses that test for specific quarter start and end dates, but that makes the query even more complex and dependent on the specific dates you would have to code. To run the query for another year, you would probably have to modify it, which could introduce errors.

A simpler solution would be to use a tally table that predefines the quarters and provides constant values 0 or 1 for each quarter column that you can use instead of a complex CASE clause to calculate the sums into the correct boxes. The tally table (ztblQuarters) looks like Table 9.16.

Table 9.16 Tally table to enable a pivot on variable quarter dates

Quarter Year	Year Number	Quarter Number	Quarter Start	Quarter End	Qtr_ 1st	Qtr_ 2nd	Qtr_ 3rd	Qtr_ 4th
Q1 2015	2015	1	5/1/2015	7/31/2015	1	0	0	0
Q2 2015	2015	2	8/1/2015	10/31/2015	0	1	0	0
Q3 2015	2015	3	11/1/2015	1/31/2016	0	0	1	0
Q4 2015	2015	4	2/1/2016	4/30/2015	0	0	0	1
Q1 2016	2016	1	5/1/2016	7/31/2016	1	0	0	0
Q2 2016	2016	2	8/1/2016	10/31/2016	0	1	0	0
Q3 2016	2016	3	11/1/2016	1/31/2017	0	0	1	0
Q4 2016	2016	4	2/1/2017	4/30/2016	0	0	0	1

In the final query, we will use the tally table in a Cartesian Product with the query that joins Agents and Engagements and filter the results on the QuarterStart and QuarterEnd dates. To make it really flexible, you could use a parameter to filter the YearNumber column. When you need to run the report for other years, simply add rows to the tally table. Listing 9.25 shows the solution.

Listing 9.25 Calculating contract totals by agent by fiscal quarter for 2015

```
SELECT ae.AgtFirstName, ae.AgtLastName, z.YearNumber,
  SUM(ae.ContractPrice * z.Qtr_1st) AS First_Quarter,
  SUM(ae.ContractPrice * z.Qtr_2nd) AS Second_Quarter,
  SUM(ae.ContractPrice * z.Qtr_3rd) AS Third_Quarter,
  SUM(ae.ContractPrice * z.Qtr_4th) AS Fourth_Quarter
FROM ztblQuarters AS z
  CROSS JOIN (
    SELECT a.AgtFirstName, a.AgtLastName,
      e.StartDate, e.ContractPrice
    FROM Agents AS a
    LEFT JOIN Engagements AS e
      ON a.AgentID = e.AgentID
  ) AS ae
WHERE (ae.StartDate BETWEEN z.QuarterStart AND z.QuarterEnd)
  OR (ae.StartDate IS NULL AND z.YearNumber = 2015)
GROUP BY AgtFirstName, AgtLastName, YearNumber;
```

Note that the query uses the 1 and 0 values in the tally table multiplied by the value being summed to put the values in the correct column. The result (using our sample database that does not have a lot of data) looks like Table 9.17.

Table 9.17 Contract totals by agent and fiscal quarter for 2015

AgtFirst Name	AgtLast Name	Year Number	First_ Quarter	Second_ Quarter	Third_ Quarter	Fourth_ Quarter
Caleb	Viescas	2015	0.00	5760.00	3525.00	0.00
Carol	Viescas	2015	0.00	12730.00	8370.00	0.00
Daffy	Dumbwit	2015	NULL	NULL	NULL	NULL
John	Kennedy	2015	0.00	950.00	21675.00	0.00
Karen	Smith	2015	0.00	11200.00	6575.00	0.00
Maria	Patterson	2015	0.00	6245.00	4910.00	0.00

Table 9.17 Contract totals by agent and fiscal quarter for 2015 (*continued*)

AgtFirst Name	AgtLast Name	Year Number	First_ Quarter	Second_ Quarter	Third_ Quarter	Fourth_ Quarter
Marianne	Davidson	2015	0.00	3545.00	11970.00	0.00
Scott	Johnson	2015	0.00	1370.00	4850.00	0.00
William	Thompson	2015	0.00	8460.00	4880.00	0.00

We know that we did the left join from Agents to Engagements correctly because the one agent who has never booked anything shows up with empty totals. As you can imagine, it is a simple matter to add a parameter to allow the user to specify the year of interest.

It is not always the best idea to use a tally table to do a pivot when other alternatives are available. But when you have several variables to use as filters for data that you need to pivot, a tally table can be a good choice because you need only add more rows to the tally table to have the query work for other values.

Things to Remember

✦ When you need to "pivot" data, your database system may have a custom syntax solution.

✦ If you want to use only standard SQL, you can pivot data using a CASE expression to provide the value from each row within your aggregate function.

✦ When the values that determine the column ranges for your pivot are variable, it may be wise to use a tally table to simplify your SQL.

10

Modeling Hierarchical Data

You already know that the relational model is not quite hierarchical, which is generally a good thing when we need to describe more complex relationships between different entities. Nonetheless, it is not uncommon to run into requirements where you need to maintain hierarchical data in your relational database. This also happens to be one of SQL's weaker areas.

Whenever you have requirements for modeling hierarchical data with your SQL database, you must make a trade-off between data normalization, and ease of querying and maintenance of metadata. There are four different models that you can use, each represented as an item within the chapter. Each model will work optimally depending on your answers to the following questions:

1. How much work do you want to invest in storing and maintaining the required metadata? Note that the metadata itself might not be normalized.

2. How efficient and fast should the queries on the hierarchy be?

3. Will queries on the tree search in only a certain direction?

In this chapter's examples we use an employee organization chart, as shown in Figure 10.1.

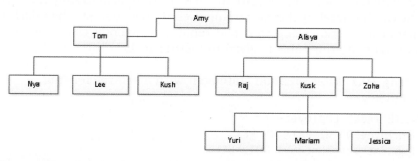

Figure 10.1 Organization chart used throughout Chapter 10

However, no matter what you ultimately choose, we encourage you to always include the adjacency list model in your database, which brings us to the first item of the chapter.

Note that certain vendors offer extensions to their products that make it easier to model hierarchy, such as Oracle's CONNECT BY clause and Microsoft SQL Server's HierarchyId data type, but the chapter focuses on solutions that work with standard SQL.

Item 58: Use an Adjacency List Model as the Starting Point

You likely have already seen an adjacency list model, even though you may not have heard the term before. All employees have supervisors. But supervisors themselves are actually employees, and they may have their own supervisors. So it is likely inappropriate to create a table named Employees and another named Supervisors—why should we have to shuttle records between two tables as people change position? Instead, what we would do is create a column on the table with a foreign key constraint that self-references its primary key, demonstrated in Figure 10.2.

ID	Name	Position	Supervisor
1	Amy Kok	President	*NULL*
2	Tom LaPlante	Manager	1
3	Aliya Ash	Manager	1
4	Nya Maeng	Associate	2
5	Lee Devi	Associate	2

Figure 10.2 Self-referencing the primary key

As you can see, we can model unlimited depths of hierarchy in a single table by creating a foreign key that refers to the same table's primary key. (In this case, SupervisorID references EmployeeID.) We can see that Lee Devi reports to Tom LaPlante because Lee's SupervisorID is 2, which is Tom's EmployeeID. In turn, Tom reports to Amy Kok, who is at the top level of the hierarchical chart because she has NULL for SupervisorID, indicating that she reports to nobody else. The statement to create this table is given in Listing 10.1.

Listing 10.1 Table creation statement with a self-referencing foreign key

```
CREATE TABLE Employees (
  EmployeeID int PRIMARY KEY,
  EmpName varchar(255) NOT NULL,
```

```
   EmpPosition varchar(255) NOT NULL,
   SupervisorID int NULL
);

ALTER TABLE Employees
   ADD FOREIGN KEY (SupervisorID)
     REFERENCES Employees (EmployeeID);
```

This model is simple to implement, and because of the way it is designed, it is impossible to build a hierarchy that is inconsistent. By "inconsistent," we do not mean that it will not guarantee that an employee will not be assigned to the wrong supervisor, but rather that we will not get different answers about who the supervisor of the employee is. Suppose for a moment that there is a reorganization of the company. We now want Nya to report to Lee, and then we want Tom to report to Aliysa. This is done with two UPDATE statements as shown in Listing 10.2.

Listing 10.2 Reorganizing the company's supervisors

```
UPDATE Employees SET SupervisorID = 5 WHERE EmployeeID = 4;
UPDATE Employees SET SupervisorID = 3 WHERE EmployeeID = 2;
```

If you are observant, you might have noticed that Lee still reports to Tom even after the reorganization. But we did not update his record. In fact, we do not have to, as you can see in Figure 10.3.

ID	Name	Position	Supervisor
1	Amy Bacock	President	*NULL*
3	Aliysa Ash	Manager	1
2	Tom LaPlante	Manager	3
5	Lee Devi	Associate	2
4	Nya Maeng	Associate	5

Figure 10.3 Employees and supervisors after the reorganization with modified records highlighted

So even though Lee's record was never directly modified, the data remains consistent. Such is the power of keeping data normalized!

And that brings us to an important point. This is the *only* model that is completely and properly normalized, requiring no metadata whatsoever. With no metadata to maintain, it is impossible to create an inconsistent hierarchy with this model.

However, the query performance required to extract data out of a hierarchy at an arbitrary depth is typically unacceptable. Listing 10.3 demonstrates a simplistic approach that works for a fixed level of depth (in this case, three levels).

Listing 10.3 Three levels of self-joins

```
SELECT e1.EmpName AS Employee, e2.EmpName AS Supervisor,
  e3.EmpName AS SupervisorsSupervisor
FROM Employees AS e1
  LEFT JOIN Employees AS e2
    ON e1.SupervisorID = e2.EmployeeID
  LEFT JOIN Employees AS e3
    ON e2.SupervisorID = e3.EmployeeID;
```

If you need to query at a different depth than three levels as shown in Listing 10.3, you would have to revise the query. A query that allows for variable depth using the adjacency list model will likely be slow and inefficient. For this reason, we suggest that you combine the adjacency list model with one of the other models described subsequently in this chapter. You would use the adjacency list model to build a consistent hierarchy, then derive the required metadata to accurately represent the other models.

Things to Remember

+ The adjacency list simply adds a column to the table and uses a foreign key that self-references the table's primary key. No metadata is needed.

+ Always use the adjacency list model to build a consistent hierarchy that is useful for the other models discussed in subsequent items.

Item 59: Use Nested Sets for Fast Querying Performance with Infrequent Updates

In the cited example of an organization chart, it might be uncommon to see the chart change frequently. The changes to the chart might be done once every few years, if even that often. In such cases, the hierarchy is a good candidate for nested sets, popularized by Joe Celko. It is easier to illustrate how it works than to describe it, so we will start with Figure 10.4. Pay particular attention to how the numbering is assigned, going from left to right, descending whenever there are children and ascending only when there are no more siblings. Note that each node gets a pair of numbers; "left" numbers are colored green, and "right" numbers are colored red.

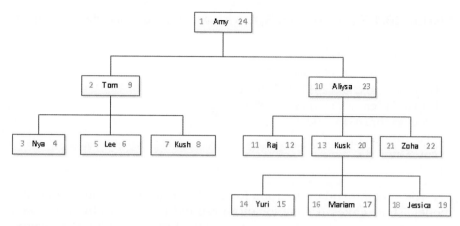

Figure 10.4 Organization chart with numbering for nested sets

Note that there are 12 employees, then consider that the topmost employee—Amy, the president—has 1 and 24 assigned to her "left" and "right," respectively. Employees who have no employees under them have numbers that are different by only one. In the case of Nya, her left-side number is 3 and her right-side number is 4. So each node in this hierarchy has a pair of numbers, and the range of numbers available to this hierarchy is 1 to 24, or double the number of nodes. The topmost node would have the difference of (<*numbers of nodes*> * 2) – 1. From this assignment, we can deduce a few things:

- A node with no children will have a difference of only 1 in its left and right numbers.

- Additionally, we can count numbers of nodes below a node with the formula (right – (left + 1))/2. In Aliya's case, it works out to be (23 – (10 + 1))/2, which is 6 nodes below him.

- We can determine all children of a given node by looking for nodes whose left and right numbers are both contained within the range of the considered node's own left and right numbers.

- Likewise, we can trace the ancestry by finding nodes whose left and right numbers are not contained within the considered node's own range.

So, if we continue with the same table structure we considered in Item 58, "Use an adjacency list model as the starting point," the only difference would be adding two more columns to provide the necessary metadata for describing the nested sets. Let's call them lft and rgt to avoid collisions with the SQL functions LEFT() and RIGHT(). Listing 10.4 on the next page shows how you can create a table that implements a nested set.

Listing 10.4 Table creation SQL with lft and rgt metadata columns for the nested set

```
CREATE TABLE Employees (
  EmployeeID int PRIMARY KEY,
  EmpName varchar(255) NOT NULL,
  EmpPosition varchar(255) NOT NULL,
  SupervisorID int NULL,
  lft int NULL,
  rgt int NULL
);
```

Per the recommendation from Item 58, we keep the adjacency list model. That makes it easy for us to rebuild the hierarchy if we need to do a wholesale change. Let's start with some examples of querying the hierarchy using nested sets.

Listing 10.5 shows how to find all children of a given node.

Listing 10.5 Query to get all children

```
SELECT e.*
FROM Employees AS e
WHERE e.lft >= @lft
  AND e.rgt <= @rgt;
```

Note that it is necessary to apply filters to both the lft and rgt columns to avoid getting nonsensical results because we want only the pair of lft and rgt numbers that is contained within the range of the given pair of @lft and @rgt. Alternatively, you can use > and < instead of >= and <=, respectively, if you do not want to include the given node for which you are finding children in the result.

Listing 10.6 demonstrates the opposite scenario where we want to find all ancestors of a given node.

Listing 10.6 Query to get all ancestors

```
SELECT *
FROM Employees AS e
WHERE e.lft <= @lft
  AND e.rgt >= @rgt;
```

Similar to what you saw in Listing 10.5, we have to apply against both lft and rgt to ensure that we do not get other parent nodes that are not the ancestors of that node.

We would need many more pages to show examples of how you can manage the nested sets using stored procedures or triggers, but the queries should at least give you an idea of how you can rebuild the hierarchy. For example, you can create a stored procedure that contains iterative logic to assign the lft and rgt numbers to each node based on the current SupervisorID value.

The biggest downside with the nested set model is that a change to the hierarchy, especially in cases of moving a node from one branch to another branch, almost always requires updating the entire table's lft and rgt metadata to stay consistent. If you anticipate that your hierarchy will change more often, consider the approaches discussed in subsequent items. The other issue to consider is that the nested sets as shown here really work only if the hierarchy has a single root node. If you have multiple hierarchies with independent roots, additional logic would be necessary to filter to only a given hierarchy.

Things to Remember

- You must maintain the nested sets model using a stored procedure to encapsulate the logic behind building the set and assigning correct left and right numbers to each node.

- The nested sets model is not good for frequent updates because changes to the hierarchy require renumbering several other nodes, likely the entire table, which makes it susceptible to deadlocking.

- Getting a count requires no lookups of other records as it can be calculated from the lft and rgt metadata columns, making the nested sets model very efficient for maintaining statistics.

- The nested sets model works best with only a single hierarchy with a single root node. If you need multiple hierarchies and therefore multiple root nodes, consider other models.

Item 60: Use a Materialized Path for Simple Setup and Limited Searching

A materialized path is relatively simple to set up and much easier to understand than nested sets. Conceptually, it is no different from what we use for file system paths. Instead of folders and files, we use the primary keys so that we can describe the hierarchy in a much more compact format. We can create the Employees table containing an extra column to hold the needed metadata for the materialized path model as depicted in Listing 10.7.

Listing 10.7 Table creation SQL with a column for materialized path metadata

```
CREATE TABLE Employees (
  EmployeeID int PRIMARY KEY,
```

```
  EmpName varchar(255) NOT NULL,
  EmpPosition varchar(255) NOT NULL,
  SupervisorID int NULL,
  HierarchyPath varchar(255)
);
```

We would then populate the data similarly to Figure 10.5.

ID	Name	Position	Supervisor	Path
1	Amy Kok	President	*NULL*	1
2	Tom LaPlante	Manager	1	1/2
3	Aliya Ash	Manager	1	1/3
4	Nya Maeng	Associate	2	1/2/4
5	Lee Devi	Associate	2	1/2/5
6	Kush Itō	Associate	2	1/2/6
7	Raj Pavlov	Senior Editor	3	1/3/7
8	Kusk Pérez	Senior Developer	3	1/3/8
9	Zoha Larsson	Senior Writer	3	1/3/9
10	Yuri Lee	Developer	8	1/3/8/10
11	Mariam Davis	Developer	8	1/3/8/11
12	Jessica Yosef	Developer	8	1/3/8/12

Figure 10.5 Employees with materialized path metadata

Note that there is no universal convention for this solution. The slash is as good a placeholder as any other for separating the primary keys, and in the interest of making the queries simpler, the example includes both root and reflexive nodes at the expense of increased storage. It is possible to omit the root and reflexive nodes, but you must revise your queries accordingly for cases where you need to include the record representing itself or the root node. As you look at the figure, note that the materialized path method makes it easy to find children and how deep a node is.

Listing 10.8 shows sample SQL for finding all children within a given node.

Listing 10.8 Finding all children for a node

```
SELECT e.*
FROM Employees AS e
WHERE e.HierarchyPath LIKE @NodePath + '%';
```

In order to find all employees under Tom LaPlante's charge, you would specify "1/2/" for the @NodePath. If you are concerned about performance, indexing the HierarchyPath column should relieve issues, at least where wildcards appear only at the end of the string. As you learned in Item 28, "Write sargable queries to ensure that the engine will use indexes," the query given in Listing 10.8 is sargable because we append the wildcard only to the end.

We can also find all ancestors of a given node, as shown in Listing 10.9, but alas, it is not sargable.

Listing 10.9 Finding all ancestors for a node

```
SELECT e.*
FROM Employees AS e
WHERE CHARINDEX(CONCAT('/',
  CAST(e.EmployeeID AS varchar(11)), '/'), @NodePath) > 0;
```

Note

The sample is specific to SQL Server; all DBMSs have different implementations of the CHARINDEX() and CAST() functions.

The @Nodepath would reference the employee's own path. So to find Lee's ancestor, you need to pass in "1/2/5." So, if your requirement is such that you need to search the tree, especially in the middle or at the bottom, extensively and fast, the materialized path may not be the best solution for you. You will run into similar problems whenever you need to deal with branches that require you to insert wildcards in the middle of the predicate value. A possible option is to create another column that stores the hierarchy in the reverse direction and index it. However, as this includes both storage for data and an index, it is quite an expensive way to do it.

Note also that we used varchar(255) as the data type for the HierarchyPath column. You will find that most, if not all, database engines place a restriction on how many characters you are allowed to index your text columns. That also places a limit on the length of your hierarchy path. The worst part is that you might break the limit because the hierarchy is too wide (e.g., there are large keys taking several digits each between each level) or because the hierarchy is too deep. So it is not trivial to proactively check whether you are in danger of exceeding the character allocation for the column. If your engine permits, a possible option is to use varchar(MAX) to allow for effectively unlimited storage and then index on only the prefix, with the caveat that queries could return strange results or have inconsistent performance.

Things to Remember

✦ Materialized path has the advantage of being fairly simple to understand and follow, because it is based on familiar metaphors such as file system paths.

◆ It is difficult to clearly identify the limit of the design because there is no simple way of knowing in advance if you will break the character limit of the index because a hierarchy is too deep or too wide. For that reason, you must place an arbitrary and conservative restriction on how large the hierarchy can be to avoid problems.

◆ The search on materialized path is effective in only one direction because you cannot create a sargable query when there are wildcards at the start or within the predicate, rather than at the end. Factor this consideration into your design.

Item 61: Use Ancestry Traversal Closure for Complex Searching

The last option available for managing hierarchical data is to use an ancestry closure table. This is basically a relational approach to the materialized path method we saw in Item 60, "Use a materialized path for simple setup and limited searching." Instead of using a string in a column of a table, we use a second table, and for each "connection" between nodes, we create a record for the metadata. Unlike the adjacency list model from Item 58, "Use an adjacency list model as the starting point," where we record only the immediate connection, we record all possible connections irrespective of how many nodes there are between the two nodes being considered. Listing 10.10 shows how we could set it up for the Employees table.

Listing 10.10 Table creation SQL with an ancestry table

```
CREATE TABLE Employees (
  EmployeeID int NOT NULL PRIMARY KEY,
  EmpName varchar(255) NOT NULL,
  EmpPosition varchar(255) NOT NULL,
  SupervisorID int NULL,
);

CREATE TABLE EmployeesAncestry (
  SupervisedEmployeeID int NOT NULL,
  SupervisingEmployeeID int NOT NULL,
  Distance int NOT NULL,
  PRIMARY KEY (SupervisedEmployeeID, SupervisingEmployeeID)
);

ALTER TABLE EmployeesAncestry
  ADD CONSTRAINT FK_EmployeesAncestry_SupervisingEmployeeID
    FOREIGN KEY (SupervisingEmployeeID)
      REFERENCES Employees (EmployeeID);
```

```
ALTER TABLE EmployeesAncestry
  ADD CONSTRAINT FK_EmployeesAncestry_SupervisedEmployeeID
    FOREIGN KEY (SupervisedEmployeedID)
      REFERENCES Employees (EmployeeID);
```

Note that, unlike in other models, the metadata is now stored in a separate table, EmployeesAncestry. We would then populate the data as shown in Figure 10.6.

ID	Name	Position	Supervisor
1	Amy Kok	President	*NULL*
2	Tom LaPlante	Manager	1
3	Aliya Ash	Manager	1
4	Nya Maeng	Associate	2
5	Lee Devi	Associate	2
6	Kush Itō	Associate	2
7	Raj Pavlov	Senior Editor	3
8	Kusk Pérez	Senior Developer	3
9	Zoha Larsson	Senior Writer	3
10	Yuri Lee	Developer	8
11	Mariam Davis	Developer	8
12	Jessica Yosef	Developer	8

Supervised EmployeeID	Supervising EmployeeID	Distance
1	1	0
2	1	1
2	2	0
3	1	1
3	3	0
4	1	2
4	2	1
4	4	0
5	1	2
5	2	1
5	5	0

Figure 10.6 Employees with ancestry metadata records; ancestry table truncated

For brevity, we do not show all records that should be in the ancestry table, but Figure 10.6 should show enough so that you get an idea of how you should populate the tables. Consider Nya Maeng, an associate, who is supervised by Tom LaPlante, who in turn is supervised by Amy Kok. That is a total of two connections among three nodes. We must enumerate all possible connections for Nya. For that reason, we create three records:

1. A reflexive record where Nya is both the supervised and supervising employee, with a distance of 0

2. A record that identifies Nya's immediate supervisor, Tom, as the supervising employee, with a distance of 1

3. A record that identifies Amy—because she supervises Tom—as the supervising employee, but with a distance of 2

Because all possible connections are enumerated in the ancestry table, you can now simply join the ancestry table to the data table to trace the complete path from a given node to whatever node interests you.

As with materialized paths, there is no universal convention for this solution, so you will see some variances out there. We decided to use Distance, though you might see others refer to Depth. We feel that the term *depth* is misleading because it implies the depth of the node from the root, but most of the time we are more interested in finding out how many levels there are between two nodes, neither of which is necessarily the root of the tree. Thus, we use the term *distance*. We also need to manually maintain that information, as certain classes of queries will depend on distance, which is useful when doing partial tree extraction. Also, it is common to call the columns in the ancestry table ancestor and descendant, but again, this is relative; one is an ancestor to the other and is equally a descendant of yet another. Also, labeling columns as SupervisingEmployeeID helps in understanding how to write the queries, as you will see shortly. Finally, there is the consideration of whether to include reflexive records—you might feel that records such as (1, 1, 0) and (2, 2, 0), which indicate that Amy supervises herself and Tom supervises himself, are superficial. However, not including the reflexive records in the ancestry table means you have more complicated queries if you need to show the sought employee within the result.

The biggest downside of using an ancestry table is that maintenance of the table is much more involved because you will likely insert and delete several records when changing the hierarchy in order to keep the metadata accurate. This can be alleviated by wrapping the logic into a stored procedure, and if you continue to use the adjacency list model, you have the option of using table triggers to monitor the SupervisorID column of the Employees table to automatically update the ancestry table. Though this is a comparatively more normalized solution, if the metadata in an ancestry table is not maintained correctly, you could potentially end up with an inconsistent hierarchy and thus obtain wrong results for your queries.

Listing 10.11 shows the sample SQL for finding all children within a given node.

Listing 10.11 Finding all children for a node

```
SELECT e.*
FROM Employees AS e
  INNER JOIN EmployeesAncestry AS a
    ON e.EmployeeID = a.SupervisedEmployeeID
WHERE a.SupervisingEmployeeID = @EmployeeID
  AND a.Distance > 0;
```

In order to find all employees under Tom LaPlante's charge, you would specify "3" for the @EmployeeID. Unlike with other methods, it is very easy to further restrict the depth. For example, we could add a criterion that Distance must be between 1 and 3 to list only employees who are supervised under Tom up to two levels apart.

We can also find all ancestors of a given node, as shown in Listing 10.12, and unlike the equivalent query for materialized path discussed in Item 60, it is still sargable.

Listing 10.12 Finding all ancestors for a node

```
SELECT e.*
FROM Employees AS e
  INNER JOIN EmployeesAncestry AS a
    ON e.EmployeeID = a.SupervisedEmployeeID
WHERE e.EmployeeID = @EmployeeID
  AND a.Distance > 0;
```

As you see, the query is similar to the one shown in Listing 10.11, the only difference being that we reference the SupervisedEmployeeID column instead of the SupervisingEmployeeID column in the join. This should illustrate the earlier point about why it might be desirable to use a more descriptive name than just "ancestor" and "descendant."

We think you will find that queries about the hierarchical model are quite straightforward and mainly are done with a join between the data table and the ancestry table, or in some cases with an existence check. For example, to find all nodes that have no children, we would use NOT EXISTS as shown in Listing 10.13.

Listing 10.13 Finding all nodes with no children

```
SELECT e.*
FROM Employees AS e
WHERE NOT EXISTS (
  SELECT NULL
  FROM EmployeesAncestry AS a
  WHERE e.EmployeeID = a.SupervisingEmployeeID
    AND a.Distance > 0
);
```

Observe that because we opted to include reflexive records in the ancestry table, we have to exclude those when we search for nodes other than the reflexive records. Had we opted not to keep reflexive records within the ancestry table, you would find that you need to UNION the results from Listings 10.11 and 10.12 with the record of the sought employee. That would make the queries from Listings 10.11 and 10.12 more convoluted, but it would simplify the queries similarly to what is shown in Listing 10.13.

Things to Remember

✦ Consider the ancestry closure traversal model for when you require both frequent updates and ease of searching, especially in the middle of a tree, to justify the extra complexity of maintaining an ancestry table.

✦ Though it is normalized, failing to keep the metadata in the ancestry table up to date could result in incorrect query results. This can be alleviated by using triggers on the `Employees` table to automatically modify the ancestry table, but this is not free.

Appendix

Date and Time Types, Operations, and Functions

Each database system has a variety of functions that you can use to calculate or manipulate date and time values. Each database system also has its own rules regarding data types and date and time arithmetic. The SQL Standard specifically defines three functions, CURRENT_DATE(), CURRENT_TIME(), and CURRENT_TIMESTAMP(), but many commercial database systems do not support all three function calls. To help you work with date and time values in your database system, we provide a brief summary of the data types and arithmetic operations supported. Following that, we have compiled a list of functions for several of the major database systems that you can use to work with date and time values. The lists in this appendix include the function name and a brief description of its use.[1] Consult your database documentation for the specific syntax to use with each function.

IBM DB2

Data Types Supported

DATE

TIME

TIMESTAMP

Arithmetic Operations Supported

Value1	Operator	Value2	Result
DATE	+/−	year duration, month duration, day duration, date duration	DATE

continues

---

1. Most of this material previously appeared in *SQL Queries for Mere Mortals, Third Edition* by John L. Viescas and Michael J. Hernandez (Addison-Wesley, 2014).

Value1	Operator	Value2	Result
DATE	+/−	TIME	TIMESTAMP
TIME	+/−	hour duration, minute duration, second duration, time duration	TIME
TIMESTAMP	+/−	date duration, time duration, date and time duration	TIMESTAMP
DATE	−	DATE	date duration (DECIMAL(8,0) a value containing yyyymmdd)
TIME	−	TIME	time duration (DECIMAL(6,0) a value containing hhmmss)
TIMESTAMP	−	TIMESTAMP	time duration (DECIMAL(20,6) a value containing yyyymmddhhmmss.microseconds)

Functions

Function Name	Description
ADD_MONTHS(<*expression*>, <*number*>)	Adds a specified number of months to a date or timestamp value specified by the expression.
CURDATE	Obtains the current date value.
CURRENT_DATE	Obtains the current date value.
CURRENT_TIME	Obtains the current time value in the local time zone.
CURRENT_TIMESTAMP	Obtains the current date and time in the local time zone.
CURTIME	Obtains the current time value in the local time zone.
DATE(<*expression*>)	Evaluates the expression and returns a date.

continues

Function Name	Description
DAY(*<expression>*)	Evaluates the expression and returns the day part of a date, timestamp, or date interval.
DAYNAME(*<expression>*)	Evaluates the expression and returns the name of the day of a date, timestamp, or date interval.
DAYOFMONTH(*<expression>*)	Evaluates the expression and returns the day part (value between 1 and 31) of a date or timestamp.
DAYOFWEEK(*<expression>*)	Evaluates the expression and returns the day number of the week, where 1 = Sunday.
DAYOFWEEK_ ISO(*<expression>*)	Evaluates the expression and returns the day number of the week, where 1 = Monday.
DAYOFYEAR(*<expression>*)	Evaluates the expression and returns the day number (value between 1 and 366) of the year.
DAYS(*<expression>*)	Evaluates the expression and returns the number of days since January 1, 0001, plus 1.
HOUR(*<expression>*)	Evaluates the expression and returns the hour part of a time or timestamp.
JULIAN_DAY(*<expression>*)	Evaluates the expression and returns the number of days from January 1, 4713 BC, to the date specified in the expression.
LAST_DAY(*<expression>*)	Returns the last day of the month indicated by the date in the expression.
MICROSECOND(*<expression>*)	Evaluates the timestamp or duration in the expression and returns the microsecond part.
MIDNIGHT_ SECONDS(*<expression>*)	Evaluates the time or timestamp and returns the number of seconds between midnight and the time in the expression.
MINUTE(*<expression>*)	Evaluates the expression and returns the minute part of a time, timestamp, or time interval.
MONTH(*<expression>*)	Evaluates the expression and returns the month part of a date, timestamp, or date interval.
MONTHNAME(*<expression>*)	Evaluates the expression and returns the name of the month of a date, timestamp, or date interval.
MONTHS_ BETWEEN(*<expression1>*, *<expression2>*)	Evaluates both expressions as a date or timestamp and returns the approximate number of months between the two values. If *<expression1>* is later than *<expression2>*, the value is positive.

continues

Function Name	Description
NEXT_DAY(<*expression*>, <*dayname*>)	Evaluates the expression and returns as a timestamp the date of the first day specified in <*dayname*> (a string containing MON, TUE, etc.) following the date in the expression.
NOW	Obtains the current date and time in the local time zone.
QUARTER(<*expression*>)	Evaluates the expression and returns the number of the quarter part of the year in which the date in the expression occurs.
ROUND_ TIMESTAMP(<*expression*>, <*format string*>)	Evaluates the expression and rounds it to the nearest interval specified in the format string.
SECOND(<*expression*>)	Evaluates the expression and returns the seconds part of a time, timestamp, or time interval.
TIME(<*expression*>)	Evaluates the expression and returns the time part of a time or timestamp value.
TIMESTAMP(<*expression1*>, [<*expression2*>])	Converts separate date (<*expression1*>) and time (<*expression2*>) values into a timestamp.
TIMESTAMP_ FORMAT(<*expression1*>, <*expression2*>)	Returns a timestamp by formatting the string in <*expression1*> using the format string in <*expression2*>.
TIMESTAMP_ ISO(<*expression*>)	Evaluates the date, time, or timestamp in the expression and returns a timestamp. If the expression contains only a date, the timestamp contains that date and zero for the time. If the expression contains only a time, the timestamp contains the current date and the time specified.
TIMESTAMPDIFF(<*numeric expression*>, <*string expression*>)	The numeric expression must contain a code numeric value where 1 = microseconds, 2 = seconds, 4 = minutes, 8 = hours, 16 = days, 32 = weeks, 64 = months, 128 = quarters, and 256 = years. The string expression must be the result of subtracting two timestamps and converting the result to a string. The function returns the estimated number of requested intervals represented by the string.
TRUNC_ TIMESTAMP(<*expression*>, <*format string*>)	Evaluates the expression and truncates it to the nearest interval specified in the format string.

continues

Function Name	Description
WEEK(<*expression*>)	Evaluates the expression and returns the week number of the date part of the value, where January 1 starts the first week.
WEEK_ISO(<*expression*>)	Evaluates the expression and returns the week number of the date part of the value, where the first week of the year is the first week containing a Thursday.
YEAR(<*expression*>)	Evaluates the expression and returns the year part of a date or timestamp.

Microsoft Access

Data Types Supported

DATETIME

Note

Although the Access user interface displays the data type name as Date/Time, the correct name for CREATE TABLE statements is DATETIME.

Arithmetic Operations Supported

Value1	Operator	Value2	Result
DATETIME	+	DATETIME	DATETIME. The result is the date and time that would be obtained by adding the number of days and fractions of a day from the second value to the number of days and fraction of a day in the second value. December 31, 1899, is day 0.
DATETIME	–	DATETIME	INTEGER or DOUBLE. The result is the number of days (if date values only) or the number of days and fractions of a day (if either DATETIME value contains a time).
DATETIME	+/–	integer	DATETIME

Adds or subtracts the number of days in the integer. 0 is December 31, 1899. |

continues

Value1	Operator	Value2	Result
DATETIME	+/−	fraction	DATETIME Adds or subtracts the time represented by the fraction. 0.5 = 12 hours.
DATETIME	+/−	integer.fraction	DATETIME

Functions

Function Name	Description
CDate(<*expression*>)	Converts the expression to a date value.
Date()	Obtains the current date value.
DateAdd(<*interval*>, <number>, <expression>)	Adds the specified number of the interval to the DATETIME expression.
DateDiff(<*interval*>, <*expression1*>, <*expression2*>, <*firstdayofweek*>, <*firstdayofyear*>)	Returns the specified number of intervals between the DATETIME in <*expression1*> and the DATETIME in <*expression2*>. You can optionally specify a first day of the week other than Sunday and a first week of the year to start on January 1, the first week that has at least four days, or the first full week.
DatePart(<*interval*>, <*expression*>, <*firstdayofweek*>, <*firstdayofyear*>)	Extracts the part of the date or time from the expression as specified by the interval. You can optionally specify a first day of the week other than Sunday and a first week of the year to start on January 1, the first week that has at least four days, or the first full week.
DateSerial(<*year*>, <*month*>, <*day*>)	Returns the date value corresponding to the specified year, month, and day.
DateValue(<*expression*>)	Evaluates the expression and returns a date value as a DATETIME data type. (See also TimeValue().)
Day(<*expression*>)	Evaluates the expression and returns the day part of a date.
Hour(<*expression*>)	Evaluates the expression and returns the hour part of a time.
IsDate(<*expression*>)	Evaluates the expression and returns True if the expression is a valid date value.
Minute(<*expression*>)	Evaluates the expression and returns the minute part of a time value.

continues

Function Name	Description
Month(<*expression*>)	Evaluates the expression and returns the month part of a date value.
MonthName(<*expression*>, <*abbreviate*>)	Evaluates the expression (which must be an integer value from 1 to 12) and returns the equivalent month name. The name is abbreviated if the <*abbreviate*> argument is True.
Now()	Obtains the current date and time value in the local time zone.
Second(<*expression*>)	Evaluates the expression and returns the seconds part of a time.
Time()	Obtains the current time value in the local time zone.
TimeSerial(<*hour*>, <*minute*>, <*second*>)	Returns the time value corresponding to the specified hour, minute, and second.
TimeValue(<*expression*>)	Evaluates the expression and returns the time portion. (See also DateValue().)
WeekDay(<*expression*>, <*firstdayofweek*>)	Evaluates the expression and returns an integer representing the day of the week. You can optionally specify a first day of the week other than Sunday.
WeekDayName(<*daynumber*>, <*abbreviate*>, <*firstdayofweek*>)	Returns the day of the week according to the specified day number. You can optionally ask to have the name abbreviated, and you can specify a first day of the week other than Sunday.
Year(<*expression*>)	Evaluates the expression and returns the year part of a date as an integer.

Microsoft SQL Server

Data Types Supported

date

time

smalldatetime

datetime

datetime2

datetimeoffset

Arithmetic Operations Supported

Value1	Operator	Value2	Result
datetime	+	datetime	datetime Value is the result of adding the number of days and fractions of a day in each value. January 1, 1900, is day 0.
datetime	−	datetime	Number of days and fractions of days between the two values.
datetime	+/−	integer	datetime Adds or subtracts the number of days in the integer.
datetime	+/−	fraction	datetime Adds or subtracts the time represented by the fraction. 0.5 = 12 hours.
datetime	+/−	integer.fraction	datetime
smalldatetime	+	smalldatetime	smalldatetime Value is the result of adding the number of days and fractions of a day in each value. January 1, 1900, is day 0.
smalldatetime	+/−	integer	smalldatetime Adds or subtracts the number of days in the integer.
smalldatetime	+	fraction	smalldatetime Adds the time represented by the fraction. 0.5 = 12 hours.
smalldatetime	+	integer.fraction	smalldatetime

Functions

Function Name	Description
CURRENT_TIMESTAMP	Obtains the current date and time in the local time zone.
DATEADD(*<interval>*, *<number>*, *<expression>*)	Adds the specified number of the interval to the date or datetime expression.

continues

Function Name	Description
DATEDIFF(*<interval>*, *<expression1>*, *<expression2>*)	Returns the specified number of intervals between the datetime in *<expression1>* and the datetime in *<expression2>*.
DATEFROMPARTS(*<year>*, *<month>*, *<day>*)	Returns the date value for a specified year, month, and day.
DATENAME(*<interval>*, *<expression>*)	Evaluates the expression and returns a string containing the name of the interval specified. If the interval is a month or a day of the week, the name is spelled out.
DATEPART(*<interval>*, *<expression>*)	Extracts (as an integer) the part of the date or time from the expression as specified by the interval.
DATETIMEFROMPARTS(*<year>*, *<month>*, *<day>*, *<hour>*, *<minute>*, *<second>*, *<milliseconds>*)	Returns the datetime value for a specified year, month, day, hour, minute, second, and milliseconds.
DATETIME2FROMPARTS(*<year>*, *<month>*, *<day>*, *<hour>*, *<minute>*, *<second>*, *<fractions>*, *<precision>*)	Returns the datetime2 value for a specified year, month, day, hour, minute, second, and fraction with the specified precision.
DAY(*<expression>*)	Evaluates the expression and returns the day part of a date.
EOMONTH(*<date>* [,*<months>*])	Adds the optional number of months to the date specified and returns the last day of that month.
GETDATE()	Obtains the current date as a datetime value.
GETUTCDATE()	Obtains the current UTC (Coordinated Universal Time) date as a datetime value.
ISDATE(*<expression>*)	Evaluates the expression and returns 1 if the expression is a valid date value.
MONTH(*<expression>*)	Evaluates the expression and returns the month part of a date value as an integer.
SMALLDATETIMEFROMPARTS(*<year>*, *<month>*, *<day>*, *<hour>*, *<minute>*)	Returns the smalldatetime value for a specified year, month, day, hour, and minute.
SWITCHOFFSET(*<expression>*, *<offset>*)	Changes the time zone offset of the expression (a datetimeoffset) value to the specified offset and returns a datetimeoffset.

continues

Function Name	Description
SYSDATETIME()	Returns the current date and time as a datetime2 value.
SYSDATETIMEOFFSET()	Returns the current date and time (including time zone offset) as a datetimeoffset value.
SYSUTCDATETIME()	Returns the current UTC date and time as a datetime2 value.
TIMEFROMPARTS(*<hour>*, *<minute>*, *<second>*, *<fraction>*, *<precision>*)	Returns the time value for a specified hour, minute, second, and fraction with the specified precision.
TODATETIMEOFFSET(*<expression>*, *<offset>*)	Converts the expression (a datetime2 value) using the specified time zone offset and returns a datetimeoffset value.
YEAR(*<expression>*)	Evaluates the expression and returns the year part of a date as an integer.

MySQL

Data Types Supported

DATE

DATETIME

TIMESTAMP

TIME

YEAR

Arithmetic Operations Supported

Value1	Operator	Value2	Result
DATE	+/−	INTERVAL: year quarter month week day	DATE

continues

Value1	Operator	Value2	Result
DATETIME	+/−	INTERVAL: year quarter month week day hour minute second	DATETIME
TIMESTAMP	+/−	INTERVAL: year quarter month week day hour minute second	TIMESTAMP
TIME	+/−	INTERVAL: hour minute second	TIME

Note

The syntax for intervals is INTERVAL *<expr>* *<unit>*, where *<unit>* is one of the keywords listed above, as in INTERVAL 31 day or INTERVAL 15 minute.

It is also legal to add an integer of decimal value to or subtract it from any of the date and time data types, but MySQL first converts the date or time value to a number and then performs the operation. For example, adding 30 to the date value 2012-11-15 yields the number 20121145. Adding 100 to the time value 12:20:00 yields 122100. Be sure to use the INTERVAL keyword when performing date and time arithmetic.

Functions

Function Name	Description
ADDDATE(<*expression*>, <*days*>)	Adds the specified number of days to the date value in the expression.
ADDDATE(<*expression*>, INTERVAL <*amount*> <*units*>)	Adds the specified interval quantity to the date value in the expression.
ADDTIME(<*expression*>, <*time*>)	Adds the specified amount of time to the time or DATETIME expression value.
CONVERT_TZ(<*expression*>, <*from tz*>, <*to tz*>)	Converts the DATETIME expression from the specified time zone to the specified time zone.
CURRENT_DATE, CURDATE()	Obtains the current DATE value.
CURRENT_TIME, CURTIME()	Obtains the current TIME value in the local time zone.
CURRENT_TIMESTAMP	Obtains the current date and time in the local time zone as a DATETIME value.
DATE(<*expression*>)	Extracts the date from a DATETIME expression.
DATE_ADD(<*expression*>, INTERVAL <*interval*> <*quantity*>)	Adds the specified interval quantity to the date or DATETIME value in the expression.
DATE_SUB(<*expression*>, INTERVAL <*interval*> <*quantity*>)	Subtracts the specified interval quantity from the DATE or DATETIME value in the expression.
DATEDIFF(<*expression1*>, <*expression2*>)	Subtracts the second DATETIME expression from the first DATETIME expression and returns the number of days between the two.
DAY(<*expression*>)	Evaluates the expression and returns the day part of a DATE as a number from 1 to 31.
DAYNAME(<*expression*>)	Evaluates the expression and returns the day name of the DATE or DATETIME value.
DAYOFMONTH(<*expression*>)	Evaluates the expression and returns the day part of a DATE as a number from 1 to 31.
DAYOFWEEK(<*expression*>)	Evaluates the expression and returns the day number within the week for the DATE or DATETIME value, where 1 = Sunday.
DAYOFYEAR(<*expression*>)	Evaluates the expression and returns the day number of the year, a value from 1 to 366.

continues

Function Name	Description
EXTRACT(<*unit*> FROM <*expression*>)	Evaluates the expression and returns the unit portion (such as year or month) specified.
FROM_DAYS(<*number*>)	Returns the date that is the number of days since December 31, 1 BC. Day 366 is January 1, 0001.
HOUR(<*expression*>)	Evaluates the expression and returns the hour part of a TIME.
LAST_DAY(<*expression*>)	Returns the last day of the month indicated by the date in the expression.
LOCALTIME, LOCALTIMESTAMP	See the NOW() function.
MAKEDATE(<*year*>, <*dayofyear*>)	Returns a date for the specified year and day of the year (1 – 366).
MAKETIME(<*hour*>, <*minute*>, <*second*>)	Returns a TIME for the specified hour, minute, and second.
MICROSECOND(<*expression*>)	Evaluates the expression and returns the microsecond portion of a TIME or DATETIME value.
MINUTE(<*expression*>)	Evaluates the expression and returns the minute part of a TIME or DATETIME value.
MONTH(<*expression*>)	Evaluates the expression and returns the month part of a DATE value.
MONTHNAME(<*expression*>)	Evaluates the expression and returns the name of the month of a DATE or DATETIME value.
NOW()	Obtains the current date and time value in the local time zone as a DATETIME value.
QUARTER(<*expression*>)	Evaluates the expression and returns the number of the quarter part of the year in which the date in the expression occurs.
SECOND(<*expression*>)	Evaluates the expression and returns the seconds part of a time or DATETIME value.
STR_TO_DATE(<*expression*>, <*format*>)	Evaluates the expression according to the format specified and returns a DATE, DATETIME, or TIME value.
SUBDATE(<*expression*>, INTERVAL <*interval*> <*quantity*>)	See the DATE_SUB() function.

continues

Function Name	Description
SUBTIME(<*expression1*>, <*expression2*>)	Subtracts the TIME in <*expression2*> from the DATETIME or TIME in <*expression1*> and returns a TIME or DATETIME answer.
TIME(<*expression*>)	Evaluates the expression and returns the time part of a time or DATETIME value.
TIME_TO_SEC(<*expression*>)	Evaluates the time in the expression and returns the number of seconds.
TIMEDIFF(<*expression1*>, <*expression2*>)	Subtracts the TIME or DATETIME value in <*expression2*> from the TIME or DATETIME value in <*expression1*> and returns the difference.
TIMESTAMP(<*expression*>)	Evaluates the expression and returns a DATETIME value.
TIMESTAMP(<*expression1*>, <*expression2*>)	Adds the TIME in <*expression2*> to the DATE or DATETIME in <*expression1*> and returns a DATETIME value.
TIMESTAMPADD(<*interval*>, <*number*>, <*expression*>)	Adds the specified number of the interval to the DATE or DATETIME expression.
TIMESTAMPDIFF(<*interval*>, <*expression1*>, <*expression2*>)	Returns the specified number of intervals between the DATE or DATETIME in <*expression1*> and the DATE or DATETIME in <*expression2*>.
TO_DAYS(<*expression*>)	Evaluates the DATE in the expression and returns the number of days since year 0.
UTC_DATE	Obtains the current UTC date.
UTC_TIME	Obtains the current UTC time.
UTC_TIMESTAMP	Obtains the current UTC date and time.
WEEK(<*expression*>, <*mode*>)	Evaluates the expression and returns the week number of the date part of the value using the mode specified.
WEEKDAY(<*expression*>)	Evaluates the expression and returns an integer representing the day of the week, where 0 is Monday.
WEEKOFYEAR(<*expression*>)	Evaluates the date expression and returns the week number (1–53), assuming the first week has more than three days.
YEAR(<*expression*>)	Evaluates the expression and returns the YEAR part of a date.

Oracle

Data Types Supported

DATE

TIMESTAMP

INTERVAL YEAR TO MONTH

INTERVAL DAY TO SECOND

Arithmetic Operations Supported

Value1	Operator	Value2	Result
DATE	+/−	INTERVAL	DATE
DATE	+/−	numeric	DATE
DATE	−	DATE	numeric (days and fractions of a day)
DATE	−	TIMESTAMP	INTERVAL
INTERVAL	+	DATE	DATE
INTERVAL	+	TIMESTAMP	TIMESTAMP
INTERVAL	+/−	INTERVAL	INTERVAL
INTERVAL	*	numeric	INTERVAL
INTERVAL	/	numeric	INTERVAL

Functions

Function Name	Description
ADD_MONTHS(<*expression*>, <*integer*>)	Returns the value of the expression (a DATE) plus the specified number of months.
CURRENT_DATE	Obtains the current DATE value.
CURRENT_TIMESTAMP	Obtains the current date, time, and timestamp in the local time zone.
DBTIMEZONE	Obtains the time zone of the database.
EXTRACT(<*interval*> FROM <*expression*>)	Evaluates the expression and returns the requested interval (year, month, day, etc.).
LOCALTIMESTAMP	Obtains the current date and time in the local time zone.

continues

Function Name	Description
MONTHS_ BETWEEN(*<expression1>*, *<expression2>*)	Calculates the months and fractions of months between *<expression2>* and *<expression1>*.
NEW_TIME(*<expression>*, *<timezone1>*, *<timezone2>*)	Evaluates the date and time expression as though it is the first time zone and returns the date and time in the second time zone.
NEXT_DAY(*<expression>*, *dayname>*)	Evaluates the expression and returns the date of the first day specified in *<dayname>* (a string containing MONDAY, TUESDAY, etc.) following the date in the expression.
NUMTODSINTERVAL(*<number>*, *<unit>*)	Converts the number to an interval in the unit specified (DAY, HOUR, MINUTE, SECOND).
NUMTOYMINTERVAL(*<number>*, *<unit>*)	Converts the number to an interval in the unit specified (YEAR, MONTH).
ROUND(*<expression>*, *<interval>*)	Rounds a date value to the interval specified.
SESSIONTIMEZONE	Obtains the time zone of the current session.
SYSDATE	Obtains the current date and time on the database server.
SYSTIMESTAMP	Obtains the current date, time, and time zone on the database server.
TO_DATE(*<expression>*, *<format>*)	Converts the string expression to a date data type using the format specified.
TO_DSINTERVAL(*<expression>*)	Converts the string expression to a days-to-seconds interval.
TO_TIMESTAMP(*<expression>*, *<format>*)	Converts the string expression to a TIMESTAMP using the format specified.
TO_TIMESTAMP_ TZ(*<expression>*, *<format>*)	Converts the string expression to a TIMESTAMP with time zone data type using the format specified.
TO_YMINTERVAL	Converts the string expression to a years-to-months interval.
TRUNC(*<expression>*, *<interval>*)	Truncates a date value to the interval specified.

PostgreSQL

Data Types Supported

DATE

TIME (with or without time zone)

TIMESTAMP (with or without time zone)

INTERVAL

Arithmetic Operations Supported

Value1	Operator	Value2	Result
DATE	+/−	INTERVAL	TIMESTAMP
DATE	+/−	numeric	DATE
DATE	+	TIME	TIMESTAMP
DATE	−	DATE	INTEGER
TIME	+/−	INTERVAL	TIME
TIME	−	TIME	INTERVAL
TIMESTAMP	+/−	INTERVAL	TIMESTAMP
TIMESTAMP	−	TIMESTAMP	INTERVAL
INTERVAL	+/−	INTERVAL	INTERVAL
INTERVAL	*	numeric	INTERVAL
INTERVAL	/	numeric	INTERVAL

Functions

Function Name	Description
AGE(<*expression*>, <*expression*>)	Subtracts expressions (both TIMESTAMP), producing a "symbolic" result that uses years and months.
AGE(<*expression*>)	Subtracts the TIMESTAMP expression from CURRENT_DATE() (at midnight).
CLOCK_TIMESTAMP()	Returns the current date and time (changes during statement execution).

continues

Function Name	Description
CURRENT_DATE	Returns the current date.
CURRENT_TIME	Returns the current time of day.
CURRENT_TIMESTAMP	Returns the current date and time (start of the current transaction).
DATE_PART(<unit>, <expression>)	Gets the subfield specified by the TEXT unit (year, month, day, etc.) from the expression (either TIMESTAMP or INTERVAL. (See also EXTRACT().)
DATE_TRUNC(<unit>, <expression>)	Truncates the TIMESTAMP expression to the precision specified by the TEXT unit (microseconds, milliseconds, minute, etc.).
EXTRACT(<unit> FROM <expression>)	Gets the subfield specified by the TEXT unit (year, month, day, etc.) from the expression (either TIMESTAMP or INTERVAL).
ISFINITE(<expression>)	Tests whether expression (one of DATE, TIMESTAMP, or INTERVAL) is finite (not +/- infinity).
JUSTIFY_ DAYS(<expression>)	Adjusts the expression (an INTERVAL) so 30-day time periods are represented as months.
JUSTIFY_ HOURS(<expression>)	Adjusts the expression (an INTERVAL) so 24-hour time periods are represented as days.
JUSTIFY_ INTERVAL(<expression>)	Adjusts the expression (an INTERVAL) using justify_ days and justify_hours, with additional sign adjustments.
LOCALTIME	Returns the current time of day.
LOCALTIMESTAMP	Returns the current date and time (start of the current transaction).
NOW()	Returns the current date and time (start of the current transaction).
STATEMENT_TIMESTAMP()	Returns the current date and time (start of the current statement).
TIMEOFDAY()	Returns the current date and time (like CLOCK_ TIMESTAMP(), but as a text string).
TRANSACTION_TIMESTAMP()	Returns the current date and time (start of the current transaction).

Index

REGISTER YOUR PRODUCT at informit.com/register
Access Additional Benefits and SAVE 35% on Your Next Purchase

- Download available product updates.

- Access bonus material when applicable.

- Receive exclusive offers on new editions and related products.
  (Just check the box to hear from us when setting up your account.)

- Get a coupon for 35% for your next purchase, valid for 30 days. Your code will
  be available in your InformIT cart. (You will also find it in the Manage Codes
  section of your account page.)

Registration benefits vary by product. Benefits will be listed on your account page
under Registered Products.

InformIT.com—The Trusted Technology Learning Source
InformIT is the online home of information technology brands at Pearson, the world's foremost
education company. At InformIT.com you can
- Shop our books, eBooks, software, and video training.
- Take advantage of our special offers and promotions (informit.com/promotions).
- Sign up for special offers and content newsletters (informit.com/newsletters).
- Read free articles and blogs by information technology experts.
- Access thousands of free chapters and video lessons.

Connect with InformIT—Visit informit.com/community
Learn about InformIT community events and programs.

informIT.com
the trusted technology learning source

Addison-Wesley · Cisco Press · IBM Press · Microsoft Press · Pearson IT Certification · Prentice Hall · Que · Sams · VMware Press

ALWAYS LEARNING   PEARSON